"In all my years of journalism, I've read few accounts so well told, so powerfully written, so deeply moving. Merrill eloquently describes the suffering that comes with love, and the love that blossoms in suffering. Be prepared to have your heart gripped—and strangely warmed."

—Mark Galli, editor in chief, *Christianity Today*

"Some stories warm your heart; others break it. *Redeeming Ruth* does both. She was the littlest, the last, and the least of all, but God used this exceptional child to change not only a family, but an entire community—and, Lord willing, you too. God said, 'A little child shall lead them,' and I pray Ruth's story will lead you into a closer, sweeter, and more intimate encounter with Jesus than you dreamed possible. I have the deepest admiration and respect for the Merrill family, and it's with great joy I recommend this book to you!"

—Joni Eareckson Tada, CEO of Joni and Friends International Disability Center

"In this riveting, beautifully written book, Meadow Rue Merrill takes us through the story of her daughter Ruth—from her unlikely adoption from Africa to her inclusion in the Merrill family to her growth and beauty as a thriving little girl. . . . It is ultimately a story about family, about faith, and about coming home. I highly recommend this book."

—Amy Julia Becker, author of *A Good and Perfect Gift:*
Faith, Expectations, and a Little Girl Named Penny

"Sure to inspire an outbreak of deepened hearts, larger families, greater love. Isn't this the kind of life Jesus has called us all to?"

—Leslie Leyland Fields, author of *Crossing the Waters: Following*
Jesus through the Storms, the Fish, the Doubt and the Seas

"Honest, painful, and full of hard-won wisdom, *Redeeming Ruth* tells the story of one family's adoption of a medically fragile daughter and how opening their home and hearts to her would forever affect their notion of who are the blessed ones in our world."

—Jennifer Grant, author of *Love You More: The Divine Surprise of Adopting My Daughter*

"Meadow Rue Merrill is a great storyteller, and she's gifted us with the story of her beautiful Ruth. You'll be glad you picked it up and won't want to put it down."

—Margot Starbuck, author of *The Girl in the Orange Dress*

"It's rare that I can't put down a book, but *Redeeming Ruth* held me captive. Evocative writing, a stunning story, and a beautiful girl kept me turning the page. For those who need to know that love is always worth it (even in loss), this book will truly help you embrace all the people God has brought into your life."

—Mary DeMuth, author of *Thin Places: A Memoir*

"Meadow captivates us with a mighty work of love the Lord called her whole family to perform. She is a powerful writer, an unashamedly vulnerable storyteller, a woman of deep motherliness, a Christian of commitment sometimes battered by doubt, and one fierce fighter to protect her family. She's also a realist and, as Ruth's redemptive story comes to its climax, she is willing to show us her sudden understanding of 'pain so deep you'd swallow razor blades to kill it.'"

—Dikkon Eberhart, author of *The Time Mom Met Hitler, Frost Came to Dinner,* and *I Heard the Greatest Story Ever Told*

Redeeming Ruth

Everything Life Takes, Love Restores

MEADOW RUE MERRILL

Library of Congress Cataloging-in-Publication Data

A catalog record for this title is available from the Library of Congress Hendrickson Publishers Marketing, LLC ISBN 978-1-61970-907-2

Jacket design by Karol Bailey

Back flap photo: Used with permission of Theresa Jackson

❧

For the five fingers of my right hand—
Judah, Gabriel, Lydia, Ruth, and Asher;
for the one man who holds it;
and for Ezra,
who reminds us that God's dreams
are always greater.

"Our sons shall be as plantings, flourishing in their youth,
And our daughters shall be as corner pillars,
Formed in the raising of a palace."

(Psalm 144:12, as translated by Lucy Lincoln)

Contents

Prologue

2011

"You are going home," I tell my daughter Ruth, worried about who will feed her on the plane. It is a long journey, and her hands are curled into fists at the end of her stiff and crooked arms. If only I could go with her or at least explain where she is going, but home is a place Ruth has never been.

At seven, she is too young to travel alone. Ruth is crying as I carry her down the center aisle of the plane, which is oddly empty. I lay her in a passenger seat and wrap her feather-light body in a sheet of white lace, soft as a bridal veil against her smooth brown skin. Dana, my husband, appears beside me.

"I want to bring Ruth back." I turn to him, pleading.

He shakes his head. "We can't."

I think he is saying this because he no longer wants Ruth, which makes me mad.

"Then I want to go with her." I raise my voice right there in the middle of the plane.

As if taking Dana's side, Ruth's special education director and physical therapist butt in. "You have three boys and two girls," they say. "White, all white."

"No!" I cry. "A part of me will always be black."

I open my eyes to see the glowing green clock on the dresser across my dark bedroom. Gone is the plane, the white lace. Dana sleeps beside me, curled toward the closet, the peak of his shoulder hiding the grassy stubble of his chin. I groan, knowing that in one week it is he who will board a plane, he who will cross an ocean and two continents to deliver our daughter's wheelchair to a child we've never met.

I once dreamed of our whole family traveling to Uganda, of driving down the red, dusty streets of Entebbe past roadside fruit sellers and outdoor furniture markets on the three-hour drive to Ruth's first home. This is no longer possible, but her absence is so new—so unreal—I imagine that Ruth is still downstairs, asleep in the bed she once shared with her sister, their legs tangled, their heads—one blonde, one black—tucked side by side beneath a mound of warm blankets.

It is not surprising that I see them this way. After all, they were twins. But I do not allow myself to dream it. I have learned that dreams are dangerous. Dreams take you places you never expected. They are difficult to control. And even when they are wonderfully, magically more fantastic than you ever imagined, eventually you wake up.

1

The Danger of Dreaming

The house was cool and quiet, the dazzling Maine summer slowly drifting toward autumn, as I slipped down the hall of our century-old New Englander—a white clapboard house that rose above Bath's busy High Street. Dana was asleep, as were our two boys. I'd peeked in their room to be sure. Five-year-old Judah lay swaddled on the top bunk, his face partially hidden by a stack of books. Two-year-old Gabriel, in the bed below, shone pink with sleep. A dandelion puff of hair sprouted from his pillow. The boys' breathing was soft, their eyes closed.

I smiled and tiptoed downstairs. I loved getting up before everyone else. Cushions on the couch. Counters clean. Mayhem mostly contained from the day before. But as soon as I turned into the narrow galley of our kitchen, I saw I wasn't alone. My mother, Lucy, leaned over the counter, rummaging through a cupboard. She'd been living with us all summer, and I was surprised to see her awake at this hour. She was a linguist and Bible translator who often worked late, hunkered over her laptop, copying ancient Scriptures into a little-known language spoken near the Caspian Sea.

"You're up early." I pulled a mug from the drying rack and made myself a cup of tea with water from the steaming electric kettle Mom had put on.

"I couldn't sleep." She sighed. Mom's long calico nightgown peeked out from beneath her short robe. Gray hair floated around her face like fog, shadowing her eyes as she made tea and carried it to the kitchen table. "I had the strangest dream."

A pang of anticipation fluttered in my stomach. Would this be like her dream in which our house burned down? It hadn't, but I'd faced an emotional inferno that year. Or like her dream where I'd bobbed in a boat over the cresting waves of an ocean on the night contractions battered my body during labor with Gabriel? I squeezed my tea bag against the side of my mug, scalding my fingers, and wondered—for some reason, I actually wondered—whether this dream had anything to do with a baby. Only Dana knew I might be pregnant. I'd whispered my suspicion to him in bed a few nights before but hadn't taken a test, wanting to savor this precious possibility like a gift.

Pale morning light filtered through the leafy lilac bush outside the window, brightening Mom's face as I sat across from her.

"Two girls were diving off a dock into the water," she said. "They were twins."

I drew a breath, clasping my hands over the soft cotton of my robe.

"They sprang up—way, way up—into the air like Olympic divers," Mom continued. "Then they crossed their arms over their chests before spinning down and disappearing into the water with a splash. They were strong and athletic and very graceful. I knew they were yours. And when I woke up, I started praying, 'Not before they're ready, Lord. Don't let them have any more children before they're ready.' "

From childhood I'd planned out my life in measured detail, plotting my future in dream-filled journals. I'd go to college, get married, and become a writer. My husband and I would have two boys and a girl—in that order. While they were little, I'd work from home, and eventually we would adopt a beautiful brown baby from Africa.

"God is going to give you the desires of your heart," three separate ministers had confirmed on three separate occasions—once during my freshman year of Bible school, once when Dana and I were newly married, and once after discovering that we were expecting our first child. And I believed them. Having grown up in Pentecostal churches, where white-haired saints often jumped from their pews to proclaim words straight from heaven, I was accustomed to hearing God speak through others. Twins, however, were not part of my plan.

"Wow, that *is* a strange dream."

"You have so much to keep up with already." Mom glanced past me toward the unfinished back hall, which was part of a two-story addition we lacked time and money to finish. "I've known couples who've had too many children too fast," she said, reminding me of a family we once knew who always had a toddler or two padding about in diapers. "It was so hard, they divorced."

Apparently, this was not the best time to reveal to her that I might be pregnant. A month or two later, after a doctor confirmed my suspicion, I remember running my hands over the drum-tightening skin of my belly and wondering just how many babies were in there.

That October, I lay on an exam table at our local hospital. Gabriel, with his floppy kitchen haircut, squirmed in Dana's arms as a technician squirted cold goo above my pelvis and pressed down with a probe. Ever eager, Judah leaned toward the snowy blur on the monitor. As a gray shadow emerged, I studied the image with extra care. One head. One tummy. One baby.

"No twins?" I questioned.

"No twins." The woman handed me a fistful of tissues to wipe the gel from my stomach. "Everything looks great."

Dana smiled. As we had with our other children, we'd chosen to wait to find out whether we were having a boy or girl. Still, I hoped the baby was a girl. My hopes to adopt didn't seem nearly as likely— although in the nine years we'd been married, Dana and I had talked about it often. Our conversations went like this:

Me: "Let's adopt."

Dana: "I don't know."

Me: "Let's become foster parents."

Dana: "Maybe."

Me: "Let's do something."

Dana: "Okay."

That was all my no-hurry, take-tomorrow-as-it-comes husband would commit to.

"Someday," he promised, "we will do something."

Adoption isn't a choice you push someone into. Even I knew that. And after hearing stories of parents who'd adopted children who were so physically or emotionally limited that they'd sent them back to the very same orphanages from which they'd tried to adopt them, I had my own reservations. Could I love someone else's child the way I loved my own? Kiss her on the mouth? Eat off the same spoon? I didn't know. Yet that didn't keep me from perusing pictures of adoptable children on the Internet after our own children were in bed.

Before becoming a mother, I'd read heartbreaking stories about neglected children and shake my head. After becoming a mother, those stories haunted me. I'd watch our boys building forts in the backyard and picture children living in garbage dumps. I'd read them a good night story and wonder how many children have never held a book, let alone had someone read to them. I'd sing, tucking them safe in their beds, and imagine children huddled in the darkened doorway of a street. I couldn't fathom how a child could grow up without the safety of a home, without the love of a parent—without a song.

What right do we have to be so content? I wondered. *And what is my responsibility for the suffering in this world?*

I thought about it again when I saw a newspaper photo of an African mother with emaciated breasts nursing a skeletal toddler in her lap; or when I watched a documentary on Eastern European teenagers sniffing toxic glue so they wouldn't feel the frozen streets where they slept; or when I read an article about Afghani women digging pits in mountainsides to shelter children who peeled bark from trees to satisfy their hunger. The realization that life could be so brutal doubled me over, summoning a grief I could express only in moans.

How can you love me? I questioned God. *How can you care about my needs when I have so much and others have so little?* I couldn't reconcile my comfort—my family's—with the utter misery of others.

"What if those were our children?" I once asked Dana, holding up a newspaper photo of children sleeping on the floor of an Indonesian airport. "What if there was no one to take care of them?"

"I don't know," he said. "I just think our own kids should be older before we think about taking care of someone else's."

Typical. While I wanted to rush out and save the world, Dana wanted to wait. We settled our conflicting desires the only way we knew how. Holding hands, we sat on our bed one night and prayed, "Lord, if you have another child for us, you will have to bring that child to us."

We wouldn't pursue it. If God wanted us to adopt, then it was up to him.

On a gray afternoon in March, I lay curled on the bed in the room at the end of our still-unfinished back hall, watching out the window as Judah and Gabriel scampered over backyard boulders. I'd been having contractions all day, but was it labor? Just before 4:00

p.m., I called Dana at his office, which was just a mile away, and suggested he might want to come home. Soon after, we gathered my hospital bags, dropped off our boys with a neighbor, and zoomed the ten minutes to the nearest hospital. Less than an hour later, it was over.

"Is it a boy or girl?" I sat up, trying to see past the nurses and midwife clustered around the squalling bundle near the foot of my bed.

Dana was barely able to contain his excitement as his eyes met mine. "A girl."

"A girl?" I sank into the pillows, overcome with joy as our daughter was finally placed in my arms. Lydia was plump, soft, and purple as a plum, with a stubborn little wrinkle across the bridge of her nose. When I held her, I was holding my dream come true: two boys and a girl.

Little did I know that halfway around the world in an overcrowded maternity ward, where women brought tarps to lie on as they gave birth on the floor, my mother's dream was also about to come true.

2

Twins?

ABANDONED BABY GIRL

*An unknown baby girl was born to Nakabuye Sharon, 19
yrs., on 17/4/2003 at 9 hrs. in Labour suite, Mulago Hospital.
Her birth weight was 1.8 kgs. She was admitted to the special
care unit for prematurity and grunting respiration. The
mother abandoned her soon after. After a long struggle the
baby girl is now stable and active at 1.38 kgs. The Medical
Social Work Department requests that the child be placed in
a baby's home for better care and protection.*

F. K. Karamagi
For Principal Medical Social Worker
Medical Social Work Department, Kampala

The sanctuary of my friend Theresa's church was sweltering. It reminded me of the weeklong revival services my mother often dragged my older brother, Sunny, and me to when we were kids—the excitement, the anticipation, and the sweat that beaded up and trickled down every available crease of skin. Air conditioners spun and fans whirled, but they did little to offset the August heat in a room packed with a hundred radiant parents and their kids on the last night of Vacation Bible School.

"Hey!" Theresa knelt on a pew in the middle of the church and waved as Dana and I towed seventeen-month-old Lydia through the crowd.

Relieved to find someone we knew, I pushed toward her while Judah, independent and sure at seven, darted up front to join a row of first graders half sitting, half tumbling off a pew. Four-year-old Gabriel cheerfully bounced along behind his brother, his golden hair glittering through the crowd. Our boys had been coming to the kids' program at Maine Street Baptist Church in Brunswick all week, and this was the grand finale: their big chance to belt out Bible songs onstage.

"I was wondering when ya'll'd get here." Theresa gave me a hug. As I scooted in beside her, my friend's long black hair brushed my cheek. An ocean wave of bangs curled over her forehead, and I caught a hint of the hair spray that held it all together. Theresa looked pressed and primped and every bit the Southerner—in a state where she'd once tried to sell Mary Kay cosmetics but quit after discovering how few Maine women wear makeup. She and her husband, Allen, had moved here from Virginia after he'd retired from the navy. Like us, they were in their early thirties, and their four children were close enough in age to ours that we sometimes swapped. Daniel, their youngest, pushed a plastic truck up the pew, and Lydia toddled off to join him.

"So—" Theresa leaned forward, dark eyes twinkling as Dana settled beside me. "Want to meet Ruth?"

"Ruth?" It took me a minute to remember the baby my friend and her family were hosting from Uganda.

A few weeks before, Theresa had called to share Ruth's story— how she'd been born prematurely, abandoned, and sent to Welcome Home Ministries, Africa, a home that cared for some of Uganda's neediest children.

"'Abandoned Ruth,'" Theresa drawled out the word as only a Southern girl can. "That's what it says on one of her papers where her name should be. Isn't that sad?"

I nodded, wondering what special qualifications her family had to care for a child with cerebral palsy. "How long will she be here?"

"Six months." Theresa scanned the crowd. "Then she'll go back to Uganda—unless someone decides to adopt her."

"You're not thinking about it?" I asked.

She shrugged. "It isn't our calling."

For being so quick to question my friend's ability to care for a child with cerebral palsy for a few months, I was even quicker to judge her for not being ready to do it for a lifetime. And I was jealous. Since that long-ago night when Dana and I had prayed about adopting, we hadn't talked about it. Not once. But in a quiet moment alone, I'd recently offered up this feeble prayer: "Lord, if you want us to adopt, you will have to put it in Dana's heart too."

If opposites attract, then Dana and I could not be more attracted to each other. While I am often outspoken and rash, he is more quiet and reserved. We met at a Bible study during our senior years at neighboring southern Maine high schools. Dana was kind, cute, and easygoing with round, metal-rimmed glasses and thick brown hair that curled at the nape of his neck. I was a socially insecure seventeen-year-old who'd moved too often to make many friends. But after our first hour-long phone conversation I thought, *If we ever start dating, we will never stop.*

Dana was my first boyfriend, my first date, my first kiss. We took long, moonlit walks on sandy beaches and slow drives home—after which he walked me over the cobblestones to my front door and kissed me good night beyond the view of my mother's window. After graduating that spring, we enrolled in separate colleges—a Rhode Island Bible school for me, and the United States Merchant Marine Academy on Long Island for him. Despite the distance, we saw each other every chance we got. In letters and late-night phone calls, we even talked about marriage. There was just one problem: while Dana planned to serve his country, I felt increasingly called to work with orphans in Africa.

"Maybe I'm not supposed to get married," I wondered aloud during one of the many times we discussed it. "Maybe I'm supposed to be one of those single missionaries who goes off and lives in a hut somewhere."

"Or maybe not," Dana countered.

Even after withdrawing from the academy and switching to a Maine university, he wasn't remotely interested in Africa or orphans. Meanwhile, I'd transferred to Gordon College, a Christian liberal arts school near Boston, to major in English. But with such differing interests, how could we spend our lives together?

The following Christmas, after ice-skating under the stars on the frozen cattail pond outside Dana's family home in Nobleboro, we warmed up beside the living room woodstove. Curled next to each other on the couch, Dana held me tight as we talked about our future. And oh, I wanted that future, but first I had to settle this question. Pulling away, I looked into Dana's gray-green eyes and said, "If I promise to marry you, you have to promise to let me go to Africa, alone if I have to. I don't know when, and I don't know why, but I know that God has a plan for me in Africa."

"Okay." Dana brushed back a tangle of my chin-length hair and said, "You can go to Africa."

On New Year's Eve, at the stroke of midnight one year later, Dana knelt in that same room while an ice storm battered the roof and windows. Above the crack and snap of freezing rain, he slipped a diamond ring on my finger and asked me to marry him. I blurted "Yes!" before he'd finished speaking. That's how eager I was to start our life together. We exchanged gold bands in my grandparents' flower-festooned church in historic York Village two weeks after my college graduation. As if underscoring our youthful optimism, two blooming mounds of white impatiens flanked the altar. Never mind that Dana was still working his way through school and I didn't have a job. We loved each other and wanted to serve God together. What more mattered?

Just before our wedding, Dana had found a tiny apartment nestled under the eaves of an old Victorian house, halfway up the Maine coast in the historic mill town of Topsham. I'd already contacted the local paper, *The Times Record*, and been told they weren't hiring. Dana worked for a gourmet pizza chain and attended school forty minutes away. Living there didn't make sense, but he felt a peace about it. So we signed the lease, and I moved in. One week before our wedding, the managing editor for the paper called back with a sudden opening and asked if I would come in for an interview. Within hours of returning from our four-day honeymoon in the White Mountains, the phone rang again and the editor offered me the job.

Like a mama bird, which sometimes pushes a baby from the nest so that it will learn how to fly, God often pushes us out of a place of security so that we will learn how to trust him. It takes practice to flap our fledgling wings of faith, but with each repeated plunge, our confidence grows. For two years, I wrote for the paper while Dana worked on his degree. Then we discovered that I was pregnant. I panicked, having always dreamed of working from home while raising our children. But how could I, when we needed my income?

"If you don't try now, when will you?" Dana asked.

Once again, I was being asked to jump.

You can either work for everything you need, and you can get it, I felt the Holy Spirit speak to my heart during a quiet moment alone, *or you can trust me, and I will give it to you.*

Judah arrived healthy and howling on a bright Monday morning in February, right on deadline. We were dazed with joy and terrified of bringing him home—this fragile seven-pound baby who depended on us for everything. Despite our inexperience and lack of sleep, I loved being a mom even more than I loved working at the paper. After a six-month maternity leave, I resigned to work from home. A couple of weeks later, my mom clipped a help-wanted ad from a publisher seeking Maine travel writers, and I had my first freelance contract.

With Judah buckled in back of our reliable Mazda, I raced up and down the coast, writing about inns and restaurants and beaches. Before long I was contributing to a growing number of regional and national publications, while folding an ever-increasing pile of laundry thanks to the happy arrivals of Gabriel and Lydia. God even blessed us with a newly renovated house—the only one we could afford—when we came up first in a public lottery for first-time homebuyers. It wasn't easy making ends meet on Dana's income as a drafter and mine as a writer, but God had truly granted the desires of my heart—with one exception.

"I guess that whole thing with Africa and orphans will never happen," I sighed to God one afternoon while heaving a never-ending pile of dirty clothes into our washing machine. "I am way too busy now."

Little did I imagine what God had in mind.

"Allen!" Theresa waved her arms like a person helping to guide in an airplane.

A balding head cut through the packed sanctuary. Broad shoulders, broad smile, broad legs a step stool longer than everyone else's—that's Allen. People squeezed against the pews to let him by. Then I saw the baby dangling from his arms. She was scrawny and limp and dressed in a shapeless pink onesie that sagged where a round tummy and chubby thighs should have stretched it tight. Dana was looking too. I couldn't see his face, couldn't guess what he was thinking, but I was thinking, *Hold her tighter. Lift her head.* My heart was doing flips. I couldn't take my eyes off her.

"This is Ruth." Theresa beamed.

"Want to hold her?" Allen dropped Ruth into Dana's arms without waiting for a reply.

Ruth's head flopped against his shoulder. Tiny fingers curled into her palms, but she was smiling—a lopsided, baby-toothed "Here I am" smile that creased her cheeks and made her dark eyes gleam. Ruth's head was fringed with a thin scrub of curls. Her skin was the color of gingerbread, and she was beautiful, stunning, with a high, rounded forehead and a fat little pucker of a nose. Dana wiggled a finger, holding it out for Ruth to grab. Instead, she wrinkled her nose and let out a deep *hee-hee-hee* that stiffened her entire body as laughter bubbled up her throat. Despite her being so weak, Ruth's happiness was so powerful it was contagious, and we all found ourselves laughing along with her.

"Can she talk?" I asked.

Theresa shook her head.

"Will she? I mean, will she be able to?"

"It's too early to tell." Theresa shrugged. "Ruth started therapy only a couple of weeks ago. At the children's home, she was kept in a room full of babies—except for the months with her foster family."

Theresa filled me in on Ruth's story. After being abandoned by her birth mother, Ruth spent one month in the hospital before being transferred to Welcome Home. At the time, she weighed three pounds—nearly a full pound less than she had at birth. Soon after, a local woman signed papers to foster Ruth and brought her home, planning to adopt her. Nine months later, she returned Ruth to the children's home. Ruth was so weak and sick that she cried constantly, unable to lift her head. Mandy Sydo, who'd arrived that week as the home's director, drove Ruth to a clinic where a doctor diagnosed malaria and prescribed medication to combat her high fever. He then diagnosed Ruth with something even the best medicine couldn't cure: cerebral palsy.

Sometime at or around birth, Ruth's brain had built a roadblock where a superhighway should have been. The desire to reach and sit and play was there, but the information couldn't get through the damaged neural pathways from her mind to her muscles. Knowing there was little help for children with disabilities in Uganda, Mama Mandy—as this California preacher's wife was now known—sought a grassroots organization to bring Ruth and Yvonne, another one-year-old with cerebral palsy, to America for physical therapy. An Ohio family volunteered to host Yvonne, while Theresa and her family took Ruth.

As my friend talked, I imagined it all: the tiny baby wailing in a hospital, the nurse or doctor in another room, the frightened mother sneaking away—so unlike my own pregnancy, the joyful anticipation with which I'd welcomed my daughter. I wondered how young Ruth's mother was and how she found herself pregnant and where she was now. But I didn't judge her. I could never judge her. How could I, given all the advantages I'd had?

"Want a turn?" Dana held Ruth toward me.

I'd been holding and nursing a baby for more than a year and liked having my lap to myself, but everyone was staring. "Sure." I nodded.

Dana slid Ruth into my arms. Nothing stayed where it should. Her body was alternately stiff and then limp, as if someone had forgotten to tighten her muscles. Her left eye turned weakly toward her nose. Ruth's head rolled forward and back, forward and back as I tried to steady her against my chest. A sudden urge to protect her overwhelmed me. *Don't say it*, I thought, quickly handing Ruth back to Dana. *Don't say a word.*

Amazingly, Dana said it for me. "So, do you want to adopt her?"

I gasped. "Are you joking?" He had to be crazy.

"Why not?"

I looked at Lydia tottering toward us and thought of a hundred reasons why not: the money, which we didn't have; the kids, who were way too little; the disabilities, the disabilities, the disabilities; the lifelong care and commitment Ruth would require. I'd read of people who'd adopted children who couldn't speak, couldn't walk, couldn't whatever. I'd been amazed and awed that anyone could spend a life willingly taking care of someone else. But I had never wanted to become one of those people. For all the times I had imagined adopting, I had never imagined adopting a child like Ruth. Not ever. Yet, there Ruth was. African. Abandoned. Smiling from the cradle of my husband's arms. And this was what else I was thinking: *If not us, who? Ruth is here, isn't she? She is on this earth, isn't she? If not us, then who should adopt her?*

"Baby?" Lydia poked the tummy of this small intruder.

"How old did you say she is?" I turned to Theresa.

"Fifteen . . . sixteen months?" Theresa ticked off the numbers on her fingers, looking to Allen. "You remember, honey?"

Everything else faded—parents filling the pews, Lydia leaning against my knee, our children lining the front of the church.

"When's her birthday?" I asked.

"April," she said. "April 17."

Two and a half weeks after Lydia's. It struck Dana the same way it struck me. "Twins?" he mouthed silently.

But it was impossible. Wasn't it? It was crazy.

Ruth was still looking at me, still smiling, as the pastor took his place behind the altar.

3

Two Dark Eyes

Lydia paints trees.

Page after page of bent and bowed trunks fill a white sketch pad. In some, a single tree fills an entire page. More often she draws two trees, limbs twisted together like knobby knees and elbows. An unseen storm bends the branches, which are full of unplucked fruit.

I do not doubt their meaning.

Dana and I encourage our children to express their sorrow however they need to—through pictures or words or climbing into bed with us at night. And I begin this journal, the smallest I can find. My thoughts are too dark to write large. I fill the pages with memories, regrets, and overheard conversations, like this:

"I want to go to Africa," seven-year-old Lydia says.

"You know you have to get shots," Gabriel, eleven, eagerly reveals.

"How many?" Her eyes widen.

"Lots."

"Never mind," says Lydia. "I want to stay right here."

"Were you serious about adopting?" I grilled Dana in our minivan, driving home after meeting Ruth while the kids were distracted by an audiobook in the back.

"Why not?" As he turned past Bowdoin College with its granite and glass buildings, I glimpsed the bronze statue of famous Civil War hero Joshua Chamberlain, hand outstretched as if to pat the head of a small child. "You're the one who always wanted to adopt."

"Yes," I protested, wondering when my husband had become so irrational. "But what if Ruth never walks or talks? Do you realize what raising a child with cerebral palsy would be like?"

"You can't tell what raising *any* child will be like." Dana picked up speed, merging onto busy Route 1, the thin highway that winds up the Maine coast from Kittery to Canada. "If a truck hit us right now, any of our kids could end up the same way. But if you really want to know, I think Ruth will be fine. Did you see the way she smiled?"

How could I forget? After church, our family had joined Allen and Theresa at Cote's ice-cream stand across from the Brunswick town green. While our kids licked their treats and raced around the weathered bandstand, I'd fed Ruth bits of my sugar cone after discovering that she wouldn't open her mouth for ice cream.

And that should have been it. After saying goodbye, Dana and I should have forgotten all about Ruth. Only, we couldn't. That night, after carrying our kids to bed, we sat at the kitchen table talking about her in the warm summer dark. We talked about her, curled side by side in our snug double bed, until Dana fell asleep and his snores drowned out the distant songs of crickets.

As soon as the morning light brightened our flowery curtains early that Saturday, I shook my husband's shoulder and asked, "Do you think Ruth is the girl in my mother's dream?"

Dana heaved a pillow over his head.

I hauled it off. "Would you want to adopt if my mother hadn't had her dream?"

"Sure," he grunted.

He's only saying that so I'll let him go back to sleep, I thought.

"Do you think we are supposed to adopt her?" I insisted. "Do you think God brought Ruth to us? Do you think this is his plan?"

I was half hoping my husband would say yes, half hoping he wouldn't. He kept snoring.

As a child growing up in the rural farmlands of Oregon, I spent Sunday mornings at the Elmira Church of Christ, a kindly congregation where Sunday school teachers told Bible stories with flannel cutouts and an old man, Uncle Dan, handed out sticks of Juicy Fruit gum after the service. Sunny and I sometimes rode our bikes barefoot to church, pedaling past our neighbor's golden hay fields. It was a wonder we went to church at all. Our mother was a Connecticut debutante who'd swapped elbow-length gloves and satin dancing shoes for a backpack and hiking boots in the mid-1960s, the height of the hippie movement, and hitched her way west.

While studying Balinese dance in Berkley, California, she met a former Marine named Larry who'd wandered into town the day she was lost and searching for the YWCA. Larry, who was working on a logging crew, pointed her in the right direction. For a while, they wandered together, hopping freight trains and thumbing rides across the country, until her mother insisted they get married. After a low-key wedding in my grandparents' backyard, they chugged off in a Volkswagen camper bus, a gift from her parents. First they explored Florida and Hawaii, where Sunny was born, before settling in Eugene, Oregon, where they opened an army surplus store, buying and selling spare military goods. When I arrived twenty-one months after Sunny, they bought a ten-acre farm in nearby Elmira with fields, barns, and a cattail pond perfect for catching frogs. My earliest memory is of riding on my father's back, fingers twisted around his curly brown hair, holding on tight, tight, tight.

But my parents clashed. By my fifth birthday, my dad was gone—driving a blue air force bus, which he'd rebuilt as a camper, out of town and down the Redwood Highway back to California.

Having lost my earthly father, I longed for a heavenly one. In first grade, when my friend Janey told me how much she loved Jesus, I wanted to love him too. I begged Mom to buy me a picture of the heavenly Savior to hang above my bed. Embarrassed, she eventually drove me to a Christian bookstore where I picked a cardboard print of Jesus sitting in a garden holding a smiling girl on his lap. How I ached to be that girl—beautiful and loved and protected.

About the same time, Mom began reading the Bible while exploring the teachings of the New Age mystic Edgar Cayce, but the words of Jesus spoke to her in a way that Cayce's didn't. So she stopped following Cayce and started following Jesus. Soon, we began going to church. At a Christian camp not long after, Mom committed her life to Christ. Some nights, I'd drift to sleep under a snug quilt made of wool from our own sheep before Mom's boots thudded down the back hall after penning our chickens, sheep, and goats. Other nights, she plunked herself at the foot of my bed, reading thin pages of Scripture in her smooth alto voice. On one of these nights, when I was about eight, Mom asked what I thought God wanted me to be when I grew up. "He has a plan for each of us," she said. "All you have to do is close your eyes, ask, and he'll tell you."

With Jesus gazing down from the wall above my bed, I closed my eyes and fired off a prayer.

Mom leaned forward. "What did God say?"

"He said he wants me to be a country western singer."

For a girl who'd spent long hours riding the backyard propane tank pretending it was a pony, it was the best life I could imagine. My favorite shoes were a pair of red vinyl cowgirl boots with clunky rubber soles. All I needed was a ten-gallon hat and a trusty pony to go with them. The following Christmas, I looked out the front window and saw not one but *two* ponies tied to the picket fence. Mr. Favor, the gentle, brown Welsh-Hackney, was mine; Barney, the gray-and-white-speckled Pony of America, was Sunny's. We rode bareback under the apple trees, around the fields, over the ridge to the pond, and down through the skunk cabbages until Mom called us in for supper. But the hat escaped me. So did the singing.

Still, I believed that God had a plan for my life. The Bible says that he created each of us with a purpose. The trick was knowing the difference between my plans—standing on a light-flooded stage crooning into a microphone—and his. If adopting Ruth was God's purpose for us, then I'd do it. If it wasn't, then I didn't want to change my life for her any more than I now wanted to move to Nashville.

"I'm waiting." I rolled over in bed and tapped Dana's back. I was waiting for him to say, "The birthdays are a coincidence." Or, "You don't change your life because of a dream."

Instead, he opened his eyes, wedged a pillow under his head, and asked, "Does it really matter?"

"What do you mean?"

"I mean, we have a home and Ruth needs one. If we are meant to adopt her, it will work out. If not, we can at least say we tried."

"But what if it works out and it's a mistake?" Once again, Dana wasn't making sense. "What if we adopt Ruth and it ruins our lives?"

I'd met only one child with cerebral palsy, Torie, whose mother's uterus had ruptured during labor, depriving her of oxygen for nearly forty minutes before a doctor performed a caesarean section. As a result, her parents had won what was then the biggest medical malpractice suit in Maine: $8.9 million.[1] They also had a daughter with a bent and crooked body who would never walk, never easily talk, never independently wrap her arms around them in a hug. Lisa, Torie's school aide, was a friend of mine. I'd spotted them at a local children's concert a few years before.

"Want to say, 'Hi'?" Lisa asked me as she leaned over the gaunt little girl with wispy brown hair who'd smiled up at me from her bulky wheelchair.

"Hi," I'd said louder than necessary as musicians tuned their instruments on stage.

Torie's head bobbed and a yawning sort of moan escaped from her mouth. She was beautiful, but caring for a child who was so weak and vulnerable scared me. Even so, I couldn't stop imagining what it would be like to adopt Ruth. I couldn't stop talking about her either—including in front of our children. "Remember the baby we met at church?" I asked later that Saturday as we sat around the table eating breakfast. "What would you think if we could adopt her?"

"We're gonna adopt her?" Judah jerked his head up from his cereal bowl.

"I didn't say 'going to.'" I buckled Lydia into her booster seat and gave her a scattering of Cheerios. "But what if we could?'"

"Oh, boy!" Judah sprang from his chair and threw his arms around me. "I've been praying for another sister!"

"We're gonna get another sister?" Gabriel blinked.

"We're not sure." Dana leaned against the kitchen counter, taking a tentative sip of coffee.

"But we might?" Judah insisted.

"It's too early to say," I cautioned. "But we're thinking about it."

The boys hopped and hollered as Lydia threw cereal on the floor. She was not even two, not even weaned. She was my baby, the daughter I'd always wanted, and I weighed how hard it would be to bring another baby into our family—especially one as needy as Ruth. Yet this same neediness drew me to her. My heart was telling me that ours was *exactly* the right family for Ruth—a big one with plenty of siblings to make up for all the things she couldn't do. But my head was telling me that I wasn't ready, that we weren't ready, and that if we did this, we would lose everything.

From the time our children could pull a shirt over their heads, I'd encouraged them to do it for themselves. I didn't care if their clothes matched. I cared that I had one less chore each morning. Adopting a child who might never dress herself was hard to envision, yet part of me felt Ruth was ours already. That morning, while out running errands, I stopped at a garage sale and came across mounds of clothes. Expensive clothes. Baby girl clothes. When I told the owner who I was buying them for, she gave them to me for free. I filled a giant garbage bag and drove to Allen and Theresa's.

"These are for Ruth," I announced, holding them out, when Allen opened the door. Only, when he reached for the bag, my fingers stiffened.

"I didn't want to give him the clothes," I later admitted to Dana.

"What did you want?" he asked.

"I wanted to dress Ruth in them. I wanted to strap her in a stroller and parade her all over town so everyone would see how beautiful she is."

Since that wasn't an option, I shopped for a brown baby doll, convinced that Ruth needed one while living in Maine, the whitest state in the nation. Only, all the dolls I found in our little strip of Maine were as white as me. So, I ordered one online. Then I e-mailed my mother, who had moved to Israel.

"What color were the girls in your dream?" I typed.

She typed back: "I didn't notice."

For someone with visions, she wasn't much help.

Searching for guidance, I turned to friends.

"Pray about it," some advised.

Pray about what? I wondered.

"Love your neighbor as you love yourself," Scripture says. "Share your food with the hungry. Give to the needy."

James, the brother of Jesus, defined pure religion as "caring for widows and orphans in their distress." Ruth was an orphan. She was clearly in distress. Yet some of the same people who believed God created the earth in six literal days seemed to question whether he literally meant for us to take care of orphans. Most disturbingly, I discovered that I was one of them. *What does it mean to love?* I wondered. *How much am I required to share? Are giving clothes and a doll enough? Or does caring require more?*

"Why don't we wait a couple of months and see if anyone else comes forward to adopt Ruth," Dana suggested. "If no one does, then we will."

"What about the money?" I asked, knowing adoptions often cost tens of thousands of dollars. "How could we afford it?"

"*Jehovah Jireh*," Dana quoted a Hebrew phrase from Scripture meaning "God will provide."

"Seriously?" I asked. "This is your financial plan?"

As a child, while I had been roller-skating around our church parking lot or crawling under the pews, Dana had been pinned in church between his mother, Patricia, and two older brothers while his father preached from a Nazarene pulpit. With the scrutiny that comes from being a pastor's kid and a stiff-collared shirt buttoned up to his chin, I imagine he never got to see the underside of a pew; but he did get a feel for the ministry. The scraping to get by part. The living in a loaned trailer on church land part. The trusting God part. As a result, he has the annoying habit of believing that God will take care of us. Me? I want proof—preferably in the form of cash.

In September, a Maine adoption agency posted Ruth's photo on its website. How many people were actively seeking a baby with cerebral palsy? A pair of women asked about Ruth but never called back. Another friend was interested but had a weak back. I was relieved. While uncertain that Dana and I were prepared to raise Ruth, I secretly believed we were the only ones who could.

"I know a mom whose daughter has cerebral palsy," said Beth, a teacher friend. "Her daughter was one of my students. There were all sorts of programs she got into. A bus even picked her up at her door."

This was new—the thought that if we did adopt, we would have help.

"What about your kids?" another friend asked. "It's not like you and Dana will be the only ones taking care of her as she gets older. Do you think adopting a child with cerebral palsy is fair to them?"

I wasn't sure.

"Do you think it's fair?" I asked Dana in bed, one of the few places we were free to talk. "I mean, sure, the kids are excited now. But what about when the excitement wears off? Or we can't go somewhere because Ruth can't go too?"

"I think adopting Ruth is the best thing we can do for them," he said. "It's what we've always talked about, remember? Teaching them to love."

Early in our marriage, Dana and I had debated how to raise our children in a way that demonstrated God's love for others. My greatest fear wasn't that they'd grow up to be addicts or dropouts or criminals. It was that they'd grow up to be selfish. Yet even I knew we couldn't adopt Ruth as some kind of Sunday school project.

That fall, I stopped by Theresa's and found Ruth strapped in a therapeutic, red-foam chair a few feet from the television.

"Cartoons?" I frowned, sitting on the floor beside her as Theresa's children played Monopoly nearby.

"Ruth loves them," Theresa called from the kitchen.

"If you were mine," I whispered, holding her tightly fisted hands, "I would read you books."

Ruth smiled, her strong eye focused on me.

I sucked in a mouthful of air, puffed out my cheeks, and then poked one cheek with a finger. Ruth giggled as I let the air out in a blast. Encouraged, I pulled her onto my lap and filled my cheeks again. This time, I widened my eyes and wagged my head like a balloon. Lifting Ruth's limp arm, I pressed her fist against my cheek. *Whoomph!* Ruth shrieked with joy.

"Let me try!" said Zachary, Theresa's twelve-year-old son. He scooted over, followed by his younger brother, Nathan, and sister, Tiffany. Monopoly abandoned, cheeks swelled and spit flew while Ruth screamed with laughter, thrashing her hands and feet in excitement.

"What's so funny?" Theresa asked, carrying in two mugs of tea as Ruth jerked her arm toward my bulging cheek. "Oh, that *is* funny!"

Clearly Ruth loved to play, but at seventeen months, she couldn't sit up or roll over. She also wasn't talking. To find out why, I telephoned Tracey, a Brunswick school aide and widow with two teenage sons who had helped bring Ruth to Maine, while also hosting a young boy from Haiti awaiting surgery to remove a tumor from his eye. Tracey and another Brunswick mom, Tammy, had picked up Ruth and Yvonne from the airport in Boston. After one night here, another volunteer had flown with Yvonne to a host family in Ohio. Meanwhile, Ruth had spent two weeks with Tracey before moving to Allen and Theresa's. What I learned about Tracey and Tammy astonished me. Both lived just above the poverty line. Both were raising children with disabilities. And in their "free" time, both helped kids with cancer, seizures, missing limbs, clubfeet, malformed hearts, and devastating burns come to America for lifesaving treatment unavailable in their own countries. It was a Wild West sort of effort, procuring visas, passports, and plane tickets from a horde of impoverished countries—Haiti, Burkina Faso, Mongolia, Sri Lanka, Iran—and recruiting local doctors to donate care. After being cured, most children returned home to their families. Only, for cerebral palsy, there is no cure, and Ruth had no family.

While talking to Tracey, I discovered that one of her students was Torie, the girl with cerebral palsy whom I'd met at the concert a few years before.

"How is she?" I pictured the girl who'd struggled to say hello.

"A riot!" Tracey laughed. "You wouldn't believe how much fun she is—and silly, like purposefully knocking everything off the tray of her wheelchair when I'm not looking. Every kid needs to be a little mischievous. Torie's great at math too, working on a computer that tracks the movement of her eyes."

"Can she walk?" I asked, hopeful.

"A few steps. If I help her."

"What about Ruth?" This was what I really wanted to know. "Do you think Ruth will ever walk or talk?"

"It's hard to say." Tracey sobered. "CP is a garbage-can diagnosis. Doctors don't always know what causes it, so they lump these kids together under one big lid. One child might have trouble holding a pencil while another struggles to speak or walk. Every kid is different. But let me put it this way: for two years Torie has been working hard on learning to drink through a straw. She won't give up."

Her answer was unsettling. Should we take on this burden? Pray for a miracle? Spend our lives caring for Ruth if the miracle didn't happen? Or should we send Ruth back to a world without mothers or fathers, brothers or sisters, full bellies or a safe place to call home? Amazingly, staggeringly, the choice was ours. If only someone could promise that Ruth would be well. Since Dana was unable to make such a guarantee and God remained silent, I tried our pediatrician. Dr. Wren was older, wiser, the father of two boys. He and his family were preparing to embark as medical missionaries to the Philippines, and he'd been our children's doctor from before Judah was born.

"We're thinking of adopting a one-year-old from Uganda," I told him while bringing Lydia for a checkup. "She has cerebral palsy."

Dr. Wren listened with one hand on his manila file and the other on his chin. *He is going to caution me,* I thought. *He is going to say it will be too hard. He is going to say we should take care of the children we already have.* Instead, Dr. Wren fingered his moustache thoughtfully and said, "I've been to places like Uganda. In a country like that, where even healthy people have a hard time getting food and medicine, a child like Ruth will never make it. If she goes back," he said as he leveled compassionate eyes on me, "she will die."

For the first time, I understood how much was at stake—not just for us, but for Ruth. That evening, while Dana got the kids ready for bed, I phoned the director of the medical organization that was responsible for Ruth while she was here and asked about adopting.

"It's easy," said the director, who had Ruth's guardianship papers and visa. "All you have to do is renew Ruth's visa every six months while caring for her in your home. After two years, you can petition a local judge to adopt. You won't even have to go anywhere."

That did sound easy. "How much would it cost?" I feared the worst.

"Less than $1,000."

"That's it?"

"That's it."

I'd never heard of an adoption costing so little. Neither had Dana. "What are we waiting for?" he asked.

That week, I called Mandy, the director of Ruth's orphanage, who with her husband, Lukas, co-pastors Calvary Life Fellowship, a small nondenominational church in Brea, California. In 1995, their friend, Jackie Hodgkins, and a coworker, Janet, had left California for East Africa with basic firstaid training, the prayers of their church, and a dream of rescuing dying babies. More than one in ten Ugandan children are orphaned, having lost at least one parent, many to AIDS. In 2012, they numbered 2.7 million in a country of 36.5 million people that is smaller than Oregon, creating an orphan epidemic.[2] In a journal, which she later shared, Janet described how the women first went to Rwanda where they were robbed, beaten, and held at knifepoint by a mob on a night when neighboring aid workers were killed. It was one year after the genocide in which members of the Hutu majority slaughtered nearly a million of their Tutsi and moderate Hutu neighbors. In the bloody aftershock, rebels ravaged the countryside, targeting civilians. Bruised and terrified, Jackie and Janet fled north to Uganda, which is located between South Sudan and Rwanda. There they rented a four-bedroom house in the ramshackle tourist city of Jinja, near the source of the Nile River. Across the street, two nurses and one doctor cared for eighty patients at the area's only children's hospital.

Clotheslines laced the dirt courtyard. Mothers hovered over small fires, stirring pots of food to nourish their ill children. Windows were shattered. Concrete crumbled from ceilings. Electric wires snaked around ancient cast-iron beds in which children lay on bare metal frames. The rancid stink of human waste and smoke drifted through the open windows, making Janet want to vomit as she followed Jackie inside.

"We want to care for dying children," Jackie told the doctor.

"Here." He lifted an emaciated boy from a crib and laid him in the stout woman's arms. "Take this one. He is going to die anyway."

Nearly three, the boy weighed less than eleven pounds. His arms were as thin as Janet's thumb, so the women called him Tommy—after Tom Thumb—and brought him home. Within months, Jackie and Janet took in five more children. Three died, but Tommy thrived. In six months, he went from bony angles and scaly skin to round cheeks and softly padded arms and legs. One photograph shows him gleefully peddling a rusty red tricycle.

Over time, the women brought home more children—rocking, praying, and spooning gruel into slack mouths. Those who recovered returned to joyous families. If they didn't have families, they went to orphanages licensed for long-term care. The rest they wrapped in blankets and buried in the bone-littered cemetery at the edge of town. It was hard, heart-wrenching work, but it was why the women had come: in a country that then had the lowest life expectancy at birth in the world,[3] they sought "to love sick and dying babies back to health or into the arms of Jesus."

So, when a social worker asked Jackie whether she had room for a premature one-month-old from a Kampala hospital, Jackie brought her to Welcome Home and named her Ruth. One month later, Jackie returned to California for a brief holiday. While there, she was diagnosed with cancer so widespread that doctors couldn't tell where it had started. Lukas visited her in the hospital. As a pastor, he had experience with the dying, but never one like this.

"You need to send Mandy to Uganda," Jackie told him.

"Okay," Lukas said, supposing she meant for a brief visit. "Someday, I will."

"You're not getting it," Jackie insisted. "I want you to send Mandy to Uganda right now. I'm giving her the orphanage."

Two weeks after Jackie died, Mandy—an Australian-born nurse—boarded a plane to collect her inheritance: seventy-five infants and toddlers scattered between several cinder-block houses surrounded by concrete walls topped with jagged glass and razor wire. After moving them across town to a cheerful pink bungalow surrounded by gardens, Mandy worked with local authorities to keep the home open, raising money for improvements and hiring and training more staff. In September, after being elected by Welcome Home's board as the new director, Mandy prepared to return home to her husband, having promised to fly back to Uganda every six months—for one month each time—to oversee the home. But first, she asked the home's driver, William, to take her to a field on the outskirts of the city. There, amid bones exposed by rain and bleached white by the scorching sun, she buried the silver urn containing Jackie's ashes.

After hearing pieces of this story, I told Mandy that we were interested in adopting Ruth. Cautiously, she agreed to let us bring Ruth home on weekends to see what it would be like to care for her. Our children were thrilled. Dana hauled Lydia's old wooden high chair up from the basement, and the boys helped wipe it down. Meanwhile, I laid a fresh sheet in the wooden cradle in the corner of our bedroom. It was the same cradle in which I'd laid each of our children—the cradle my father had built for me. And even though I hadn't seen him in two decades, the tulip he'd cut in the headboard still made me feel loved.

Smoothing the calico sheet, I glanced up to see Lydia standing in my doorway, soft belly peeking below the bottom of her shirt. My heart dropped. If we adopted Ruth, I would lose a little of Lydia, and Lydia would lose a little of me. She would lose a little of my lap, a little of my hugs, a little of my good night songs, a little of my attention. And I would lose a little of this time rejoicing in the daughter I loved. But if we did nothing, Ruth would lose the most of all.

"Come see Mommy." I opened my arms.

Lydia hurtled across the room, ramming into me so hard I fell backward on the bed.

"Who's my girl?" I inhaled the soft, soapy scent of her.

"Me! Me!" Lydia squealed.

Judah I slowly weaned a few weeks before his first birthday, just like the books said, and we were miserable. He didn't understand my arbitrary rebuttals, and his sorrow afflicted us both. Gabriel I nursed until two. At eighteen months, Lydia showed no signs of stopping, but since our lives were about to get much more complicated and I might not have the energy to continue, I didn't resist when she blinked her big blueberry eyes and asked, "My juice?"

On a cold, clear Saturday in October, I backed our minivan out of the driveway. Judah and Gabriel played on the back hill, red jackets darting through the woods like cardinals. I hadn't resolved my conflict over wanting to protect Ruth and wanting to protect myself, but there wasn't much risk in one weekend—or so I told myself. Unlike when Dana had driven me to the hospital while I was in labor with Lydia, this time I drove myself. There were no bags to pack, no hand to hold, and the only baby was the one I was going to pick up.

"Judah, Gabriel, Lydia, and Ruth," I recited aloud, surprised by how right it sounded as the rhythm rolled off my tongue.

Like those of our children, Ruth's name was from the Bible. In the ancient Hebrew book by the same name, Ruth the Moabite lost her husband and traveled with her mother-in-law, Naomi, to a foreign country to live among strangers. Homeless and destitute, Ruth survived through the help of a wealthy neighbor, who fell in love with her and redeemed her through marriage. Would our Ruth's story end so happily? As I parked at the bottom of Allen and Theresa's steep driveway in nearby Topsham and walked up the hill toward their snug, clapboard home, I hoped so.

"Hi, Miss Meadow," said six-year-old Tiffany, straddling her bike by the garage, blonde ponytail snapping in the wind. "You here to get Ruthie?"

I nodded. "Yep."

"You gonna keep her?"

"Maybe."

"Why maybe?" She eyed me doubtfully as Theresa poked her head out the side door of the house and waved me inside.

"We're not sure yet if we can," I confided. "But if we do, you can come see her."

"When?"

"Anytime you want."

Tiffany grinned and coasted down the drive.

As soon as I stepped into Theresa's brightly painted kitchen, I smelled the tangy scent of cinnamon.

"Apples?" I sniffed, spying a large pot boiling on the back of the stove.

"We took little Miss Ruthie apple picking yesterday." Theresa pointed toward two bulging paper bags on the counter. "I'm making sauce. She loves it!"

Across the double room, Ruth lay on a blanket beside the doll I'd bought her.

"Hey, little Miss Ruthie." I imitated my friend's Southern lingo as I knelt beside her. "You ready for some fun?"

Ruth's cheek dimpled, but she didn't make a sound.

"What language do they speak in Uganda?" I asked, wondering whether Ruth understood English. If not, it might explain her lack of language.

"I don't know." Theresa packed Ruth's overnight bag at the kitchen table. "But come see this." She held out a can of infant formula, sounding out the words printed on the side. "*Nestlé Lactogen, maziwa ya ufuatilizi yenye iron.* What language do you think it is?"

I had no idea.

"It came in Ruth's bag." Theresa pointed to a brown and black backpack with a torn zipper as I joined her at the table. Ruth's name was printed in large, black letters on the front. "I'm saving it for whoever decides to adopt."

Curious, I pulled out several crumpled summer dresses followed by a rich burgundy gown with a white satin collar and pink rosettes. Beneath were two thickly woven blankets, one red and one white. Who had chosen them? Someone who cared—that was obvious.

Someone who wanted Ruth to be warm and well-loved when she arrived among strangers in a foreign land. Someone who hoped she'd be redeemed.

While Allen carried Ruth's bags and foam chair to my van, Theresa handed me a thick binder filled with travel documents, contact numbers, and instructions on everything from how to warm Ruth's bottle to how often to feed her. Then she zipped Ruth in a warm pink jacket, wiggled on her black patent-leather shoes, and placed her in my arms. I worried that she would cry, but Ruth didn't make a sound as I carried her down the driveway and buckled her in the van. Every few seconds on the ten-minute drive to Bath, I glanced in my rearview mirror.

I couldn't believe what I had back there. I just couldn't believe it.

Two dark eyes stared back at me all the way home.

4

Considering the Cost

"Come on, Ruth! Race you, Ruth!" Lydia rides an invisible horse beside her equally invisible sister.

I smile sadly, unable to ask who is winning.

"When I wake up in the morning," she later confides, "I lay in bed and do flashcards in my head so I can remember Ruth and all the things we did together."

It is the same trick I practiced at age ten after moving from my childhood farm to Maine, closing my eyes to walk through each room of our little yellow ranch so I wouldn't forget.

Losing someone you love is like moving to a new house, a house where they are not.

At lunch, I reach toward Ruth's place at the kitchen table, opening and closing my fingers as if to feel her own small hand. The memory is so strong that I almost can.

But what about when I cannot?

Or when Lydia no longer rides imaginary horses?

"Hey, Ruthie!" I sat on the worn living room carpet, jingling a dog-shaped rattle above her tightly coiled fist while Judah and Gabriel crouched beside me. "Hear the doggy? Hear the pretty doggy?"

Ruth's eyes lit up. Her arms jerked. But instead of opening, her fist squeezed tighter, sharp fingernails piercing the soft skin of her palm. I straightened Ruth's fingers and slipped the rattle inside, but she didn't seem to realize it was there.

"Now what?" I asked as Dana sat on the couch with Lydia, watching. Ruth had been with us for an hour and I was already running out of ideas.

"I know!" Judah popped to his feet, tucked his chin to his chest, and waddled around Ruth like a penguin as if channeling his own inner Charlie Chaplin.

Hee hee! Ruth expelled a sharp laugh.

Not to be outdone, Gabriel shook his hair, which poofed like a pom-pom as he flailed his arms and legs in a wiggly dance. It was a fearsome new form of sibling rivalry, a competition to see who could make Ruth laugh loudest. Gabriel won, thanks to his hair, which shimmered like sunshine.

"What about taking Ruth outside?" Dana glanced out the large window facing our backyard.

While the other kids scrambled into coats and boots, I threaded Ruth's rigid arms into her snug jacket and tugged on her shoes. She was lighter than Lydia but harder to hold because every part of her moved in a different direction. I struggled to balance Ruth on my hip. As I carried her down the hall toward the backdoor, her head curved backward toward her heels as if pulled by an invisible thread.

Bath is a vast riverbank of timeworn shipbuilders' houses tightly anchored above the swift-flowing Kennebec River, one of the longest and widest waterways in Maine. Like most homes in the neighborhood, ours was built on a ledge. It had grass when we bought the place, but seven winters of sledding and seven springs of mud boots had trampled every cheerful blade into extinction. Autumn sunlight dappled the bright canopy of trees overhead as our kids waded through an ocean of crisp, multicolored leaves, plunging beneath the surface like deep-sea divers. Dana took Ruth from my arms and buckled her into the red plastic swing hanging from a sturdy maple. Ruth slouched sideways, legs sticking straight out.

"Are you sure it's safe?" I asked as Dana pulled back the swing.

In answer, he let go. Ruth's eyes popped wide, and she shrieked, shiny black shoes rocketing past our heads.

"Too high!" I hollered. Then I saw her cheeks, which were taut with excitement. She loved it!

As Dana gave Ruth another push, Lydia and the boys tromped over, and we all stood with our chins pointing up, captivated by Ruth's astonishing joy. I could only imagine the freedom she felt, shooting toward the sky.

When it came time to eat, however, her struggles came crashing back to earth. "How did a baby from a children's home in a developing country get to be so picky about the temperature of her milk?" I asked Dana as he cradled Ruth on the couch, feeding her a carefully warmed bottle after lunch.

"Beats me." Dana shook his head.

With one arm he held Ruth's bottle. With the other, he gently supported her chin and cheeks while Ruth hungrily slurped milk and air. Give Ruth cold milk and she forced the nipple from her mouth. Lukewarm and she let it dribble down her chin. The temperature had to be exactly right: "Hot like coffee," as Theresa had carefully instructed, or Ruth refused to swallow.

Solid food wasn't any easier. Offer Ruth food she liked—sugary muffins, thickly buttered toast, pancakes dredged in maple syrup— and she mashed each morsel against the roof of her mouth until it dissolved. Offer her a food she didn't—nearly everything else—and she'd grit her teeth and grin. The "anti-Atkins" diet we jokingly called it. Unless it was a carbohydrate, Ruth wouldn't open her mouth. Feeding her one bottle took nearly an hour, after which she fell asleep, nipple drooping from her mouth. Small beads of sweat dotted her head from the effort. As Dana carried Ruth upstairs and gently laid her in the wooden cradle, I stood beside him, studying the high slope of her forehead, the tight curl of her lashes, the plump pout of her lips and wondered, as I had with each of my babies, what Ruth would look like when she grew up. Then I considered another question: "How will we know when she wakes up?"

Dana was as stumped as me. All morning, Ruth hadn't cried—a condition I'd read about with babies from orphan homes. With so many children to care for, the workers aren't always able to respond, and the children learn to stop crying. Was that the case with Ruth? As if in Jacob's ancient dream of the ladder from heaven, we ascended and descended our steep wooden stairs in an ethereal rotation. A couple of hours later, I discovered Ruth quietly staring at the ceiling. That was how we knew when Ruth woke up. That was the only way. Her eyes were open.

All weekend Dana and I watched our children for signs of jealousy. Perhaps because Ruth could not knock over the boys' rows of green army men or destroy their Legos or steal their stuffed animals, they adored her. Surprisingly—since they were the same age, and Ruth required our constant care and attention—so did Lydia, who heaped toys in this newcomer's lap and kissed her warm, brown cheeks.

Wherever we went—the boys' soccer practice, the neighborhood playground, our little church—we found ourselves surrounded by constellations of people asking where Ruth was from, what was wrong with her, and why she was with us. Planets could not resist her gravitational pull. When we said that we were thinking of adopting, some shook their heads as if we were crazy. Others called us angels. *Angels!* Crazy was more likely. Serving others comes hard for me. Like a flower planted in the sewer of selfishness, I am growing toward God. When it comes to putting the needs of others before my own, I struggle. Yet Christ asks his followers to love others unconditionally—the way that God loves us. This requires grace beyond my natural abilities. It also requires sacrifice.

By Sunday afternoon, Dana and I were exhausted. Sprawled on the living room floor, we watched our children skip and twirl to a song reverberating from the CD player. Ruth lay beside us, arms and legs crooked as a cricket, twitching to join in.

"Release me, O Lord, from everything that hinders me," folk artist Nancy Honeytree sang. "Release me, O Lord, and I will preach your word."

"Listen." I turned up the music as the chorus flowed around us. "This is Ruth's song. Maybe she'll be an ambassador."

Dana looked at me funny. "What do you mean?"

"I mean, maybe God sent Ruth here for a reason. Maybe she has a message to share."

Dana pulled himself from the floor and wrapped his strong hands around Ruth's chest, swinging her in time to the music. "You are going to preach, aren't you?" he said. "You are going back to Uganda someday, and you are going to preach. You are going to walk. You are going to talk."

"Do you really believe that?" I asked, hoping it was true.

Dana twirled Ruth's legs over the floor. "Absolutely."

If so, it would take a miracle. Fresh in my mind were the words of a pediatric neurologist who'd examined Ruth a couple of weeks before and proclaimed that she would be permanently stuck with the physical abilities of a two-month-old.

"That man is a liar!" Zachary had protested to Theresa, after hearing his words. "That man is lying about Ruth!"

I wanted to believe Zach. I wanted to believe that with therapy and love and prayer, Ruth would overcome her limitations. But there was no way to be certain, and the uncertainties were nagging.

The following weekend, Lydia and I picked up Ruth. While Dana watched the boys, I drove the girls downtown, past the cast-iron lampposts lining Bath's old-fashioned brick storefronts. The granite blocks of City Hall sparkled silver in the morning light as I parked on Front Street and tucked one girl, football-style, under each arm, and trudged up two impossibly long flights of stairs to the ballroom overlooking our small city. I imagined that shipbuilders' kids once trod these same stairs to practice the waltz and foxtrot in preparation for dances at nearby Morse High, but the group gathered today was visibly younger.

Preschoolers slid across the polished wood floor on well-padded rears and slippery-socked feet while their mothers chatted nearby. Sharon Pyne, with a gently lined face and streaks of silver in her soft-flowing hair, glided among them strumming a guitar. Both of our boys had attended Sharon's music playgroup and loved it. I hoped the pleasant rhythms would unlock a door in Ruth's brain—a door that would allow her to talk. Feeling self-conscious, I picked a spot on the colorful blanket spread on the floor and balanced one girl on each knee, trying to keep Ruth from falling off. Soon, we were surrounded by a squirming ring of children and parents. One curious tot peered at us from the safety of her mother's arms, and I smiled back before her mother steered her gaze away.

"Hel-lo, everybody. So glad to see you!" Sharon joined us with her guitar, leading the first song. "Hel-lo, everybody. So glad to see you too!" Going around the circle, she welcomed each child by name. "Hel-lo Abby, so glad to see you."

Encourage Ruth to respond to her name, I'd read a therapist's note in Ruth's big binder. *Speak her name with your voice while stroking her face until she turns her head.*

"Hel-lo, Lydia!" Sharon sang, causing shy Lydia to bury her face in my shirt. "So glad to see you!" Then it was Ruth's turn. "Hel-lo, Ruth! So glad to see you too!"

Nothing.

"Ruth," I spoke close to her ear.

Still nothing.

Surely at eighteen months Ruth should recognize her name.

"Ruth." This time I stroked her cheek, and the corners of Ruth's mouth turned up in a grin so big, my heart swelled with hope. Ruth would learn. She'd get it. Maybe she just needed more time.

Unfortunately, Ruth's visa expired in early January, three short months away, and I still didn't know whether adopting Ruth was the right decision. Dana had made up his mind. The kids had made up theirs. But I was plucking petals. Adopt her? Adopt her not. Adopt her? Adopt her not. One moment excited, the next terrified, until I was clutching a nearly empty stem.

"Sometimes I think we are meant to adopt her," I confided to Dana's eighty-six-year-old grandmother, Josephine, a soft peach of a woman who still played the organ every Sunday at the little Nazarene church thirty minutes up the river in the rural town of Richmond. "Other times I think it would be too hard."

"You might be right." She nodded, leaving me to wonder: *About which option?*

Our parents nudged us neither one way nor the other. My mom, in the States for a brief visit to speak at churches, stopped by on a drive up the coast but avoided telling us what to do. Dana's parents, who still lived forty minutes north in Nobleboro, brought Ruth gifts along with treats for our other children, but I noticed apprehension in his mother's eyes—the concern of one who had worked hard and sacrificed much to care for her own family.

The real test was Dana's grandfather.

"What do you think Grampy will say?" I asked Dana, cruising down Interstate 95 with all four kids in our van on a Saturday night to visit his grandparents, Ken and Betty, in South Portland.

"I told him we were bringing her." Dana frowned in the passing glow of a car's headlights. "He didn't say anything."

"About what?" Judah piped up from the back.

"Oh, nothing." I dismissed his question while recalling the Martin Luther King Jr. Day I'd first met Dana's grandparents. While sitting in their snug kitchen enjoying Nana's tasty ham sandwiches and macaroni salad, a news report celebrating the slain Civil Rights leader had come on the television booming in the front room.

"That man got what he deserved," Grampy griped.

The food stuck in my throat. "Everyone dies," I said, abandoning any hope of making a good impression. "At least that man died for something he believed in."

We'd finished eating in splintery silence. In the decade since, I'd learned to dodge Grampy's sometimes blistering barbs, but I worried he'd say something offensive about Ruth. From the time our children were little, Dana and I had educated them against racism.

"Name all the colors you see," I'd once instructed Judah, standing outside our local supermarket under a brilliant sky.

"Blue, white, green—" he began.

After he'd finished, I said, "Now imagine if God had made everything white—white clouds, white trees, white grass, white everything."

"That would be a lot of white," he responded.

"Exactly. That would be boring. Aren't you glad God made so many colors?"

Judah nodded.

"God was just as creative when he made people," I went on. "The Bible doesn't say what color the first man and woman were, but it says God made them in his own image. So who are people really insulting when they are mean or call someone names because of the color of their skin?"

Judah was stumped.

"God," I said. "They are insulting God."

As soon as Dana parked under his grandparents' sprawling chestnut tree, the boys raced up the steps to the house. Light spilled out around Nana. Tall and thin as a cornstalk, she smiled as she held open the front door. The boys darted under her arm to see whether she'd baked sugar cookies.

"Aren't those children cold?" Nana asked as I carried in Lydia, who'd fallen asleep. "It's the middle of October, and they aren't wearing jackets."

"They're used to it." I hugged Nana, making her hearing aid squeal.

The syrupy scent of baked beans and yeasty aroma of Nana's legendary fresh-baked rolls welcomed us inside. Dana followed with Ruth, who was also sleeping. The house was so warm I imagined wavy heat lines rising from the radiators. Dana laid Ruth on a recliner across the room from Grampy, who was stretched out on the sofa with his eyes closed. Five and a half feet tall and built like a barrel, he'd been in the hospital more times than I could count. Each time, we nervously wondered whether it would be his last, and each time he made it home.

"They say it's going to be a cold winter." Nana spoke loud enough to wake Lydia, who clung to my neck as we stood in the front room. "You're not afraid of your Nana!" she chided. "A big girl like you? My, but you've grown!" Nana hobbled around the mirrored coffee table to shake Grampy's shoulder. "You're not planning to sleep through Dana's visit, are you?"

"What?" His eyelids popped open.

"Dana and his family are here," Nana repeated as the boys appeared in the dining room doorway, golden crumbs clinging to their cheeks.

"I wasn't sleeping." Grampy lifted one swollen, diabetic leg and then the other to sit up. Then he looked across the room and saw Ruth, who was still curled up on the recliner, wide-eyed, looking around. "Who's that?"

"Ruth," Dana said.

"I know who that is." Grampy scowled. "I was asking her." Then he poked his tongue between his missing front teeth and let out a loud *Blaahhhh!*

"Kenneth!" Nana scolded.

"Can't I have fun?" Grampy poked out his tongue again.

I was ready to grab Ruth and march out the door, when suddenly she giggled.

"See! She thinks I'm funny!" Grampy grinned and slapped his gut. "Give her to me."

For the next twenty minutes Grampy bounced Ruth on his knee, smacking his lips, twitching his stubby eyebrows, and wrinkling his nearly bald head while peppering Dana with questions about Ruth.

"So tell me," Grampy demanded as Nana called us to dinner. "What happens if no one adopts her?"

"She'll go back to the orphanage," Dana said.

"Then what?"

"No one knows."

"No one knows!" Grampy bellowed. "What do you mean no one knows? Anyone can see she can't go back." His lips folded inward, and I thought he was going to cry. "I'll tell you what. You've got to keep her. That's what."

Of all the people who'd shared their opinions about Ruth, I never expected Dana's church-eschewing, eighth-grade educated, Coast Guard veteran, tattooed, former truck-driving grandfather to be the one person to insist we keep her. His blunt honesty cut through all my pious flimflamming. Still, I hesitated, afraid of what committing to Ruth would cost me.

Having once considered becoming a missionary, I'd imagined giving up my life to save hundreds or thousands. "But do you make this kind of sacrifice to save one?" I asked God during a rare moment alone while driving home after doing errands.

I left the ninety-nine to save one. The answer came to mind as clearly as if God were seated beside me. The parable of the lost lamb. I knew the story well. In Luke 15, Christ spoke of the shepherd with one hundred sheep who'd left them all to save the one in danger.

"But do you make this kind of sacrifice to save one *like this*?" I asked, knowing that Ruth might never walk or talk or even understand what we'd done for her.

I left the ninety-nine to save you, I heard.

My eyes filled with tears. There was nothing I could do to earn God's love either, nothing in me to merit the sacrifice that had redeemed my life. So how could I refuse to share his love with another? Slowly, surely, God was peeling back the protective layers around my heart so he could fill it with his love.

The third weekend I arrived to pick up Ruth, Theresa's eyes were red and puffy.

"What's wrong?" I asked, immediately concerned that something had happened to Ruth.

"My doctor called yesterday." Theresa sank into a kitchen chair, wiping her eyes as a cascade of black hair hid her face. "I had a test last summer. The result came back suspicious. A couple of weeks ago, I had more tests."

"And?" I sat beside her, afraid of what might come next.

"I have cancer."

The word filled the room. Theresa was my first friend to get cancer. She was so young. Her children were so young. I didn't know whether to give her a pep talk or wrap my arms around her and cry. Afraid to do or say the wrong thing, I did nothing.

"When my doctor called for more tests, I kind of knew." Theresa exhaled. "My mother had the same thing—cervical cancer—when she was my age."

"What's your doctor recommending?"

"A full hysterectomy. If they get it all, I can skip chemo."

"When?"

"November. I'll be in the hospital a couple days, then in bed for a week, but I won't be able to lift anything for a month."

"How will you take care of Ruth?"

"I haven't had time to think about it." Theresa's swollen eyes stared into mine.

"We could take her," I blurted. "If it will help you get better, Ruth can live with us."

Dana readily agreed. So did Mandy at Welcome Home and the medical aid organization that had brought Ruth here. A few days later, Allen, Theresa, and their four kids tromped up our porch steps with bags and boxes of Ruth's belongings. Our living room looked like a giant yard sale. Kids pried lids off plastic bins and pulled out toys while Ruth excitedly watched from her chair.

"When does Ruth have physical therapy?" I asked Theresa, flipping through her big black binder.

"It's been a couple of weeks," Theresa admitted. "There was some confusion, and the agency that was helping stopped sending someone. You might want to call them."

"Ready?" Allen scooped up busy little Daniel and smacked Dana on the back. "Holler if you need anything."

"Will I see her again?" Tiffany bent to kiss Ruth.

"You'll see her," Theresa promised.

Zach, burly and tall like his dad, stood near the door, hands in his pockets while ten-year-old Nathan playfully scrubbed Ruth on the head. "Bye, Little Miss Ruthie. Stay cool!"

As the kids and Dana followed Allen into the chill October dark, talking on the porch, Theresa lingered behind with me. "There's just one more thing," she said, standing near the door. "You should check Ruth's ears."

"Her ears?"

"Zach came home from school last week and blew his trumpet behind Ruth's head. I thought the noise would scare her. But Meadow—" Theresa held my arm. "Ruth didn't blink. We think she might not be able to hear."

Of course Ruth can hear, I thought, angry at the suggestion that anything else might be wrong. Didn't Ruth have enough to deal with? With four kids to get ready for bed, I quickly pushed the possibility from my mind. Dana fed Ruth her bottle, while I wrangled our remaining kids upstairs.

"Does this mean Ruth is our sister?" Judah asked as I tucked him into the upper bunk.

"She's your Jesus sister." I chose my words carefully, knowing that even if we decided to keep Ruth, we might not be able to. "We're all brothers and sisters in Jesus."

"When will she be our real sister?" Gabriel demanded from the bed below.

"It isn't just up to us," Dana explained, joining us after laying Ruth down. "There's still lots we need to figure out."

Down the hall, Lydia slept in her big-girl bed, a Beatrix Potter book open on her chest. She had fallen asleep while waiting for me. Feeling guilty, I kissed her cheek and closed the book. A few feet away, Ruth stared quietly upward in her crib beneath a snug fleece blanket.

"The desire of your heart." Dana pulled me against the warm flannel of his shirt.

I sighed. "If only she wasn't disabled."

"If she wasn't disabled we never would have met her."

The irony seemed so cruel.

"Good night, Little Miss Ruthie." I switched off the light.

A frightened wail pierced the dark.

Shhhh—I tried to calm her as I flipped on the light.

Ruth quieted down, but she didn't turn toward my voice.

5

A Jar of Faith

"How are you?" friends ask.

"It depends," I say, "on whether I'm focused on my regrets or the things I'm grateful for. But the hardest part is wanting to know where Ruth is."

Is the belief I've built my life around real?

Or is faith an antianxiety pill for the soul, a lie I've swallowed to keep from losing my mind?

Dana doesn't bother with such questions.

And I don't share them with our children.

Instead, I stand on our front deck one night and watch the half eclipse of the moon. I know it is still there, even though part is concealed by Earth's shadow.

Unseen is not the same as absent.

Object permanence—one of the first lessons learned by babies.

I struggle to grasp what most one-year-olds know.

Still, I am praying.

"Rooooooth!" I called each morning before lifting Ruth from her crib.

"Rooooooth!" I bellowed in the kitchen while washing dishes.

"Rooooooth!" I hollered as she lay on the living room floor surrounded by toys.

I stood just out of sight, clapping, singing, banging pots, and shouting while searching Ruth's face for the twitch of a smile, the lift of an eyebrow, for some sign that she'd heard. Sometimes Ruth smiled. Sometimes—even when the noise rattled the teacups in my grandmother's antique hutch—she didn't. I repeated this daily. Testing. Always testing. The kids did too, whooping and smacking their small hands until I'd cover my ears and shout, "Stop! You're hurting my ears!"

Then I'd start over.

One morning Ruth fell asleep on the floor while I was vacuuming. Seizing our heavy upright twenty-year-old Hoover with both hands, I pushed the rumbling vacuum right up to Ruth's toes, around the outstretched bud of her hand, in a halo around her head—all without waking her.

"Maybe Ruth's used to loud noises," I suggested to Dana that night at dinner. "Maybe at the orphanage there were so many, she learned to tune them out."

"Maybe," he said, but in the silence that followed I heard his doubt.

Since Ruth was no longer receiving physical therapy, I scheduled an evaluation for her with our local Child Development Services—the agency that identifies and treats developmental delays in Maine's youngest children. The Brunswick office adjoined an auto repair shop, as if fixing sputtering, broken-down children should be so simple. On the morning of Ruth's appointment, the stench of grease and exhaust followed us inside.

"I wasn't expecting such a crowd!" A caseworker stepped into the mirrored room where I sat holding Ruth on the floor while the boys dug through buckets of toys. Lydia curled against my knee like a kitten. "You kids have the day off from school?" she asked them.

"We're homeschooled!" Judah answered, clanging the keys of a plastic piano while Gabriel tried to tug it away.

I cringed, hoping she wouldn't ask why my second-grader was here, fighting over a toy, instead of at home practicing arithmetic. While I shot the boys a look to stop, a slender woman with stylishly cropped red hair squeezed through the door.

"Peggy," she said over the shrill jangle, holding out her hand. "The PT."

"PT?"

"The physical therapist."

We were joined by a blonde woman in jeans carrying a canvas tote overflowing with more toys.

"I'm Jan, the occupational therapist," she introduced herself and then reached for Ruth. "What a cutie! May I hold her?"

For the next hour, the two therapists sat on the floor, plying Ruth with toys—hiding a ball under a sheet of tissue paper, helping her push buttons, offering her the piano. While they gauged her responses,

I answered the caseworker's questions, ranging from where Ruth was born, which I knew, to who had pierced her ears, which I didn't.

Then Peggy turned over Ruth's left arm. "What's this?"

Two long jagged scars skipped up the underside of Ruth's skin from her wrist to her elbow.

"No one knows." I shook my head, having asked Theresa the same question. "Do you think she could've gotten them from an IV at the hospital when she was born? She was there for a month."

"Not likely." Peggy glanced uneasily at Jan.

The scars looked ugly. Cruel. Maybe even intentional. But who would hurt a baby? Like so many details about Ruth, the wounds remained a mystery—a part of Ruth's life that she could neither explain nor likely recall. Equally puzzling were the strange scallop-shaped grooves notching her baby teeth just below her gums, which looked like cavities but weren't. Could they be from nutritional deficiencies when Ruth's mother was pregnant? No one recognized their significance. Not the therapists. Not the local doctor who'd volunteered to treat Ruth. Not even the dentist who later repaired them. At the time, the indentations didn't seem important. I was more concerned about getting Ruth therapy. Peggy, Jan, and a speech therapist, Lisa, would come to our house in alternating pairs twice each week.

"Any more concerns?" The caseworker glanced up from her file as the kids grew bored, pestering me for a snack.

"Just one." Then I mentioned Ruth's hearing.

Jan suggested they try a simple test. "Do you mind waiting outside?" she asked.

Despite my desire to get going, I carried Lydia toward the door, followed by the boys. Snuggled in Peggy's lap, Ruth arched her neck to keep her eyes on me. I smiled, promising we'd be right back, and closed the door. A few minutes later, Jan ushered us back in. As soon as she saw me, Ruth squealed.

"Ruth is so alert that it's hard to tell what she's hearing and what she's picking up from environmental cues." The caseworker handed me a slip of paper with a name written on it. "So I'm referring you to an audiologist."

I shoved the paper in my pocket, unsure whether to feel grateful—because Ruth qualified for therapy—or worried because of what further tests might reveal.

&

....

In many ways, bringing Ruth home was like bringing home any new baby. Taking care of her took most of our time, and we were exhausted. Only, unlike with the arrivals of our other children, we had no time to prepare and Dana received no time off work. Getting through each day was a challenge. Some mornings the boys sat side by side at small wooden desks pulled close to the woodstove, or Judah wrote spelling words that I dictated while feeding Ruth her bottle. Other mornings, when Ruth pursed her lips like a fish and her tightly knotted fists cut through the air like an infant boxer and more milk ran down her chin than into her mouth, I sent the boys outside to play. Then there was Lydia, who got lost. Literally. One afternoon after laying Ruth down for a nap, I came downstairs to discover that my twenty-month-old daughter was gone.

"Lydia! Lydia!" I ran through the house, afraid that she'd wandered out the back door into the woods or down the porch stairs to our busy street. I found her curled behind an overstuffed chair in the living room, guzzling one of Ruth's half-finished bottles.

Even a simple trip to the library or post office became an exercise in frustration. Put Lydia down and she ran off. Put Ruth down and she couldn't sit up. Often I wanted to quit. But then I'd see Ruth, lying on the floor, swinging her stiff arms at a toy she could not reach, and I knew that quitting wasn't an option. So I quit everything else. I quit teaching Sunday school and visiting friends and going out with Dana. I quit exercising and walking to the playground with my kids. I let all the nonessentials go. I barely had time for the essentials: make breakfast, feed Ruth, clean up breakfast, math, grammar, spelling, start laundry, feed Ruth, drive Judah to public school for art and music and Spanish, pick up Judah, make lunch, feed Ruth, clean up lunch, read to the kids, history, science, finish laundry, snacks, feed Ruth, pop in a movie, make dinner, crash. And that was on a day when I didn't have a writing deadline or Ruth didn't have therapy.

Twice a week Peggy, Jan, or Lisa climbed our porch stairs with exercise balls, mirrors, and bags of toys. For Ruth, these hours were magic. She squealed when her new friends walked through our door, eager to see what they'd brought. The therapists' goals for Ruth were simple.

When looking in a mirror, she would smile to show she recognized herself. When holding two objects, she would drop one to reach for the other. When sung to, she would vocalize to indicate she wanted more. It felt good to have something on paper, as if Ruth would actually be able to do these things simply because someone had written them down.

"What do you call yourself?" Jan asked me on her first visit, blowing a string of bubbles.

"I'm sorry?"

Peggy stretched Ruth's arms toward a shiny orb. Slowly one tiny pointer finger uncurled while Lydia leaped through the air, light as a dancer, clapping bubble after bubble.

"When you talk about yourself to Ruth," Jan asked, "are you 'Meadow,' or 'Mom,' or do you go by something else?"

"I—uh—I don't know."

I didn't call myself anything in regard to Ruth. On the few occasions I took all four kids out together and needed to introduce them I said, "This is Judah and Gabriel and Lydia. And this is Ruth, who we are thinking of adopting," as if she was a prosthetic, an appendage attached to and yet not quite part of our family since there were no legal ligaments joining us together.

"'Mom,'" I said, uncertainly.

"Do you see Mom?" Jan asked Ruth, tapping her thumb to her chin with her fingers spread wide. "That's the sign for 'Mom,'" she turned to me. "It may help, since we don't how much Ruth is hearing. Mom," she repeated.

The word seemed dangerous, as if I'd opened a gate and didn't know what lurked on the other side. I was equally unprepared when Peggy suggested we get Ruth a wheelchair.

"She's not even two!" I protested, preferring to let Ruth explore the limits of her body unhindered on the floor, where she enjoyed scooting on her back while pushing with her legs.

"Why don't I bring a loaner?" Peggy said. "We'll see how Ruth likes it."

The following week, Peggy and Jan dropped a two-foot metal contraption in the middle of our living room. The kids crowded around, pulling straps and snapping buckles, but I was afraid that once Ruth was in a wheelchair, she'd need it, as if by some evil enchantment the chair would suck the potential from her already weakened limbs. Then she'd no longer be Ruth, the cute one-year-old who couldn't walk. She'd be disabled.

"Let's see how this fits." Peggy propped Ruth in the brightly padded chair while Jan pinned back her shoulders with a Velcro vest. A thick belt snaked around Ruth's middle. Side supports, like blinders on a horse, stuck out on each side of her head. Even Ruth's feet were strapped down. Only her hands fluttered free.

"What do you think?" Jan stepped back and smiled.

I thought I wanted to rip Ruth out of there, but Judah grinned.

"Look, Mom!" he said. "Ruth's sitting up just like a regular kid!"

Then I saw what Judah did. Not the chair, but Ruth smiling and sitting upright and on her own for the first time.

The chair stayed.

Despite her limitations, Ruth fit right into our family, shrieking gleefully when Dana tucked her under his arm to chase the kids around the yard in a game of tag or when he wrestled with them on the floor, carefully supporting her head. Our kids invented their own ways of playing with Ruth. If Judah spotted Ruth sitting in her high chair, he would lean forward until she tapped his cheek. Then he'd topple to the floor like a drunken sailor before popping back up so she could do it again. When we pushed Ruth in the backyard swing, Gabriel would spring up beneath her, just out of reach, as she shot through the air. And at night, I often found Lydia snuggled up beside Ruth in her crib.

Even I was getting the hang of things. One Saturday morning, while Dana helped coach Judah's soccer team with Gabriel in tow, I gamely buckled the girls in the van and drove to our local grocery store. After climbing out of the van, I tucked Ruth in a fabric sling. Beside me, Lydia carried Ruth's brown baby doll, which she'd dubbed "Ruffie." Catching our reflection in the sliding glass doors, I laughed. So what if I couldn't reach half the items on my grocery list, maybe we *could* do this, I thought, enjoying the curious looks on the other shoppers' faces. On another weekend, I excavated the double stroller from our garage and plopped the girls inside—one blonde head sturdily upright, one black slumped to the side.

"Are they both yours?" a neighbor asked, raking leaves as we rattled down the street.

"They're twins," I answered, savoring her expression as I rounded the bend.

Dana later suggested adding, "You should have seen the look on the doctor's face."

In November, he took a morning off work to watch our kids so I could drive Ruth to the audiologist, thirty minutes south in Yarmouth.

"What's this little bump here?" Dr. Lisa Klop asked, touching a knob of skin beside Ruth's left ear as I steadied her on my lap.

"I don't know," I said, having noticed the odd bump before. "Is it important?"

"Maybe. We often see these in children with hearing loss. Or it could be nothing. Let's get started."

In a soundproof room down the hall, I buckled Ruth into a high chair while Dr. Klop sat in an adjoining room behind a darkened window. *Ah-Ah-Ahhh—Ah-Ah-Ahhh*, she breathed into a microphone while an assistant sat beside Ruth, watching her reaction. *AH-AH-AHHH!*

Ruth's head jerked forward. Had she heard? Her lack of physical control made it hard to tell. After thirty minutes, Dr. Klop suggested an additional test, for which Ruth needed to be asleep. Commonly performed on newborns in American hospitals, the otoacoustic emissions test gauges how well the inner ear echoes back sound. I held Ruth in the darkened room, softly singing until her curly lashes fluttered closed. Then Dr. Klop twisted a rubber plug into Ruth's ear and connected the attached wire to a computer. Thankfully, Ruth was a sound sleeper. After a few minutes, Dr. Klop repeated the test on Ruth's other ear.

"Here's what we know," she said in her office after it was over. "Ruth failed the test. Her hearing loss could be minor, or it could be serious. To find out, she needs a test that's performed under general anesthesia in a hospital. I know this is difficult news. Would you like the name of a counselor?"

"That's okay." I held Ruth tighter. "If Ruth can't hear very well, that explains why she's not talking. Once we know what's wrong, maybe we can fix it."

Dana was equally optimistic, but first we had to figure out how to keep Ruth here. I called Mandy, hoping that we could extend Ruth's visa for up to two years while we decided whether to adopt, the way we'd been instructed.

"No way," Mandy firmly replied. "It's too risky. The government could change the rules and send Ruth home at any time. If your family is serious about adopting, you need to hire an agency and figure out how. If not, Ruth returns to Uganda in January as planned."

"But that's in six weeks," I protested. "What about Ruth's hearing test?"

"I'm more worried about her emotions," Mandy said. "This little girl has already lost her mother, her foster mother, and the only real home she's ever known. I don't want her getting attached and losing you too. If you decide to adopt, I'll help you extend Ruth's visa until July so that you can put together a plan. But I have to warn you, because of concerns about child trafficking and not wanting to lose their young people to foreign countries, adoption isn't really part of the Ugandan culture. That's one reason we've never done a proper adoption before, but I've been talking with Peter, our lawyer in Kampala. To adopt, it turns out that you must first live in Uganda for three years while fostering a child."

"Three years!" I leaned against the kitchen wall, clutching the phone with both hands. Here I thought we could play it safe and protect Ruth while also protecting ourselves. Now I saw how wrong I'd been.

"The government may make an exception because of Ruth's medical needs," she went on. "To find out, you and Dana will need to bring Ruth back to Uganda and go to court. Everything needs to be done by the book. If you succeed, it may open the door for other children to be adopted."

After getting off the phone, I talked it over with Dana. "What should we do?"

"Call an adoption agency," he said. "We might as well find out what it would cost."

The following morning I phoned the Maine agency that had posted Ruth's picture on its website.

"You need to think very seriously before adopting a child with disabilities," cautioned the director. "Why don't you look at photos of other children on our site? We have many who need homes. There's no reason you should feel the need to adopt this one."

"We aren't interested in adopting any child," I said. "We are interested in adopting Ruth. Can you help?"

"We could do your home study."

"Home study?"

"Every family that adopts has to have a home study. A social worker has to interview you. You have to be approved."

"How much will it cost?" I asked.

"Through us? Two thousand five hundred dollars, which includes putting together your dossier."

"Our what?" My ribs seemed to constrict.

"Your family file. Birth certificates. Marriage licenses. Criminal background checks. That sort of thing. You'll need to present it when you go to court. Where is Ruth from again?"

"Uganda."

"Oh! Well, that's different." For a moment I began to hope, and then she said, "We don't work in Uganda. No agencies do."

International adoptions, I learned, are governed by the Hague Convention on Intercountry Adoption, which lays down rules to protect children, birth parents, and adoptive parents from child trafficking and abuse. Licensed adoption agencies typically work only with countries that have ratified the convention. At the time, sixty-eight countries had done so. Uganda wasn't one of them. Why the agency had posted Ruth's photo, I didn't know, but I wasn't ready to give up.

"What can we do?" I asked.

"If I were you, I'd hire myself one really good lawyer." She gave me the name of an adoption attorney near Portland.

I jotted down her name, fearing the cost.

"Two hundred dollars an hour," the attorney said.

Because of Ruth's disabilities, however, the lawyer offered to cut her fee in half. Still, this added $3,000 on top of our home study, anticipated travel expenses, and needing to hire an additional lawyer—Peter in Uganda. In one week, our projected adoption costs had rocketed from $1,000 to a whopping $15,000. That night, Dana and I held a convention of our own around the dining room table.

"Maybe this is the answer we've been praying for," I suggested weakly. "Maybe we're not meant to adopt Ruth after all."

"What are you suggesting?" Dana tipped back in his chair. "That we just let Ruth go?"

"We can't abandon Ruth," Judah protested. "She's already been abandoned."

"Maybe we could sponsor her." I glanced at Ruth, slumped in her high chair at the end of the table, oblivious to how our conversation would affect her. "You know, pay the orphanage or someone in Uganda to take care of her."

It sounded feeble, even to me.

"Please, can we adopt Ruth?" Gabriel squeezed his small hands together while Lydia played nearby.

"Adoptions cost money," I explained. "And we don't have the kind it takes."

Without a word, Gabriel, who'd just turned five, scooted off his chair and disappeared down the still-unfinished back hall. A few minutes later he returned holding a mayonnaise jar of coins he and Judah had been saving to buy a dog.

"We have this money," he said.

Dana's eyes widened. "You want to spend your money to adopt Ruth instead of buying a puppy?"

Gabriel nodded.

Judah grinned. Jumping up, he raced upstairs to their room. A minute later, he was back, waving two crumpled bills that he stuffed in the jar. "And this!"

"Are you sure?" Dana asked.

Two small heads bobbed. Dana poured the money on the table, sorting pennies, nickels, dimes, and quarters. It came to around five dollars. Then I got an idea.

"There's that antique bedroom set that was my grandmother's," I said. "We could sell it. And with Christmas coming up, we could raise money at craft fairs."

"Then we could adopt Ruth?" Judah leaned forward. Our children were Ruth's biggest advocates, always eager to help, hold, and cheer her on. "Then Ruth would be our sister?"

Dana and I looked at each other. Wasn't this the love Christ talked about?

"We can try," Dana said. "The rest is up to God."

6

A Raw, Choking Wail

"Be still and know," you say.
But I question everything I thought I knew.
I blame myself for letting Ruth down.
For letting you down.
How easily shattered life is.
One test,
or phone call,
or slip can steal it away.
Her life was literally in my hands.
Limbs stiff,
heart hard-beating.
I have never felt so fallen,
so in need of grace.
Be near, O God.
Be near, O God.
Be near, O God, to me.

Rally 'round Ruth. I taped a sign to a sawhorse table in the gymnasium at Fisher-Mitchell Elementary School just down the street from our house early one Saturday before Thanksgiving. *Donations welcome. All proceeds benefit a special-needs adoption.*

Christmas carols streamed over the public address system while I set up for our first fund-raiser. Down the long rows of tables, crafters hauled cases of hand-knitted mittens, button-eyed dolls, jars of jam, chunks of fragrant soap, and trays of homemade treats across the basketball court. I unpacked a framed photo of Ruth, shot by a photographer friend, Jackie, the night before, and set it beneath a three-foot plastic Christmas tree I'd bought from the drugstore. Beside it, I filled a basket with Marys, Josephs, and wise men—an entire pageant of olive-wood ornaments that my mother had mailed from Israel. We'd bought five hundred—at about thirty cents each—plus a hand-carved nativity to raffle, hoping that people would be generous. After all, it was nearly Christmas.

One thing was certain. To adopt Ruth, Dana and I couldn't borrow money. With me freelancing and him working for a small Maine company, our family walked a tight financial rope. If God truly wanted Ruth to join our family, then we had to trust him to provide. So there I sat, vinyl money bag at the ready, as the first shoppers straggled through the open doors.

"How much?" A silver-haired woman stood at a distance, eyeing the ornaments.

"A donation." I pointed to the sign. "We're raising money to adopt an abandoned baby from Uganda. She has cerebral palsy."

"Oh, well, I wouldn't know." The woman frowned and kept walking.

Soon after, two more ladies stopped and asked the same question.

"A dollar?" I suggested hopefully.

They promised to come back later.

As the hands on the clock above the basketball hoop circled the hour, I hung more ornaments on the tree and arranged a row of plastic gift bags—each containing six of the most beautiful pieces—at the front of the table. Within minutes, a girl with fat black braids sprinted over, followed by her mother.

"Look, Mommy!" the girl, who looked around nine, said as she dug through the basket. "Aren't these pretty?"

"They're olive wood, from Israel," I jumped in, encouraged by her enthusiasm. "We're raising money for a special-needs adoption."

"Can we buy some? Please?" the girl begged as Mary on her donkey dangled between her fingers.

"You really want that?" Her mother pulled a stick of gum from her purse and wove it into her mouth.

"We could paint them." The girl's black braids bobbed.

Paint them! I bit my tongue.

"What are you asking?" the woman asked.

"A donation." I forced a smile. "Every bit helps."

The woman dug through her purse again, this time pulling out a green folded bill. When she placed it in my hand, I smiled, seeing that it was a five. "Thank you!"

Only, instead of picking a single ornament, the mother grabbed two plastic bags—twelve ornaments all together—and stuffed them in her purse before strutting across the gym after her delighted daughter. I wanted to chase after them and demand that they give the ornaments back. Instead, I picked up a pen, turned over our sign, and wrote *Christmas ornaments: $2 each or one bag for $10* before sitting back to seethe.

Six hours later, as the fair was winding down, I was relieved to see Dana pushing our double stroller with Lydia and Ruth across the gym. Floppy-haired Gabriel danced along beside them, while Judah raced off to check out the tail end of a book sale.

"How much did we get?" Gabriel asked as he slipped behind the table and eyed my money bag.

I unzipped the pouch and sorted bills on my lap while a small crowd gathered around Dana and the girls—clearly the feature attraction I'd been missing. "Eighty-five, eighty-six, eighty-seven dollars," I counted. "Plus change."

"Wow!" Gabriel's eyes widened.

I didn't have the heart to tell him that after subtracting our expenses, we were more than two hundred dollars in the negative.

"Why don't you take these for your fund-raiser?" Julie, a member of the school's parent-teacher association, stopped by with a bulging garbage bag of soda cans as vendors began to pack up.

"Thanks," I said.

It looked like we were going to need all the help we could get.

The following weekend, Dana removed the seats from our minivan and loaded in my grandmother's seven-piece, early nineteenth-century cottage bedroom set—the one hand-stenciled by my grandfather. I'd been storing the two twin beds and matching bureau, blanket chest, bedside table, writing desk, and chair to use in a guest room since the summer I was eleven. One year prior, Mom had sold our Oregon farm and driven my brother and me—along with our short-haired collie, Halo, and two lovebirds—three thousand miles across the country to live with her mother, Ginny, who was alone in Maine and dying of cancer. My grandfather, Spencer, who had once taught me the foxtrot by dancing me down the hall to bed, had died of a heart attack a couple of summers before. Living clear across the country, I hadn't spent much time with either of them. Mom, who was in her early thirties, had just graduated from the University of Oregon. Despite her love of farming, she felt God calling her to move back home to care for her mother. "Everyone who has given up house or brothers or sisters or mother or father or children or property for my sake and for the Good News will receive now in return a hundred times as many," she read Jesus' words aloud to us from Mark 10:29–30, explaining her decision. And so she left her fields.

For nine months, we lived in my grandmother's elegant house overlooking the bold Atlantic Ocean. An accomplished pianist and artist who'd once shown her work in the nearby Ogunquit Barn Gallery, my grandmother taught me to play backgammon, made me grilled cheese and tomato sandwiches, and lay on the couch in the den calling out the answers to game shows. Mom drove her to appointments, massaged her feet, and shared the love of Jesus. The following spring, one week before dying, my grandmother declared her faith in Christ, rasping from her hospital bed, "That one you believe in? I believe in him too." This was the reward my mother had been seeking.

Sorting through my grandmother's belongings, Mom asked what I wanted to keep. Unwilling to let another precious thing slip from my grasp, I wanted it all, but I'd settled on the bedroom set.

"I'd never sell," I'd confided to the antique dealer who'd come to make an offer, standing beside me in the dim light of our shed, "but we're raising money to adopt a baby with disabilities from Uganda."

The woman ran her hand over a bed's round finial. "Twelve hundred."

I hesitated. "Is that the most you can offer?"

"Beds are hard to sell," she said. "Take it or leave it."

I took it. Later, strolling past the dealer's downtown storefront, I spotted the writing desk in the window. The sales tag looped over the knob said $650, and that was without the chair.

To pay for our home study, I cashed in a straggling retirement fund and appealed to family and friends, who gave generously. Meanwhile, Dana took a second job, pacing the aisles of a warehouse in nearby Freeport to fill Christmas orders with thousands of other seasonal employees. After racing home from his day job, he had just enough time to scarf down dinner and sprint off to work again, stumbling home between 12:00 and 2:00 a.m. before rising several hours later to rush back to work.

"You know you are broke," I said one night, only half joking while serving dinner, "when you have to split two hot dogs between three kids."

Luckily, Ruth wouldn't yet eat hot dogs, so I scooped her extra homemade macaroni and cheese—a favorite.

When friends asked how we were doing, I took a deep breath. "Okay," I said. "We're doing okay." But I felt like a turtle being slowly crushed by the weight of the load on its back. Mornings were madness. Dana stumbled out of bed with deep pockets under his eyes. I awoke, not wanting to wake at all. Clothes matched by chance. Pajamas lay crumpled on bedroom floors. "Bath time" was whatever time anyone happened to take one. Kids slept in what they were wearing or in nothing at all. And despite a month of therapy, Ruth remained physically trapped at two months old, just as the neurologist predicted. The more Ruth wanted something, the more rigid she became, tightening her fingers instead of opening them. To help Ruth make choices, Lisa, her speech therapist, took photos of household objects that we attached to a Plexiglas rectangle with Velcro dots, but the process was achingly slow. Maybe adopting was too hard after all.

"Do you think it's worth it?" I asked Dana when he arrived home from work in the wee hours of the morning to find me still awake in bed.

"My second job only lasts until Christmas." He pulled back the quilt and climbed in beside me.

"I'm not talking about the job." I sat up. "I'm talking about the stress, the medical appointments, the lack of money, the all-out effort to get through each day. Do you realize how much adopting Ruth has cost us?"

"A few thousand?" He pulled up the covers and closed his eyes.

"Everything," I answered, staring into the dark.

One night that December, I sank into bed beside Lydia, so tired from carrying Ruth that I wished someone would carry me.

"Dis one." Lydia pushed a lift-the-flap version of the Christmas story onto my lap as Ruth slept a few feet away in her crib, arms outstretched, hands relaxed. Asleep, she looked perfectly healthy. Yet, as soon as she woke up, her joints would stiffen. Without continued therapy, this would lead to contractures that would permanently lock her arms and legs in painful positions, making movement impossible.

Ruth was also growing more attached to our family, just like Mama Mandy had said, crying now when I left to go somewhere and didn't bring her too. What were we to do? I sighed and turned to the first page of the book.

"Long ago, in a city of Galilee called Nazareth, there lived a young woman, and the woman's name was Mary," I read, pointing to the people on each page. "That's the angel and that's Mary. There's Joseph and these are the shepherds." On the last page, I pointed to the baby lying in the manger. "And that's Jesus."

"No," Lydia, not yet two, shook her head and touched the picture. "Dat's Ruffie."

In her words I heard an ancient echo from Matthew 25:

> *"For I was hungry, and you gave Me something to eat," Jesus said. "I was thirsty, and you gave Me drink; I was a stranger, and you invited Me in; naked, and you clothed me; I was sick, and you visited me."*
>
> *"When?" the people asked.*
>
> *"Truly I say to you," Jesus answered, "to the extent that you did it to one of these brothers of Mine, even the least of them, you did it to Me."*

One day, Dana and I would stand before God and answer for how we treated the people he brought into our lives. The hungry. The stranger. The poor. The sick. This was the greatest truth that mattered. And it took my twenty-one-month-old daughter to remind me.

Mandy thought our trip to Uganda could be brief, just enough time to petition a judge to become Ruth's legal guardians and get permission to take her back to the United States. Then, after a brief trip to Nairobi where her visa needed to be finalized, we would complete her adoption in Maine. So far, most of Ruth's medical care had been donated, but no one was lined up to provide the additional $3,000 test that would tell us what she could hear and what she couldn't.

"Leave it to me," offered Tracey, who often climbed our porch steps with steaming boxes of pizza, bags of battery-operated toys that Ruth could activate with the swing of a fist, and jumbo cases of diapers. For three weekends that January, she even watched our children so that Dana and I could complete the extensive interview process to be approved as adoptive parents. Tracey's generosity was not lost on me. While Scripture commands that we protect widows and orphans, even placing a curse on those who don't, here was a widow caring for orphans.

By February, Tracey had enlisted Maine Medical Center, the state's largest hospital, and a team of specialists to administer Ruth's hearing test for free. Meanwhile, I posted fliers and collected raffle donations for our biggest fund-raiser yet: a dessert and family folk dance at Sharon Pyne's music studio. The first week of March, I baked cookies, brownies, and cakes. Then, on the day of the big event, disaster descended in the form of the biggest snowstorm of the season. One hour before the dance, fat flakes plunged to the ground. The roads were solid white, our windshield a slippery smear as we coasted downtown and parked on the mostly deserted street. After hauling boxes up the two flights of stairs, I peered out a window from the dance hall to the parking lot below. Streetlamps revealed white lumps that I knew to be cars. I imagined their owners shrugging off heavy jackets in the surrounding second-floor apartments, heating hands over hot radiators, going nowhere.

"What if no one comes?" I asked Dana, who was busy unfolding metal chairs with Judah and Gabriel.

"They'll come," he said.

Hoping he was right, I set out raffle items and desserts. Lydia twirled across the ballroom like a storm-tossed leaf in the holly-green dress that I had sewn her for Christmas, while Ruth, enveloped in a cloud of matching berry-red tulle, watched from her specialized foam chair. And I prayed the snow would stop.

It didn't.

Fifteen minutes before the dance was to start, Sharon and her piano-playing husband, Doug Protsik, tromped up the stairs. Their accordion-, fiddle-, and pennywhistle-playing friends soon followed, trailing small glaciers of snow. They gathered around the piano, blowing hands, coaxing strings. And still the flakes kept falling.

As the minute hand on the clock above the door ticked past 7:00, we were the only family there. *We might as well go home,* I thought as Gabriel pushed Ruth around the room in her chair, chasing Lydia like a musher pursuing prey. Their happy screams filled the hall while Judah eyed the desserts, but I was growing more miserable by the moment, sure that our best efforts had failed. Then the thump of boots sounded on the stairs. A moment later, Ron and Mona—volunteer firefighters from our church who lived all the way down the long, isolated peninsula of Harpswell—lumbered through the door.

"Sorry we're late!" Mona unzipped her jacket and threw her arms around me in a hug. "You should see the roads!"

Mustache hung with icicles, Ron dropped a bundle of bills in the basket by the door. Soon, two more church families, the Evans and Smiths, bustled into the hall with their children, exclaiming, "Weren't sure we'd make it!" "Where's Ruth?" and "You sure picked a night!"

Close on their heels followed our pastor, Rev. Dana Lindsey, and his wife, Lynne, and then Jackie, who had snapped Ruth's picture for our fund-raiser, carrying an enormous framed photo of the Paul Revere bell atop City Hall to add to the raffle.

"You made it!" I gasped, amazed at how many people from our little nondenominational church were here. "I'm so glad to see you!"

As I greeted people, an arm wrapped around my shoulder. I looked up to see a dazzling smile half-hidden by long black hair.

"Theresa!" I cried.

"Didn't think we'd miss all the fun, did ya?" my friend asked as Allen and their kids fanned out around us.

Now strong and healthy, Theresa was cancer free—a gift as great as the love sparkling in her beautiful brown eyes.

Gritty as snowplows, people pushed in from the furthest corners of our community, braving slick roads and deep winter dark. Some Dana and I recognized. Some we didn't. With each arrival, Ruth squealed, as if aware each and every one was there for her. Lisa, Ruth's speech therapist, scooped her up for the first dance. A bow slid across a string, and a storm was stopped by the feet of many dogged dancers.

"I danced all night! I danced all night!" Lydia gleefully exclaimed as we carried her up the stairs to bed four hours later. Ruth, who was already asleep, had made the rounds thanks to many eager arms. And we were nearly $2,000 closer to our goal.

Two weeks later, I cradled Ruth, dressed in a cotton Johnny small enough to fit a doll, on my lap in a drab waiting room at Maine Medical Center's Brighton Avenue campus. Her fuzzy yellow hospital socks bunched around her ankles, and she stared at me, dark eyes questioning as an anesthesiologist squirted bubble-gum-scented goo around a clear rubber mask and held it to her face, checking the size.

"It's okay." I rocked her on the bed, humming a lullaby if only to soothe my own anxious heart. "Mommy's right here."

None of my kids had ever been sedated, and I wasn't sure what to expect. The procedure, an auditory brainstem response test, was noninvasive but required Ruth to be absolutely still and make no noise, thus the anesthesiologist.

"Ruth?" A nurse poked her head behind the curtain a few minutes later.

I nodded.

"Follow me," she said.

I carried Ruth through a pair of double doors and down an empty corridor, turning left and right and left so many times that I lost track, ending in a sterile room where several nurses stood waiting. White walls. White floor. White sheet on a gleaming metal bed. Gently, I laid Ruth down, her body so tense that her skinny legs stuck straight up. Ruth's eyes darted wildly as the nurses gathered around, taping electrodes to her head.

Shhhh. I cupped Ruth's fist with my hand, bending down to brush her cheek with my lips. "Relax."

As the anesthesiologist held the mask above Ruth's nose and mouth, her eyes locked on mine and a bitter mist enveloped us both.

"You're okay." I stroked her hair. "Everything's gonna be okay."

Ruth's eyes glazed over. Her legs dropped, and her arm went limp. She was so tiny, her toes barely reached the middle of the bed.

"Okay, Mom. Time for you to go." A nurse pointed toward the door. "Can you find your way out?"

I nodded, not wanting to leave but knowing I had to. Right. Left. Right. Pain throbbed behind my eyes and in my heart as I zigzagged my way to the waiting room, overwhelmed with worry. Through all the weeks of caring for Ruth, I had stationed guards around my heart, knowing we might not be able to keep her. Now, I realized that the guards were gone. I loved Ruth, more than I meant to. I loved her in spite of what loving her would cost me. And this made me afraid for her as well as for myself.

For the next hour, I sat in the waiting room while a computer shot bullets of sound into Ruth's brain, measuring how her cochlea— the tiny, snail-shaped part of her inner ear—responded. When the audiologist, Bethany, finally called my name, I tripped over my bag in my eagerness to find out. Down the hall in an empty conference room, she closed the door and picked up a dry erase marker, drawing undulating lines across a giant whiteboard, one wave above another with corresponding sound frequencies.

"We tried this. And this. And this." Bethany pointed to the lines one by one. "Our equipment didn't pick up any response."

"What do you mean?" I asked.

"I mean." Bethany paused. "Ruth is profoundly deaf. She can't hear a thing."

"Can we fix it?"

She shook her head. "Either the tiny hairs in her inner ear aren't working, or they aren't there at all."

I heard Ruth before I saw her. A raw, choking wail echoed down the corridor as a nurse led me to her room. Tangled in a jumble of tubes and wires, Ruth lay in a metal crib. Needles poked through the thin skin on the back of her hand. Her eyes were clenched clam tight, and she was screaming. Tears streamed down my cheeks and onto Ruth's as the nurse placed her, still wailing, in my arms. I nuzzled her hair, her cheek, her neck, but Ruth kept screaming.

"It's okay. It's okay. It's okay," I whispered over and over.

But it didn't make any difference.

Ruth couldn't hear my words.

7

Reservations and Preparations

This grief is too heavy.
It buries me like a mountain with its deep, dark weight.
I failed to see the signs, to recognize
that something was wrong.
No sorrow can change it.
No words can bring her back.
I am alone with my responsibility and my regret.
Do not tell me how lucky Ruth was to have us.
Do not tell me what a good job we did.
Don't muffle my agony with well-meaning words.
Dig down deep to where I am.
Show me love in a place where words no longer matter.

"How'd it go?" Dana raced down the porch steps to meet us in the driveway as soon as Ruth and I arrived home.

"She can't hear," I said.

"Nothing?" He looked as shocked as I felt.

"Nothing." I walked up the stairs, through the front door, up more stairs to our room, slammed the door, and collapsed on the bed, pulling up the covers.

All my hopes for Ruth were shattered by one word: *deaf.* Face toward the wall, I burrowed beneath the swell of blankets as gale-force sobs bent my body in two. When I could no longer cry, I stared out the window, watching our children run through the woods, waving sticks and shouting. Ruth was not with them. And I realized that Ruth would never be with them. Never run. Never shout her siblings' names. I hadn't questioned why God had allowed Ruth to have cerebral palsy or why she'd been abandoned. That was how we'd met her. But how could he have also allowed her to be deaf? The combination was devastating.

"Meadow?" Dana called through our door. When I didn't answer, he opened it anyway. Footsteps crossed the floor, and the edge of the bed dipped down as he sat beside me. "Ruth's asleep. I fed her a bottle. Do you want anything?"

"I want Ruth to hear." I refused to look at him, as if he were to blame. "I want her to run. I want her to sneak out her bedroom window when she turns sixteen to meet a boyfriend."

"So do I." He stroked my hair. "So do I."

Finding out Ruth was deaf was like an amputation. Part of her was cut off from me. My shock was so severe that I no longer spoke when lifting Ruth from her crib each morning, no longer read aloud when turning the pages of a book. I made funny faces or sad ones and offered toys and food without making a sound. For months I stopped talking to neighborhood cats and dogs and to friends' babies in the bizarre belief that they all must be deaf too.

Not so our children, who accepted Ruth's deafness the way they accepted everything in their rapidly changing lives. One day they were sledding through our woods dodging snowcapped rocks and trees. The next, they were turning over logs in search of salamanders. One day we were convinced Ruth could hear. The next we knew with devastating certainty that she could not. Judah still clowned around. Gabriel still danced. Lydia still heaped toys in Ruth's lap, and Ruth still shrieked with joy. Only now we knew that she couldn't hear the sound ringing from her own throat.

"Is she blind?" Strangers stopped us on the street, in the library, at the playground as Ruth's left eye quivered on its seemingly cosmic course toward her nose.

"Her eyes are fine," I snapped.

Tired of other people's unceasing curiosity, I kept everything that was wrong with Ruth to myself. Yet, far from tempting me to reject her, this new vulnerability—hers and mine—made me want to love and protect her all the more. Having filed preliminary papers at our local courthouse declaring our intention to adopt, we added Ruth to our health insurance. Soon after, I scheduled an appointment with a Portland ophthalmologist who surgically tightened the muscles in Ruth's wandering eye, a condition called strabismus. After a couple of weeks wearing a pirate patch, her eyes moved together. Next, Dr. Klop fitted her with hearing aids.

"These may allow Ruth to detect the presence of certain sounds," Dr. Klop said, twisting a pink plastic mold into Ruth's ear.

"Speech?" I asked.

"Fire engines," she said. "Lawn mowers."

In April I loaded all four kids in the van and drove to the Maine Educational Center for the Deaf and Hard of Hearing, forty minutes south on Mackworth Island. While I sat on the floor of the infant and toddler room with Ruth in my lap, the children around us waved their hands and fingers in the most animated rendition of "Old MacDonald Had a Farm" I'd ever seen. The effect was startling and beautiful, but I had never seen Ruth's hands move like that. How would she preach now?

She will preach if she never speaks a word, the answer came tenderly to my heart. Would God heal Ruth? I'd often asked him too—sometimes shouting, sometimes begging for a miracle. And I wasn't the only one. "Please help Ruth walk and talk," Gabriel prayed each night before bed.

"Wouldn't it be great if we read the newspaper and saw that Jesus was coming to Bath?" I asked the children one morning, reading them a Bible passage in which Christ healed a man who couldn't walk. "Then we could bring Ruth to him." Even as I spoke, I knew we had the same opportunity through prayer, the chance to bring people to Christ—the lover, the life giver, the healer. Still, it would be easier if we could see him.

Twice a week, I drove the children to the school for the deaf. Lydia joined Ruth in class, while the boys sat in the lobby with their matching red backpacks stuffed with books. We also began learning American Sign Language (ASL). Dana, who couldn't take time off of work, borrowed sign language videos from our library and held me at night while I wept. Ruth adeptly responded to our gestures by smiling and glancing at what she wanted, but signing seemed unlikely.

Then one evening Dana shouted, "You've got to see this!"

I raced downstairs to find my husband holding Ruth on the couch.

"Watch." Dana squeezed his fist open and closed, open and closed—the sign for milk. Then he held up Ruth's arm.

Slowly, one tiny pointer finger uncurled halfway before curling again. Dana squeezed his fist again, and Ruth curled her finger again. "Milk." The movement was so small I might've missed it except for Ruth's delighted grin. She was there, a fully functioning little girl imprisoned in an unresponsive body, and she was trying to communicate.

That spring, robins filled the backwoods. Tender green shoots poked through needle-brown soil. The apple tree blossomed beside our front porch, and we celebrated the girls' second birthdays. Lydia's fell on Easter—the same day we carried Ruth to the front of our church and dedicated her to the Lord. Two weeks later, to celebrate Ruth's birthday, Tracey, Tammy, and Theresa arrived with a veritable merry-go-round of kids—some adopted, some with special needs, some here for medical treatment, including an Iraqi toddler with a damaged heart and her mother, neither of whom spoke English. Ruth sat in her high chair on our back deck, playing with a helium balloon. The children took turns helping Ruth open her gifts, including a banana-leaf ball and two hand-sewn Ugandan dolls that Mandy had mailed from Welcome Home, along with a card.

"Our beloved Baby Ruth Alyssia," I read the card aloud. "How we miss you so much. It hasn't been easy to believe you have gone, but it was all due to your well-being in that your dear life continue. The Bible says in Jeremiah 29:11, 'The good job God started in you, He shall accomplish it.' We love you and pray for you so much. We praise God for the family that took you and accepted you as you are. God richly bless them. Be blessed always, Mummy Joy."

Forty-six names, some squeezed sideways, filled the card, signed by the home's workers. Soon Dana and I hoped to meet them. I'd been piecing together our travel plans with Mandy. Yvonne, who had arrived with Ruth from Welcome Home, had also found an adoptive family. In January, one day before she'd returned to Uganda, a Wisconsin couple and their two teenage daughters had driven all night through a snowstorm to meet her. That spring they traveled to Uganda and Nairobi to finalize Yvonne's immigration and receive the papers she needed—all in just two short weeks. Dana and I would follow the same route with Ruth. Only, because we couldn't apply for her new visa until Ruth left the country, our trip would take longer, Mandy explained after consulting several immigration lawyers.

"How much longer?" I asked.

"A month. Maybe two."

"That's impossible," I protested. "Dana would lose his job."

"There's only one other way," Mandy said. "You could bring Ruth back to Uganda on your own."

You have to promise to let me go to Africa, alone if I have to. My words from a decade before returned with stunning clarity, but now I no longer wanted to follow through on them.

"It's too dangerous," our Maine attorney said. "If you bring Ruth back to Uganda and her visa application is denied, you'll be forced to leave her."

Over the following days, Dana and I debated what to do.

"I could go," Judah volunteered. "You could take me to Uganda with you. That way if Ruth can't come home, I could stay at the orphanage with her."

For a moment, I actually considered it. Then I realized the sheer lunacy. Leave my eight-year-old son in an orphanage? Yet I couldn't imagine leaving Ruth there either. As surely as I once felt God calling me to Africa, I felt him calling me now.

Come away. Come away. Come away with me, my love. The words of an old Keith Green song inexplicably filled my mind. Lying on the floor of our little Oregon ranch, feet propped on the record player, I'd been captivated by the message of God's love for the lost through the Christian folksinger's music.

Do you see, do you see, all the people sinking down?
Don't you care, don't you care, are you gonna let them drown?
How can you be so numb, not to care if they come?
But you close your eyes and pretend the job's done.

Maybe adopting Ruth wasn't about my dreams after all. Maybe it was about God's dreams for me and my family. His dreams for all of the abandoned, sinking-down children like Ruth—to welcome them, to raise them up, and to redeem them with his love. Whenever I began to panic, whenever I began to doubt, I heard this same persistent call: *Come. Come. Come.*

In mid-May, I gave Mama Mandy my answer. "I'll go, but only for three weeks. That's the longest I can leave my family. If God wants Ruth to be with us, he will make a way for me to bring her home."

"How do you feel?" she asked.

Only one word came to mind. "Terrified."

"What country are you going to again?" my doctor asked when I stopped by her office for a list of medicines and required vaccinations.

"Uganda," I said.

"Uganda?" She jerked her head up from her chart. "That's a place people disappear from."

She didn't need to remind me. As a student at Gordon College, I'd studied African literature, including the brutal history of Uganda's civil wars in which at least 800,000 people were murdered over two decades, beginning soon after the country gained independence. At least 300,000 were victims of Idi Amin, the military dictator who had declared himself president in 1971. Eight years later, Amin was ousted by rebels, who fought one another for power. The most notorious, the Lord's Resistance Army, or LRA, had been killing and kidnapping people in the country's rural north ever since. Like some grim nightmare, LRA soldiers stole into villages under the cover of dark to massacre civilians and snatch children from their beds. Some they butchered. Some they made into soldiers. Others they forced into sexual slavery.[4] And it was still happening. I knew from glimpsing a news broadcast in which a child soldier had triumphantly displayed a woman's severed breast in his hand.

I took back everything I'd ever said about wanting to go to Africa. I no longer wanted to go anywhere. I wanted to remain safely cocooned with my family. The thought of leaving Lydia was the hardest. But Lydia could be without a mother for a month, I told myself, or Ruth could be without a mother for a lifetime. The boys, on the other hand, thought my leaving was great. While Dana worked, five friends and both of our moms would take turns watching our children. I charted each day on the kitchen calendar, but with Lydia, who was too young to understand, I simply pointed to the sky.

"See the plane?" I asked as P3-Orion from the nearby Brunswick Naval Air Station rumbled over our backyard. "Mommy has to go on a plane."

"I go on a plane too?" Lydia twined her arms around my neck.

"No. Mommy has to take Ruth far, far away to a place called Africa."

"I go to Africa too?"

I shook my head. "Mommy has to go alone."

Each night I read Lydia a book about an owl mommy who flies off, leaving her three little chicks. When the mother doesn't return, her babies are sure she is gone forever. Finally, she returns soft and silent, swooping through the trees.

"Do Mommies come back?" I asked Lydia.

She nodded.

"Mommies always come back," I said, praying my words were true.

Knowing I wouldn't be able to heat Ruth's milk while we were traveling, Dana and I gave her one fractionally cooler bottle at a time until she grudgingly swallowed her milk cold.

Mama Mandy gave us as much advice as she could—and a warning. "You can eat with the workers," she said in her lilting Australian accent as we talked one night on the phone, "but the food is awful."

"That's okay," I assured her. "I grew up on a farm. We ate everything."

"No, really," she repeated. "It's awful. AW-FUL."

"How awful can it be?"

"O-F-F-A-L," Mandy spelled. "Offal. Organ meat from cows and pigs. The cooks wash the intestines, boil them in a pot, and serve them on rice."

I packed a two-pound bag of trail mix, a dozen cans of tuna, ten boxes of brownie batter, a case of powdered milk, and two canisters of instant lemonade along with a jumbo box of disposable diapers, cartons of boxed milk, a flashlight, batteries, and an ultrasonic bug repeller guaranteed to scare away insects with silent sound waves. All I needed now was our plane tickets, but without a court date, I couldn't buy them. Finally, in late June, Peter e-mailed me the time: Monday, July 11, 2005, at 9:00 a.m. Immediately, I called our travel agent and booked two seats on a plane flying from Boston to London on Wednesday, July 6. After a twelve-hour layover, we'd land in Uganda early Friday morning—plenty of time to settle in before going to court on Monday. The only hitch was that because we'd been forced to buy our $3,400 tickets so close to departing, they weren't changeable, and Ruth's hearing was one of the last scheduled before the court recessed for the month.

"Whatever you do," Mandy warned, "don't miss your flight."

I didn't plan on it. With each passing day, I felt like God had placed me in the center of his slingshot and was slowly pulling back the band. One week before leaving, Dana and I collected letters from Ruth's doctors and therapists describing why she needed ongoing medical care in the States. We also took her back to the neurologist who'd predicted that she wouldn't progress. While Dana sat in the lobby with our kids, I held Ruth in his cramped office, running down the list of Ruth's accomplishments as well as the results of her hearing test and eye surgery. When the doctor swung his stethoscope back and forth like a pendulum, Ruth's eyes tracked it perfectly.

"Isn't she doing great?" I boasted. "Ruth loves taking steps if we hold her, and she even moves her arms and legs as if she's trying to crawl."

"Does she go anywhere?" He palpitated her arms and legs.

"Backwards, a little, when she's lying on the floor. And look—" I opened my mouth, and Ruth opened hers. I stuck out my tongue and Ruth's stuck out back. "She loves imitating us. She even understands sign language." I waved my pointer finger to sign "Where?" and squeezed my fist for milk.

Ruth grinned and glanced at the bottle poking out of my bag.

"To be honest?" The doctor tilted back in his chair, finishing the exam. "I don't see significant progress. The only real change is knowing that Ruth is deaf. When combined with cerebral palsy, this indicates that her mother likely contacted some kind of virus while pregnant. The result is usually severe mental retardation." He paused, tapping his pen. "In my opinion, it won't matter whether you adopt Ruth or leave her in Uganda. She won't know the difference."

Speechless, I gathered Ruth and hurried out.

"Won't know the difference?" Dana fumed when I repeated the doctor's words to him in the lobby. "How can he say that? It makes a difference if you leave the room."

It was true. Over the past months, if I pulled on my jacket without getting Ruth's, she wailed like a fire engine, knowing that I was going somewhere without her. Something had to be missing, something that explained Ruth's cerebral palsy and deafness that neither we nor the neurologist recognized. But what?

Before driving home, we stopped by the South Portland immigration office to ask about expediting our application for Ruth's permanent resident visa, or "green card," once I took her out of the country.

"Why not apply now?" the immigration officer asked.

"Because she's still here." I pointed to Ruth, slumped in the umbrella stroller beside me.

"So?" The officer slid a form for Ruth's permanent resident visa across the counter, saying that we didn't have to wait.

Who was wrong, the immigration attorneys we'd consulted or this man? Either way, after filling out the application, inking our fingertips, and paying more than $600, we were assured that Ruth's visa would be waiting for us when we arrived in Uganda.

Our final weekend together, our family hawked Shain's of Maine ice-cream sandwiches under a tent during Heritage Days, Bath's annual Fourth of July celebration, to raise the remaining money for our trip. After Lydia ran off to dance to a reggae band, Tracey came to the rescue again by volunteering to watch our kids. The afternoon before we were to leave, she stopped by the house one final time.

"Hey, baby girl." Tracey snuggled Ruth on the couch, reaching into her pocket. "I brought you a present."

Body stiff with anticipation, Ruth squealed as Tracey pulled out her fist to reveal a small, silver bracelet stamped with hearts.

Sliding the thin band over Ruth's frail wrist, Tracey said, "In case you can't come back, this is so everyone in Uganda will know that you are a loved baby."

My heart broke at the possibility. Dana and I both knew that Ruth's future lay beyond our control. All we could do was to keep trusting, keep beating our wings of faith, believing that God would be there to catch us. After a somber dinner, Dana returned to his office so he could take time off to drive Ruth and me to the airport the next afternoon. Tucking the boys in bed, I asked what each of them wanted me to bring back—a banana-leaf ball for Judah and a cloth doll for Gabriel. By the time I reached her room, Lydia was already asleep. I lingered longest over my daughter, running my fingers through her corn-silk hair and resting my cheek on her chest to memorize the rhythm of her softly beating heart. Then I walked down the hall to start packing.

My room was a mess. A borrowed suitcase lay on my floor and laundry covered the bed. To quiet my anxious heart, I pushed aside the clothes and picked up my Bible, which fell open to the second chapter of Ephesians. Glancing over the page, I read the first verse I came to: "For we are His workmanship, created in Christ Jesus for good works, which God prepared beforehand that we should walk in them."

Suddenly, it all seemed clear—why I had long dreamed of going to Africa to work with orphans, why I yearned to adopt, why God had brought Ruth to us.

This is what we'd been made for.

Now it was time to walk.

8

Soaked

Ruth's silver bracelet is missing.

I have searched her backpack, her dresser, her bookcase, beneath her bed and come up empty.

Does everything vanish so easily?

I once believed that having a large family would protect me from loss.

Now, I see that I will lose everyone I love anyway, either one at a time or all at once, depending on whether they go first or I do.

At night, I close my eyes and see my family and everyone I love being sucked down a rushing river toward a waterfall. The closer we get, the faster the river flows, until it pulls us over the edge—one by one.

How do I go on when all I see is water?

"Keep my side of the bed warm for me," I said as I ruffled Gabriel's hair, standing in our living room on the Wednesday afternoon we were to leave.

Ruth squealed with anticipation as the other kids wrapped us in hugs. Having seen Dana carry down our mounds of luggage, she knew we were going on a trip, something she loved—even to the dentist. Little did Ruth know that this was a trip from which she might not return. The van was packed. Our boarding tickets were waiting at the airport in Boston. And I was petrified. Ever since terrorists hijacked four planes on September 11, 2001, and used them as weapons, I'd dreaded flying. If I kept my family together with our feet on the ground, I somehow believed that we'd all be safe. But to redeem Ruth, I had to get on a plane. Once more, God was asking me to trust that he was still there, still leading, still in control.

"Ready?" Dana lifted Ruth as the kids jostled around us.

Mom, who was visiting friends, had driven up the coast just that morning. One of the most courageous people I knew, for her traveling was nothing. The year that I'd transferred to Gordon College, she'd enrolled at Gordon-Conwell Theological Seminary, just up the road, earning a master of divinity degree. To pay for it, she sold our family home. When I was pregnant with Judah, she'd helped me set up my father's cradle before moving to Moscow. Although I was sorry to have her so far away, I admired her steadfast determination to follow God wherever he led—the same determination I now needed.

"I'm proud of you," Mom said, wrapping me in a hug. "I'll be praying."

Summoning more courage than I felt, I picked up my pack. Stuffed inside were Ruth's medical reports, legal documents, a copy of our home study, and letters from doctors, all of which we hoped would convince a judge to let me bring Ruth home. After a final round of hugs, I stepped outside and started down the porch stairs with Dana, trailed by Mom and the kids.

"Wait!" Gabriel raced after us. "I want to go with you!"

"Are you sure?" I looked up to where Mom and the kids stood watching. "It's a three-hour drive to Boston. Once Daddy drops us off, he's just turning around and driving home again."

"Please?" Gabriel begged.

"Anyone else want to come?" Dana asked, buckling Ruth into the van.

Judah shook his head while Lydia clung to Mom.

"Okay," I told Gabriel. "Climb in."

Gabriel wiggled in beside Ruth. As Dana backed out of our driveway, I flicked on our local Christian radio station, astonished to hear the Watoto Children's Choir, a group of orphans from near Kampala, the city where Ruth was born. Because Welcome Home is licensed to care for children only through age six, some children transfer to Watoto for continued care in a village of traditional African houses where they are raised and educated in a family-like atmosphere. We'd heard them at a local church several weeks before. Now there they were, all these waiting-to-be-redeemed children, raising their voices in praise to God as we drove out of town.

Several hours later, dark clouds threatened rain as we pulled up to the departures terminal at Logan International Airport. To save money on parking, I'd suggested that Dana drop us off, but he insisted on coming inside. While we stood in line for our boarding passes, Dana kneaded my shoulders. A few feet away, Gabriel pushed Ruth in giant figure eights inside the nearly empty terminal. Knowing how hard it would be for me to carry Ruth for our thirty-hour trip, Dana had ordered a special car seat with retractable wheels and a pull-out handle that converted into a stroller, but it hadn't arrived.

"Everything will be fine," Dana promised as I eyed the clock behind the counter. A little past 4:00, two hours before our flight. But suppose everything wasn't fine? Before leaving home I'd written Dana a letter that I'd left on his pillow. With the words *Just in case . . .* written on front, it held detailed instructions for what to do and how to raise our children if I didn't make it back. That's how scared I was.

"Passports?" the ticket agent called when it was finally our turn.

I placed them on the counter, waving Gabriel over.

"This is Ruth Alyssia Hodgkins?" The agent peered over the counter, comparing the somber, bald-headed baby in Ruth's passport photo to the child grinning up at him with bright bows in her softly curling hair.

"Yes." I nodded.

"May I see her transit visa?"

"Her what?" I asked.

"Her British transit visa."

I knew we were in trouble when the agent directed the people in line behind us to the next counter.

"Because this child is an African national," the agent explained, "she needs special permission to fly through England. Your travel agent should have told you. Without it, I can't let her on the plane."

"Can't let her on the plane?" A wave of heat flashed up my neck. "She's an orphan, and we are flying to Uganda to complete her adoption. Our court date is in five days. Can you make an exception?"

"Unfortunately, this happens all the time." The man slid a piece of paper across the counter with a list of phone numbers. "Drive to the British Embassy in New York. If you apply for the visa in person you should get it tomorrow. I'll reschedule you to fly from New York."

"But our tickets aren't changeable," I protested.

"I'll make a note in the computer giving you special permission." He waved us on with a grim smile.

Too upset to look at Dana, I helped push our two luggage carts piled with totes full of gifts for the orphans toward a row of pay phones at the back of the terminal.

"Maybe there's a reason you weren't on that plane," he suggested.

"I don't see how," I grumbled.

While Dana fed Ruth graham crackers and juice, I called our travel agent, my mom, and Mandy. Neither Ruth nor Yvonne had needed special permission to fly through England before. Even so, we were stuck. As we piled back in the van for our four-hour drive south, the first drops of rain splatted across our windshield. Shortly before midnight, we stopped at a roadside hotel in New York. When Dana pulled out our credit card to pay, I winced. All our cash—thirty crisp one hundred dollar bills—was stuffed in a money bag strapped to my leg. Since credit cards aren't usually accepted in Uganda, I needed every cent. From now on, every dollar we spent here was a dollar we wouldn't have over there. Gabriel and Ruth slept on the floor while Dana and I climbed in the bed—all of us still wearing our clothes.

Thursday morning, we ate breakfast in the hotel lobby before wearily climbing back in the van. With Dana behind the wheel, I cranked back my seat and closed my eyes. A short time later, I woke to words blaring from the radio: "Explosion . . . number of dead . . . London."

"What is it?" I shot up, wide awake. "What happened?"

"Bombs," Dana said. "Last night there was a terrorist attack in London."

The details were sketchy, the reports just coming in, but explosions had ripped through three British subway cars and a double-decker bus, killing fifty-two people and injuring more than seven hundred. Airports were on high alert, flights delayed, transportation at a standstill.

"Imagine if you were there right now," Dana said.

I did.

As news of the attacks flooded the airwaves, we drove in shocked silence. New York City was on high alert for a terrorist attack. We squeezed into Manhattan during rush hour. Cars and pedestrians crammed the streets, but we had no problem finding the British Consulate General. A wall of armed police lined the glass and concrete building. Commuters streamed past, chatting on cell phones as if oblivious to the guns at the officers' sides. Remarkably, Dana found a parking spot right around the corner.

"It's a miracle!" I hoisted my pack and stepped onto the sidewalk, plopping Ruth in her stroller. Together, we approached a grim-faced guard.

"Name?" He glanced up.

I gave him mine.

"Do you have an appointment?"

"It's an emergency." I explained our situation.

"The embassy is locked down." The guard shook his head. "Go home and make an appointment."

"You don't understand," I said. "We're from Maine. Isn't there someone we can talk to?"

"This is the best I can do." The officer handed me a card printed with embassy phone numbers.

While Dana walked the kids up the street in search of coffee, I fed coins into a corner pay phone. For the next hour, I dialed number after number, only to reach voice mail. Three times I went back to the guard. Three times he pointed toward the phones. After another hour, I reached a sympathetic receptionist who gave me the phone number for a courier service that helped travelers obtain travel documents. After booking the earliest afternoon appointment, we fed all our remaining coins into our parking meter, grabbed a couple of sausage rolls from a street vendor, and walked to the Lincoln Building, nearly a mile away on East 42nd Street.

"How can I help you?" Lissette, a young Latina with ringlets of dark hair, pushed a stack of books off a chair so I could sit in the agency's crowded office.

While Dana entertained the kids, I repeated our story, which sounded more pathetic each time. "Can we get Ruth's transit visa today?"

"Not today." Lissette drummed her long nails on the desk. "Our carrier goes to the embassy once each morning. Today, he's already gone and come back, but for two hundred dollars, he can get it tomorrow."

All she needed was Ruth's passport and her current American visa. My heart sank. The director for the medical aid organization had mailed us her passport the week before but not her visa.

"See if someone can overnight it," Lissette said, handing me a business card with the agency's address. "If not—" She waved her glossy nails as if to indicate that it was out of her hands.

I phoned the director, who was out of the office, and left a message. It was already well past 2:00 p.m. Our chance of receiving Ruth's visa by Friday was shrinking by the minute—as was our hope of arriving in Uganda in time for Ruth's hearing. We trudged back to our van in weary silence to find a note tucked under our windshield wiper—a $115 parking ticket. Turned out the miracle we'd discovered was only for delivery trucks.

Friday morning, New York City was drowning. Rain sliced across the window of our hotel room. Several stories below, streets ran like rivers. People hoisted shopping bags, newspapers, and flaps of cardboard over their heads in a futile effort to stay dry.

"We should buy you and Gabriel clothes," I said as Dana pushed Ruth past a fancy boutique, looking for a place to eat. Unlike Ruth and me, who'd scavenged clothes from the van, they'd been wearing the same outfits for three days. To keep Ruth dry, I tucked my sweatshirt over her body.

"We're fine. Aren't we, Gabe?" Dana insisted while Gabriel skipped through the downpour in sandals and shorts.

While buying hamburgers for dinner the night before, Dana had splurged on deodorant and a toothbrush, but I knew he was right not to waste money on clothes—especially in posh Manhattan. By the time we ducked into a crowded café and settled at a table, poor Ruth looked as if she'd gone swimming. Damp curls clung to her forehead, but she was still smiling, happy to be out on even this dreadful day. Across from us, a teenage boy with untied sneakers lay sprawled over the neighboring table, asleep. He looked as if he'd had a harder night than we had.

"What will we do if this doesn't work?" I mopped Ruth's face with a napkin while Gabriel eyed a glass case of pastries.

"Drive home." Dana studied the menu. "It's not like we can afford another night in New York."

"Then what?" I moaned.

Dana clamped his lips, unwilling to say what we both knew. If Ruth's transit visa didn't arrive when the courier's office opened at 9:00, we'd miss her hearing. Later that morning, Gabriel and Ruth lay side by side on the bed watching cartoons while Dana reloaded the van. As soon as the courier's agency opened, I dialed the number and asked for Lissette.

"You're all set," she said. "Ruth's visa arrived first thing this morning. We'll bring it to the British embassy in an hour, and we should have her papers ready this afternoon."

"She got it!" I jumped off the bed as soon as Dana returned.

He was as stunned as I was. A quick call to our travel agent, and we were assured that she would book our flight from New York that evening. With nothing left to do after updating my mom and Mandy, we spent the morning exploring the Natural History Museum. Pushing Ruth into a room full of African animals, I finally began to get excited. After all these years, I was really going to Africa!

"What's that?" I signed as Ruth stared up at the long face of a buffalo. "Cow." I extended my thumb and pinky beside my forehead like a horn.

For "zebra" I wagged two fingers like ears, signing "horse."

But even Ruth looked puzzled, gazing at the stalky legs of an ostrich, when I tapped my thumb and index finger beside my mouth and signed, "Big chicken."

After lunch at a pizzeria, Dana dropped me off at the Lincoln Building. Rather than risk another parking ticket, he circled the block in the van with the kids while I rode the elevator to the seventh floor and picked up Ruth's passport with the freshly stamped transit visa.

All I had to do now was confirm our flight. Passport in hand, I rode the elevator to a bank of phones in the basement and called our travel agent. And that is when one of the last things that could possibly go wrong did.

"Your trip to London is all set," our agent said over the phone. "I can put you on any flight you want from Boston or New York. Once you get to London, however, all the seats on your carrier are booked solid for the remainder of the month with the exception of first class. Would you like me to upgrade your tickets?"

"How much would it cost?"

"Three thousand five hundred dollars."

"That's it?" I could hardly believe it. "Just one hundred dollars more than our original tickets?"

"No," she said. "Three thousand five hundred dollars in addition to your original tickets. Would you like to reserve them?"

Through the narrow window above, a steady stream of vehicles splashed past. In one of those was Ruth, her life literally resting on my answer. I thought of the hundreds of Christmas ornaments we'd sold, of my grandmother's furniture, of the dance and raffle, and the ice-cream sandwiches—plus a last-minute garage sale. I thought of Dana's and my agreement not to go into debt to fund Ruth's adoption and of all our remaining money strapped to my leg.

"Can I call you back?" I asked.

After calling Mandy and my mom, both of whom urged me to charge the tickets, I gave our travel agent my answer. Then I rode the elevator to the lobby. Within minutes, our blue van pulled up to the curb, and I stepped out into the soaking rain.

"You should be proud of me!" Dana leaned across the passenger seat and opened my door. "I cut off a taxi!"

Then he saw my face. "Did you get Ruth's visa?"

I nodded and climbed in as traffic swooshed past, splattering the windshield with a sheet of water. Exhausted, Gabriel and Ruth slept in back, heads tilted toward each other. Over the squeak of windshield wipers, I told Dana what had happened.

"The only way was to charge our tickets," I said.

"And did you?" he asked, eyebrows raised.

Slowly, I shook my head. "I told her that unless God provides the money, we're not going."

Here we were trying to rescue an abandoned baby, and I couldn't even get her on a plane. I had never felt so devastated. After driving all night, we pulled into our driveway around 2:00 a.m. on Saturday morning. Mom helped Dana carry the sleeping kids inside, while I climbed in bed, sobbing. Had God led us this far only to fail?

The next thing I knew, someone was speaking close to my ear. "It's for you."

Bright light shone through my window. I squinted through half-closed lids to see Mom standing beside my bed with a telephone. She propped the receiver next to my chin.

"Hello?"

"The church talked it over, and we'd like to give you five hundred dollars," said our pastor's wife, Lynne.

After thanking her, I turned to my mom. "How did she know we needed money?"

"I phoned a few people last night." Mom smiled. "Another family from your church pledged an additional five hundred."

The effect was as strong as coffee. I pulled on my robe and staggered downstairs, where Dana was gathered with our kids in the living room.

"Mommy!" Lydia barreled into my arms.

While we were talking about what to do, the phone rang again.

"Aloha!" It was my brother, Sunny, calling from his home in Hawaii during what must have been the middle of the night for him. "Heard you were having a little trouble getting to Uganda. I'm sending a check for five hundred."

As soon as I said goodbye, I turned to Dana. "If God can supply that much money that fast, I know he can supply the rest!"

I phoned our travel agent and reserved two first-class seats on the last plane able to deliver Ruth and me to Uganda in time for our hearing. This time, all of our children squeezed into the van for the drive back to Boston, with Ruth securely buckled in her new travel chair, which had arrived while we were gone. Only Mom stood on the porch, smiling and waving goodbye. Three hours later, I pushed Ruth toward the ticket counter at Logan while Dana and the kids pushed our carts of luggage.

"Looks great." The agent checked our passports, shaking her head in sympathy as I recounted our crazy trip to New York. Then she lowered her gaze and picked up the phone. "Just a moment." She waved the people in line behind us to a different counter, making my heart beat faster. "I need to talk to my supervisor." A moment later, she put down the phone and said, "There's a problem with your tickets."

"What?" I yelled. "What could possibly be wrong with our tickets? We drove to New York. We got the travel visa. I'm paying first class. All I want is to get on that plane!"

"I'm sorry." She sighed. "But your tickets aren't upgradable to first class. It says so right on them. Travel agents do this all the time, hoping we'll overlook it."

"Can't you?" I pointed to Ruth. "If we miss our flight, this child is going to spend the rest of her life in an orphanage!"

"I'll see what I can do." She directed us to sit in the same row of chairs where we'd waited three days before.

"Want to pray?" Dana asked.

"No!" I shouted. "I do not want to pray! I want to get on that plane!"

While the kids climbed over and under chairs like a jungle gym, I bored holes in the clock above the ticket counter, counting down the minutes until our plane left. Forty. Thirty. Twenty. The line of passengers dwindled until we were the only ones left. Ten minutes before our flight was to leave, the ticket agent motioned me over.

"There is no way I can sell you these tickets," she said. "I tried everything. Our computer won't accept a payment. But I know you need to get on that plane, so I am upgrading your tickets for free." She slid two boarding passes over the counter and reached down to tag our luggage. "Quickly! Run straight to the front of the security line and tell them your plane has already boarded."

"Hurry!" I wheeled Ruth around in her travel chair and started to run.

Dana snatched Lydia, and we raced toward the crush of people waiting at the security gate. Lydia shrieked, reaching for me from Dana's arms as I kissed each child goodbye.

"Take care of each other." I tore myself away. "I'll see you soon!"

After pushing our way through security, Ruth and I were the last ones to board our plane. I was in such a hurry I slammed my leg against the armrest of our middle row, leaving a purple bruise that lasted for weeks. Only as we began our slow taxi down the runway did I begin to relax. Leaning back in my seat, I squeezed Ruth's hand, realizing with remorse that I had forgotten to kiss Dana goodbye. Why had it been so difficult to get on this plane?

Everything you have just been through, I felt a silent whisper, *was to prepare you for what lies ahead.*

9

Welcome Home

"The way to a stronger faith," the great preacher Charles Spurgeon once wrote, "usually lies along the rough pathway of sorrow. . . . I am afraid that all the grace that I have got out of my comfortable easy times and happy hours, might almost lie on a penny. But the good that I have received from my sorrows, and pain, and griefs, is altogether incalculable."

I do not want the rough pathway.

I do not want sorrow and pain and grief.

I yearn for comfortable, easy times and happy hours.

Sitting in the wood-paneled church, seventeen miles up the river in Richmond, Dana's father picks up his saxophone. His grandmother, Josephine, sits at the organ—short-heeled pumps on the pedals, knotty hands hovering over keys. Aunts, uncles, and cousins fill the pews, while Gabriel slides onto the piano bench.

Clear, familiar notes fill the room as three generations play "Amazing Grace."

How sweet the sound.

"Hold this." I wrap my arm around Judah's broadening shoulders as he sits beside me. "Hold this inside you. Nothing else lasts."

"Ladies and gentlemen," the captain's voice crackled over the intercom as I sat beside Ruth in our plush, first-class seats at London's Heathrow Airport, "please disregard the commotion in the main cabin."

I gripped my armrest as shouts rang from the back of the plane. Moments before, while we were preparing to board, a flight attendant had asked Ruth and me to step aside to make way for a priority passenger. *Who?* I wondered. *Elton John on safari? Angelina Jolie on her way to aid refugees?* A side door opened and through it walked a tall, powerfully built black man with his ankles and wrists shackled to two undersized security guards. He was visibly angry.

"Is he safe?" I asked as the trio rattled past.

"Probably," the flight attendant said. "He's a Ugandan national who overstayed his visa. They usually calm down once we're in the air, but this is one of the worst I've seen."

What kind of place were we headed to that people would risk imprisonment to stay away? I was about to find out.

Nine hours later, our plane touched down in the early morning dark of Entebbe. Out the window I glimpsed something I'd never seen in another airport: *United Nations* painted on the fuselage of a nearby plane. Part of me wanted to stay in my first-class seat where I would be safe and comfortable and cared for; but when I glanced at Ruth, sleeping peacefully beside me, I knew that my welfare was no longer my main concern. As passengers filled the aisle, I slipped my arms through my pack and lifted Ruth in her seat, carrying her toward the door and down the stairs to the tarmac below.

In the vast, hangar-like terminal, insects droned beneath fluorescent lights while I stood in a long customs line with Ruth. The loud jangle of metal made me turn. Head bent and eyes down, the prisoner from our plane shuffled across the floor with his guards and disappeared through a door, which closed ominously behind them. I said a quiet prayer before moving on. After a clerk stamped our passports, I retrieved our luggage, which filled two carts. Unable to push them and Ruth, I asked a female security guard for help. Together we wheeled the carts and Ruth toward a pair of sliding glass doors at the end of the terminal—while I desperately hoped someone from Welcome Home was there to meet us.

"How will I recognize them?" I'd asked Mandy before leaving.

"Don't worry," she said. "They'll recognize Ruth."

As soon as we stepped outside, the guard disappeared. Ruth and I met a wall of silent, staring faces. No one smiled. No one greeted us. I was about to duck back inside when from the rear of the crowd a voice called, "Alyssia!" A stout middle-aged woman with short hair pushed toward us, calling Ruth's middle name. Behind her appeared a meticulously dressed Ugandan man in dark trousers and a crisp white shirt.

"I'm Janet." The woman grasped me with one hand and pounded my back with the other. "This is William."

Janet, I remembered from conversations with Mandy, *the woman who'd helped start Welcome Home. William, the driver.*

William welcomed me and then stooped to take Ruth's hand, telling her how beautiful she was. As if understanding every word, Ruth grinned up at him.

"She is good?" William looked at me.

"Very good," I said. "But hungry. She slept right through breakfast on the plane."

"Let's go." Janet grabbed one luggage cart while William took the other. "I know a great place we can stop to eat."

Pushing Ruth as I followed them toward the parking lot, I glanced at my watch. A little past 6:00. Just three hours before our hearing. "That's okay." I struggled to keep up. "I saved some rolls to feed Ruth from the plane. How far to Kampala?"

"Not far." William stopped at a rusting white van with the words *Welcome Home* painted on the sides.

After helping stow our luggage, I retracted the wheels on Ruth's chair, slid her across a plastic-covered bench seat, and climbed in beside her. William and Janet sat up front, a cage of metal bars between us. After searching for a seat belt, I realized the van didn't have them. Every part of the vehicle shuddered and shook as William steered away from the airport on our way to the capital. Crowds lined the red dirt road, but my eyes were fixed on the trucks and buses barreling toward us at terrifying speeds. Heart pounding, I fought the urge to scream as William swerved into oncoming traffic to avoid a pothole so big it would've been considered a tourist attraction back home.

"Lake Victoria." Janet pointed out the window toward a gray glimmer at the edge of a scorched field.

The name of Africa's largest lake, named after Queen Victoria, explained the preppy plaid uniforms of the children walking beside the road toward school. Their neat-pressed clothes clashed incongruously with the surrounding earth shaved bare of trees, the unfinished mud-brick houses, the mounds of burning garbage, and chickens, goats, and cows foraging alongside the road. In the 1500s, European traders had descended on Africa, filling the holds of their tall-masted ships with gold and ivory and people—the beginning of the African slave trade in which at least 12 million Africans were captured and shipped across the Atlantic.[5] Three centuries later, Scottish missionary and anti-slavery advocate David Livingstone cut a swath north from Cape Town through the African jungle in search of a path to the interior. More missionaries followed, bringing medicine, education, and the good news of the gospel, but the countries from which they came held less altruistic aims.

During the 1800s, England, France, Portugal, and other wealth-hungry European countries divided the continent into colonies, devouring its abundant resources and forcing its people to toil on tea, coffee, and sugar plantations or to dig for gold and diamonds beneath its sun-cracked soil. Uganda, a British protectorate since 1894, declared its independence in 1962, but the name of the great lake that forms its southern border still bears the imprint of the crown, as does its official language—English—and the uniforms of its schoolchildren.

As we rattled toward Kampala, Ruth's head jerked forward and back, forward and back in her seat beside me. I placed my hand on her sweaty brow, slipping soft bits of bread into her hungry mouth. Out the sliding glass window, cows and goats continued foraging along the road, unfazed by oncoming traffic. I gaped at outdoor furniture markets and rickety fruit stands displaying neat pyramids of tomatoes, avocados, and mangoes. Most astonishing were the bicycles loaded with baskets of bananas, crates of live chickens, and trays of eggs and bread in astonishing feats of height. In and among the swirling rush, businessmen in dark suits and ladies in vibrant dresses rode on the backs of bicycle taxis.

"Why are so many people waving?" I asked as a cluster of people raised their hands in a silent salute as we clattered past.

"The van," William said. "It used to be a taxi."

Angry clouds darkened the horizon, followed by a streak of lightning. Raindrops pummeled the dry, dusty ground like bullets, soaking everything in sight. William and Janet rolled up their windows as the road turned to mud, and my window quickly steamed over.

"There are two things you should know." Janet hefted her weight to face me through the metal bars. "One, you are *Mzungu.*"

"*Mzungu?*"

"White. Two, everywhere you go, you will pay the white tax."

"There's a tax for the color of your skin?"

"Officially? No. Unofficially? Everything you buy will cost more because people assume you have more money."

But I do have more money, I thought, feeling the stiff bundle of cash strapped to my leg. "I'll be like a walking bank," I'd joked to Dana before leaving. "I might as well wear a neon sign flashing above my head that says, *Rob me*." Now, as we passed a windowless house with a sheet for a door, I saw how truly wealthy I was, how wealthy my family was. I'd never felt so powerful. Or conflicted, knowing that the fortune I carried could change the life of any one of the people lining this busy road. I could help only the little girl nodding to sleep beside me.

As we neared Kampala, traffic slowed to a crawl. Beads of sweat dotted Ruth's forehead and pooled in her ears, slicking her springy curls. She always seemed a little hotter than the rest of us, even in winter, prompting us to take off her jacket before buckling her in the van, but here there was no way to cool off. Eyes and throat stinging from exhaust, I slid open my window to let in some fresh air only to discover the odor was the air—diesel fumes mixed with burning garbage and thick clouds of dust. Gritty granules lodged between my teeth and clogged my nostrils. I stuck my face near the window anyway, rain pelting my skin as we inched past a traffic circle filled with people holding picket signs. Janet explained that they were marching in opposition to a change in the country's constitution that would extend term limits in the upcoming election.

"Very dangerous." She nodded at a man clutching a wooden club.

By the time we reached the city center, the rain had stopped. William parked along a narrow street lined with low concrete buildings and offered to stay with Ruth, who had fallen back asleep. Hoisting my pack, I followed Janet across the street and inside a dim parking garage where she gave our names to a female security guard with a military-style gun slung over her shoulder. Checking our names on a list, she motioned us toward a dingy stairwell. Several floors above, it opened to a modern office with floor-to-ceiling shelves of manila folders.

"Welcome. Welcome." A Ugandan man wearing a navy-colored suit greeted us with an outstretched hand. "I am Peter. How are you? How was your journey?"

"It was good." I shook our lawyer's hand, suddenly aware of the red road dust covering my filthy khakis and wishing I'd changed.

Peter didn't seem to notice. From his paper-strewn desk, he picked up a file, peering at me over his silver glasses. "You are here to apply for guardianship of Ruth Alyssia Hodgkins? She is with you?"

"Sleeping in the van with our driver."

Peter held out a photograph I'd mailed three months before. "This is your family?"

Cheeks smudged with chocolate from Ruth's birthday party, Judah, Gabriel, Lydia, and Dana smiled at me from our backyard. Missing them, I nodded.

After a few more questions, Peter confirmed that we were ready for our hearing, which began in less than an hour. "Now there is only one other matter." He held out his hand. "You have brought payment?"

Embarrassed at needing to unbutton my pants, I turned toward the wall and reached down my left pant leg to pull out my money bag and hand Peter a crumpled envelope containing twenty crisp one hundred dollar bills—all of our in-country court and legal fees. I knew that international adoptions often cost much more, but in the midst of such poverty, the amount now seemed staggering.

Half an hour later, we met Peter a few blocks away at the High Court of Kampala. The white polished stones gleamed magnificently in the bright morning light. Carrying Ruth, I followed Peter and Janet up a twisting flight of stairs to an outdoor portico, imagining the stately rooms inside. Instead, a single lightbulb dangled from a bare wire above a long wooden table. At the far end sat the judge, an imposing man, with a miniature Ugandan flag fluttering beside a table fan. The only other equipment was an old-fashioned black dial telephone.

Peter sat at the table, while Janet, Ruth, and I squeezed against the wall in a crowded room. The growl of engines and grind of brakes from the street below carried through the room's only window. It was so hot, sweat dripped down the backs of my legs as we sat through the first case, involving land. The man's lawyer spoke with such a heavy accent, I caught only a few words. To keep Ruth from fussing, I pulled a children's board book from my pack and helped her turn the pages. Finally, after a couple more cases, Peter stood and reviewed Ruth's history of abandonment along with our efforts to find her birth mother by placing ads in Ugandan newspapers, something we'd done before coming. After asking several questions, the judge turned to the clerk, a woman who sat beside him jotting notes in a stenographer's book. Before I understood what was happening, Peter gathered our papers and motioned for us to leave. Worried we were being dismissed, I grabbed Ruth and scrambled after him.

"What happened?" I asked, squinting in the blinding morning light as we stood outside.

"Congratulations." Peter shook my hand. "The judge approved your guardianship. Your papers will be ready in three days."

Just when I thought nothing could shock me more, I noticed birds—bodies as big as bloodhounds—swaying in the tops of the nearby palm trees.

After climbing back in the van, we careened across the city toward the US Embassy. William dropped Janet, Ruth, and me off at the base of a hill surrounded by a security fence. High above rose a concrete building with narrow windows, which had been constructed a few years before after terrorists had blown up the US Embassy in Nairobi, killing two hundred people. After confiscating my camera and Ruth's bottle, a guard let us through. "Wanted" posters for Osama Bin Laden decorated the waiting room. Others advised us to seek shelter in case of an explosion. Looking at the room filled with flimsy chairs and weary passengers and the long row of embassy officials working behind a wall of protective glass, I plunked down in the nearest chair and wondered where we were supposed to hide. When my name was called, I carried Ruth in her sling into a closet-sized booth segregated by more glass. Across from us stood Peter Hancon, a young consular section chief with a British accent, who'd been expecting us. While I signed the register, he stepped away to search for Ruth's visa.

He returned, frowning. "Nothing yet. But I'll keep an eye out for it. How long are you here?"

"Two weeks." I adjusted Ruth on my hip. "Then we're headed to Nairobi."

"Two weeks?" Mr. Hancon raised his eyebrows. "The last family that was here for a visa had to wait two months."

Two months? I felt like such a fool as I stammered my thanks and followed Janet outside.

"It will be okay," William assured me as we settled back in the van for the two-hour drive to Welcome Home. "God will take care of it. You will see."

He said this with the same certainty with which he rubbed Ruth's frail legs and said, "She will walk. She will be strong." But I, who had left my family and carried Ruth halfway around the world in the hope that God would allow me to bring her home, wondered how William could be so sure and whether he was right.

The road to Jinja was so rough and our speed so fast that Ruth began to wail. I unbuckled her chair and hoisted her onto my lap. If we crashed, we were all going to die anyway. And I was tired, tired, tired as I leaned my head against the window, teeth rattling so hard that I thought they might break. Mile after mile, we passed open-air markets, chickens, goats, bicycles, mud houses, and mounds of hand-made bricks drying alongside the road. More than the poverty, it was the vast throngs of people dressed in Western castoffs that really surprised me. With our charitable donations, it seemed we had clothed an entire continent, devastating the domestic clothing industry in the process. With this uncomfortable realization rattling through my head, I gave in to sleep as Ruth snuggled beneath my chin.

Two sharp beeps of the horn. I opened my eyes with a start to find Ruth already awake, our sweaty skin plastered together. Through the front windshield rose a solid metal gate with a hand-carved wooden sign shaped like Africa. *Welcome Home*, it read. A small window slid open. White eyes flashed in a dark space, and the window slid closed.

"Who was that?" I leaned forward.

"The *askari*," Janet said as the gate swung inward with a screech. "Our watchman."

On the other side, dozens of toddlers dragged toy trucks and rusty tricycles to the edge of the pavement alongside a rambling pink bungalow and ambling gardens. *Boys?* I looked out the window as they lined up, bald faces watching us as William inched the van up the drive. *All boys?* Then I spotted a ruffled shirt and a faded bow and realized that the girls' clean-shaven heads only made them look like boys.

"Uncle William! Uncle William!" As soon as our driver opened his door, the children pounced.

"You want to have fun, eh? Like this?" William picked up a barefoot boy and swung him over the heads of the other children, who ducked and shrieked.

"Play! Go play! Rhoda! John! Juliet!" A young woman with ginger skin and dark springy curls appeared around the corner of the house, shooing the children behind a white picket fence. "Welcome." She wiped her hand on the frilly apron covering her flowered skirt and then held it toward me. "I'm Esther."

"You're Esther?" I gasped, trying to match her girlish face with the name of the California social worker who Mandy said supervised the home. "I thought you'd be seventy!"

"Hardly." Esther laughed and hoisted my heavy pack onto her slim shoulders. "I'm twenty-five. Come on, I'll show you your room."

Hoisting Ruth, I followed this spunky college grad across the cement-tiled courtyard, around tarps covered with cloth diapers drying in the sun. I thought it was laundry day, but with sixty children to care for, I quickly learned that *every* day is laundry day. While the home now has industrial-sized washing machines and dryers, at the time of my visit, each soiled diaper and article of clothing had to be scrubbed and rinsed by hand. Esther led me behind a cinderblock wall to our room: a concrete shed with a two-by-four bed and a bare mattress. The only other furniture was a changing table and a crib. A plastic tarp covered the floor.

"Sorry it's a little rough." Esther dropped my bag on the bed. "This is the isolation room where we keep sick children." *Click. Click.* She tried turning on the fan beside the door and frowned. "It must be broken."

Exhausted, I sank on the bed with Ruth. Our room might not be luxurious, but at least it was in our price range: free. When I looked up, a crowd of women blocked the doorway, peering over one another's shoulders.

"Come in!" Esther waved them in. "Meet our Mamas."

Clicking tongues and covering their shy grins with worn hands, the women swarmed around us, filling every remaining inch of space. "Alyssia!" they cried. "You are so beautiful! So big!"

Why did everyone keep calling Ruth by her middle name? I was confused until Esther explained that while Jackie Hodgkins, the home's founder, had given Ruth her first and last names, her Ugandan foster mother had named her Alyssia.

"She is tired from your journey." A woman knelt by my feet with a pink plastic washtub and a box of rose-scented soap. "You would like for me to give her a bath?"

"No thank you," I said, too exhausted to undress her. "I will give her a bath later."

"Alyssia is well?" Another quizzed.

"Very well," I said. "Ruth cannot walk, but she is stronger. And she cannot hear, but we are learning to talk with our hands."

"Sorry. So sorry." Their voices surrounded us like a song.

Before leaving, the Mamas formed a line. Stepping forward one at a time, each took my hand. "Thank you, Mama Alyssia." They bowed their heads. "Thank you for loving one of our babies."

Their gratitude touched me deeply. Welcome Home employed about thirty Mamas—one for every two or three children. Ask a little one "Who's your Mama?" and a tiny finger would instantly point her out. This system, designed to help the children feel secure and loved, was perhaps one reason Ruth had bonded with us so easily.

Just outside our shed stood "God's Glory Kitchen," an open shed where enormous pots boiled over open fires. Crossing the tiled courtyard with Ruth, I ducked to follow Esther beneath long rows of laundry lines. On the other side, several Mamas sat in the shade of a sprawling mango tree swishing flies away from a circle of babies propped in bouncy chairs. The flies aimed for the children's moist eyes and mouths. Seeing us, a stout woman pushed to her feet and smiled. "Alyssia!" She stretched out her arms.

As soon as Ruth saw her, she twisted her body, thrusting herself away from me with a kick. The movement was so forceful, I nearly dropped her. *She doesn't want me*, I thought with a pang, passing Ruth into this other woman's arms. *She belongs here.*

"This is Mama Joy," Esther introduced the woman who had taken care of Ruth as a baby, the woman who had written her birthday card.

As Ruth snuggled against Mama Joy's bosomy chest, she squealed with pleasure as if remembering the woman who had nursed her back to life. Then she rolled her head and locked her eyes on mine, making sure I was still there. When Mama Joy passed Ruth back, I held her tighter, certain that she'd chosen me after all.

After walking through the babies' cottage, where Ruth had spent her first months with the home's youngest and frailest children, we crossed the courtyard to the main house. Inside, double-decker cribs lined room after room with small mounds of sleeping children, diapered bottoms poking up in the air. On the floor beside them, several Mamas slept on woven mats. The only trace of opulence from the Indian family that rented the house to Welcome Home was the dining room's elaborate parquet floor, now covered with tot-sized picnic tables. In the enclosed porch hung a framed photo of a weighty woman wearing clown makeup and a rainbow wig while hugging several children to her chest.

"Mama Jackie," Esther said.

Before leaving, I silently thanked the woman who'd rescued Ruth. When our tour was over, Esther stepped outside, and I laid Ruth on a mat in the corner of the dining room.

"I go. Come back. Go. Come back." I signed, but as soon as I stepped into the hall where I'd spotted a telephone, Ruth wailed, having no way to gauge how far I'd gone since she couldn't hear my steps. "Surprise!" I jumped around the corner, opening my fingers next to my eye and making Ruth grin—a game I often played at home to reassure Ruth that I was nearby. After a few rounds of peekaboo, I pulled my international calling card from my pocket and picked up the phone, dialing a long string of numbers.

"Hello?" Dana's voice crackled across nearly 7,000 miles. Seven hours ahead, I'd caught him eating breakfast. Our children's voices echoed in the background.

"I'm here," I said.

He shushed the kids. "Quiet! It's Mom. How was your trip?"

"Good." I pressed the phone against my ear, struggling to speak. "The court gave us guardianship."

"That's great! What about Ruth's visa?"

I swallowed, swallowed, swallowed.

"Meadow?"

I gripped the phone with both hands, but my mouth wouldn't form the words.

"Are you there?" Dana asked.

All I could see were those babies covered with flies, the mud houses and mounds of burning garbage. The shaved heads and cribs full of children. For the first time I realized the full measure of jeopardy I'd placed Ruth in by bringing her back and what her life would be like if I could not bring her home. Partly choking, partly sobbing, I forced out each word, "We—can't—leave—her—here." With tears streaming down my cheeks, I described everything I'd seen.

"Know what this sounds like?" Dana asked, trying to comfort me.

"What?"

"This sounds like the start of something bigger."

10

Waiting

"What are we going to do?" I ask Dana—ten, twenty, thirty times a day.

"Keep trusting. Keep moving." He grabs his workbag and coffee and kisses me goodbye before moving right on out the door.

I envy him the option.

My days spin in an endless cycle of laundry, work, and children. Judah skateboards and strums guitar. Gabriel shoots hoops. Lydia withdraws into her art and imagination. And I throw dice at the kitchen table in a solitary game of Yahtzee, always hoping for a better score.

"I wish everything was pluses," Lydia says one day, practicing subtraction at the kitchen table. "Everything would be so much easier."

Me too.

My life plus family, plus health, plus success equals happiness.

Yet my algorithms—my rules for solving problems in a finite number of steps—are often flawed.

Too many factors lie beyond my understanding and control.

At night, I climb the stairs and shut the door to our room. Dana grieves however it is that fathers grieve. In the morning, the circle spins all over again, and I gather dice.

Motherless children coughed and cried in their sleep. Their thin wails echoed across the dark courtyard and pierced the isolation of my shed where I lay fully dressed under a mosquito net—one arm holding Ruth, the other a flashlight. A row of termites climbed up the wall near my head. So much for my bug repeller. As soon as I'd found my adapter and plugged it in, sparks had shot from the electrical socket, forcing me to yank it from the wall.

From beyond Welcome Home's cinder-block walls came angry shouts followed by raucous laughter and the loud barking of dogs. Knowing that Janet and Esther had gone for the night, my ears strained to identify each unfamiliar sound. Something heavy dropped on the roof, dragging itself over the ridged metal. A cat? A burglar? A few minutes later, flip-flops slapped across the concrete courtyard, stopping just outside my door. Was it a Mama on her way to the babies' cottage? The *askari* on his rounds? I held my breath and stared at the heavy metal bolt, wishing I'd also closed and latched the wooden shutters beside the iron-barred window. Eventually, the footsteps moved on, and I let out my breath, relieved, and gripped my flashlight tighter. Not that I needed it. On this, my first night in Uganda, I was too scared to turn off the light.

"Does the *askari* carry a gun?" I asked Esther as she drove Ruth and me to town the next morning in Welcome Home's scrappy Datsun, which the government taxed as a "luxury" vehicle despite a cracked windshield and jammed rear doors.

"He carries a bow and arrow." She swerved to avoid a bicycle piled with mattresses rolled like giant sausages.

"A bow and arrow?" She had to be kidding.

"We don't have violent criminals like they do in Nairobi," Esther explained, passing a building that appeared pocked by bullet holes. Nearby, soldiers stood on a street corner with assault rifles slung over their shoulders. "Here it's mostly people looking to steal something they can eat or sell. Last month the night watchman caught a robber sneaking over the wall. He didn't even try to run away."

I wasn't sure whether to believe her. After our trip to the bank and a stop to buy a case of bottled water, we returned to the home, where Esther led me to a back shed. Through the darkened door, she pointed to a tightly strung bow and several homemade arrows leaning against a wall. They looked like something my boys might make to hunt imaginary beasts in the woods back home. Even though the police station was right next door, this did not make me feel safer. I hadn't seen an emergency vehicle since arriving.

"What do people do when there's an accident?" I asked, knowing that traffic accidents are a leading cause of death across Africa.

"They lay the bodies beside the road and wait for someone to claim them."

Death lurked everywhere here it seemed. One day during our first week, Janet and Esther took Ruth and me out for lunch at Ozzie's, an open-fronted café squeezed between the bars and souvenir shops on busy Main Street. As soon as we found a table, the sinewy owner, Jude, hustled over. With white, short-chopped hair and sunbaked skin, she looked every part the Australian expatriate who'd come to Uganda to do missionary work, adopted several children, and stayed.

"Did you hear?" She leaned over our table, breathless with excitement, as traffic whizzed past.

"Hear what?" Janet glanced up from her menu.

"A car hit a little girl out front this morning." Jude gushed. "Didn't even stop. It was good a group of medical missionaries had just sat down for breakfast. Everyone ran out, and they drove the girl to the hospital. I don't know whether she survived. It's been so busy, I haven't even had time to go home and change."

Planting a foot on the rung of Esther's chair, the café owner tugged at the leg of her pale khakis to show us the spattered blood before asking what we wanted for lunch.

On another day, we returned from a trip to find the Mamas, heads bowed, filling long rows of wooden benches in the shade alongside the driveway.

"What are they doing?" I asked.

"Praying," Janet said. "A Mama's one-year-old daughter died this morning."

"How?"

"She had a fever." Janet shrugged. "That's all anyone knows."

My heart ached, wondering how a child could die from such a simple illness. It seemed unfathomable. After laying Ruth down for a nap, I walked to the edge of the driveway and sat on a back bench, bowing my head to pray for one whose pain lay deeper than I could imagine.

Toward the end of our first week in Uganda, William took a taxi to Kampala to pick up Ruth's guardianship paper and returned empty-handed.

"Do not worry," he assured me. "I will go again. A few days, and the paper will be ready."

I did worry—about getting Ruth's visa too. Each day I called the embassy, and each day it wasn't there. To keep busy, I stuffed my pockets with toys from Ruth's therapists and pushed Ruth down the driveway to play with the children. Fascinated by her stroller, they swarmed, poking the wheels and grabbing the handles. They even poked Ruth, yanking the soft brown tufts of her hair. Unable to push them away, Ruth began to fuss.

"Do you want to play?" I brushed away their fingers and pulled a red rubber ball from my pocket, bouncing it on the pavement.

The children pressed closer. Small hands searched my pockets. One boy, with warts protruding from the corners of his eyes and mouth, spit on my shirt.

"No spitting." I shook my head.

He grinned, wound up another glob of spit, and did it again.

A small girl with solemn eyes stood quietly watching from the edge of the garden. I tossed her the ball. "Now bounce it to me." I patted my chest.

She caught it and scampered off to hide behind a tree, clearly afraid to lose her prize. The other children pushed in tighter, hands reaching. There were too many children, too few balls. Beneath their weight, Ruth began to wail. Not knowing what else to do, I pulled the two remaining balls from my pockets and hurled them down the driveway. As the children raced after them, I spun Ruth around and ran up the driveway, ducking behind a metal gate and yanking it closed behind me.

Other days, I joined Esther and William on bone-jarring drives to distant villages, searching for children's relatives. Mandy's first priority was to reunite children with surviving family members, often providing small business loans or goats and chickens to help them, plus paying the children's ongoing medical and educational fees. But in a country where roughly half of the population is younger than fifteen, the second lowest median age in the world,[6] adults willing to raise someone else's child are often hard to find.

Some children, like Ruth, had no known family members. Others had parents too troubled to care for them, due to untreated mental illness or extreme poverty. Part of Esther's job was to find long-term homes for children without able parents. After turning seven, some transferred to Watoto Child Care Ministries in Kampala, one of the largest child rescue organizations in Uganda.

One quest led down a grassy train track to a one-room shelter made of mud and sticks. As we walked down a thin trail, chickens scratched in the dirt yard near a smoldering fire, and children scattered into the brush. A woman, thin as the clothes hanging off her body, pulled a bench from her house and set it beside the fire. Gesturing for us to sit, she knelt in the dirt.

"Jeremiah and Jonah are getting big." Esther held out two manila folders with records of the woman's five-year-old twin sons, who'd been starving before arriving at Welcome Home. "It has been many months since you came to see them. Do you have any plans for them? Any idea where you want them to live?"

"Eh?" asked the mother, who had two additional sets of twins plus a nursing baby.

"Do you want your children to come home?" Esther tried again while William translated. "Because if you do, you need to visit them so they will know you. We can take care of them only a little longer. If you cannot take them, they can go to Watoto, but you must decide. Would you like to see Jeremiah and Jonah's photos?"

The mother's worn face lit up in a smile. She embraced the folders, caressing her sons' faces with a dirty thumb. Peeking around the corner of the house, a girl of about nine watched while balancing a naked baby on her hip.

"I can visit them?" the mother asked.

Esther nodded. "If they are allowed visits, do you want them to go to the other children's home?"

"Yes," the mother whispered, eyes toward the ground.

The ride back to the children's home was somber.

"I feel very bad for that mother," said William, explaining that she did not even own the land on which she'd built her house. "I grew up like that, without even covering my body. No blanket. Nothing. If it rained we did not sleep. We stood because of the water. My mother, she dug the food we ate from the ground with a stick. When I see that lady, my mind goes home."

"Do the rich in Uganda share with those who have nothing?" I asked.

William shook his head, telling of a wealthy uncle to whom he'd once walked a long way, asking to borrow money for school fees. The uncle had chased him away with a stick. How could anyone be so coldhearted?

That night Janet and Esther drove Ruth and me to the Kingfisher Resort on Lake Victoria where a boatman rowed us in a wooden canoe to the underwater spring that forms the beginning of the White Nile. Small whirlpools churned around us as glossy kingfisher birds dove into the water, coal-black backs burning bright in the light of the setting sun. Along the shore, monkeys swung from tree to tree. The beauty was overwhelming. No wonder Winston Churchill had called this country "The Pearl of Africa."

By the time we returned to shore, I was famished. For dinner, I ordered avocado stuffed with tomato salad, creamy potato soup, marinated pork grilled over a fire, fresh-baked flatbread, warm tapioca pudding, and an icy bottle of Coca-Cola—all for less than five dollars. We ate beneath a private, grass-roofed cabana near a glimmering pool where guests frolicked beside a man-made waterfall.

An hour or so later, we climbed back in our car, sleepy and satisfied. Ruth and I hadn't even been able to finish our meal. As we thudded over the railroad tracks on the ten-minute drive back to Welcome Home, I cradled a container of leftovers. Only after slipping my bag of unfinished food in the refrigerator back at the children's home did I realize—with a sudden sickness—that Jeremiah and Jonah's hungry mother and siblings, whom we'd visited hours earlier, lived only a few minutes' walk up those same tracks. And I—I had taken home my leftovers.

If we think we understand the need but do nothing, then we are without a heart or we do not understand, I wrote that night in my journal. *We are like the Pharisee, who seeing the wounded man along the road crossed to the other side and went on his way. It does not matter where we are going. It does not matter what our plans may be. We must stop. We must use all we have to help those who are most wounded.*

In Welcome Home's library, I read a biography about Bob Pierce, the preacher who founded World Vision. Echoing his words, I prayed, "Let my heart be broken by the things that break the heart of God"—little imaging how God would answer this prayer.

Each child at Welcome Home had a story as unique as it was heartbreaking. Four-year-old Raymond had HIV, the virus that causes AIDs, which infects an estimated 7 percent of Uganda's population—a success compared to the previous infection rate of about 15 percent.[7] Both of Raymond's parents had died from the disease. With a round face and belly, Raymond often squeezed close to me as I read to the children on the porch. He especially loved playing with a book shaped like a telephone that I'd brought in a rubber tote full of books.

"Hel-lo!" Raymond puffed out his bare tummy one afternoon, punching plastic numbers on the phone. "This is Raymond. You are there?"

"Hello, Raymond!" I stuck out my thumb and pinky to sign "phone" as Ruth squealed with laughter, watching from her chair. "I am here! How are you?"

"I am *gooood!*" Raymond drew out the word importantly before pretending to hang up and quickly redialing. Every time he saw me, Raymond played this game, and every time he asked the same question, "You are there?"

Grace was a chubby baby with wispy black hair whose mother had given birth to son after son after son. She had prayed for a daughter, only to die while delivering her. Two-year-old Timothy was born with a damaged heart. Too weak to use his legs, this inquisitive little tot pulled himself over the tiled courtyard commando-style, using only his arms, to investigate each bright blade of grass. John was four and had spent the first two years of his life in prison alongside his mother, who was still awaiting trial. Then there were three-year-old sisters, Lora, Lisa, and Lois, whose quadruplet brother had died shortly after birth, mere days after their father. Unable to produce enough milk to feed them and too poor to buy any, their mother lay beside them on the dirt floor of her house, waiting to die, when Mama Mandy found them. Now, with a loan from Welcome Home, their mother ran a vegetable stand and was preparing to bring her daughters home.

Each day brought a new knock at the gate. One Esther told me about was for a one-year-old boy found crawling in a garbage dump. Another was a newborn rescued from a sewage pit. Seeing how loved and looked after these children were, it was easy to forget that most were orphans. Welcome Home resembled any well-run day care I'd ever visited, with one exception: rarely did anyone come to take a child home. Occasionally, a parent or relative arrived to hold a small tot in the quiet of the garden, but many children had no one—a reality as haunting as the silence on the other side of Raymond's question, "You are there?"

As I pushed Ruth around the garden, or bounced her on the trampoline filled with squirming, wriggling babies, or pushed her on the bench swing with toddlers piled two rows deep, the children carefully watched Ruth and me with somber faces as if wondering what special claim she had on me. One Mama for one child? How could this be?

Pick me, four-year-old Cissy seemed to ask, slipping her small hand into mine. She was bright and clever and easy to love. I found myself watching her too, until I realized her eyes were asking for something I couldn't give. From then on I spent more time shaking rattles and singing silly songs with the babies, who were too young to ask. Propped in their circle of bouncy seats, they stared at me with unblinking fascination.

"How old is this one?" I asked Mama Joy, picking up a feather-light girl in a frilly blue dress. No bigger than a newborn, she had enormous brown eyes beneath a thin felt of hair.

"This one?" boasted Mama Joy, who had no children but knew each baby's story like it was her own little one. "This one is Agnes. She is nearly one year old."

"But she's so little!" I gasped.

Mama Joy sucked her teeth in disapproval, telling how Agnes's mother, who suffered from a mental illness, had run away after her birth. The girl's father was so poor he filled her bottle with black tea and sugar. When she was nine months old, he brought her to Welcome Home.

"How much did she weigh?" I asked.

"Seven pounds," Mama Joy said.

Was it possible? How could a nine-month-old baby weigh less than my own children had at birth?

Because of its limited size, Welcome Home could help only the neediest. Before admitting a child, Esther would phone Mama Mandy, who asked, "How starving are they? Is his hair turning orange? Is her skin peeling off?"

When I heard this, I closed my eyes, imagining what might have become of Ruth had the home's beds been full on the day she'd arrived. As I sat with Mama Joy under the mango tree, I discovered more about Ruth, including that her foster mother had pierced her ears—and possibly more.

"Do you know how she got these?" I turned over Ruth's wrist one day to reveal the rough raised scars. "Did Ruth have them when she arrived from the hospital?"

Mama Joy's face hardened, and she shook her head, saying that Ruth had the scars after returning from her foster family. As if holding a knife, she turned over her own arm and drew a long slit. Then she touched Ruth's limp legs. "To make her strong."

"What do you mean?"

Mama Joy suspected that Ruth's arms had been ceremonially cut by a traditional healer—or witch doctor—to remove whatever curse kept her from growing. The idea cut my heart.

Uganda held great beauty—the white rushing Nile, the bats that swooped through the gardens at night, the men singing on their way to work each morning as they walked past the front gate—but great sorrow too. One night while I was reading on the porch, I heard a soft wail. The Mamas sat on the floor outside the kitchen, eating dinner and speaking in soft tribal languages. Not wanting to disturb them, I set down my book and crept from room to room until I found Juliet, Cissy's twin sister, weeping with her face pressed against her mattress on the upper level of a row of cribs.

"What's the matter?" I reached through the wooden bars to rub Juliet's back. Shoulders trembling, she turned away.

All around, small faces pressed against the wooden bars of double-decker cribs, watching to see what I would do. I did what I would have done with my own children. I did what my mother did for me, long ago and far away when the stars shone down on our Oregon fields. "Hush little baby, don't say a word," I sang. "Papa's gonna buy you a mockingbird."

Cissy, in the adjoining crib, lifted her head.

"And if that mockingbird won't sing, Papa's gonna buy you a diamond ring."

Across the room I spotted a long row of stuffed bunnies and bears on a high shelf above the window. Hoping it was allowed, I crossed the room and jumped, pulling down a bear and dropping it over the top of Juliet's crib. She grabbed it with both hands, burying her face in its fur. Instantly, Cissy sprang up. Eyes wide with anticipation, she pointed to the shelf. Quietly as I could, I tiptoed back and jumped, grabbing a bear for her. Suddenly, every child was sitting up, every finger pointing. I jumped, jumped, jumped. Missed! Giggles filled the room. I jumped and missed again, this time on purpose. More giggles. Only when the shelf was empty and every child held a stuffed bear or rabbit did I tiptoe toward the door.

"Quiet." I pressed a finger to my lips. "Go to sleep."

As soon I stepped into the hall—*thunk!* A bear hit the floor. I turned and handed it back to the child who'd accidentally dropped it, starting toward the door again. *Thunk!* Another bear hit the floor. Cissy's impish face grinned through the bars at me.

"No throwing." I handed Cissy her bear.

Thunk! Thunk! Thunk! Bears and bunnies rained down, filling the floor. I scrambled after them, tossing stuffed animals into cribs as fast as I could, but not fast enough. Each time I rescued one floppy animal, another hit the floor. Finally, I stood in the middle of the room, arms raised like a traffic cop.

"No. No." I said. "If you throw the animals, you will not get them back. You must hold on, like this." I picked up a bunny and hugged it to my chest before walking around the room returning each child's prize—Cissy's last of all.

"Hold on." I looked deep into her questioning brown eyes. "Do not let go."

As I stepped into the hall, one final bear hit the floor. I stopped, longing to turn around, yet knowing I couldn't. An hour later, sneaking through the rooms of sleeping children, I saw that each child still clutched a furry friend—all except one. From the middle of the room, I rescued Cissy's stuffed bear and tucked it securely beside her, willing her to hold on.

While waiting for Ruth's papers, I took her for walks down Jinja's dusty streets to shop for baskets, dolls, banana-leaf balls, and animal carvings for family and friends. I baked the brownies and mixed the lemonade I'd brought for the children; worshiped in a church without walls; held Ruth's wobbly head steady to have her hair braided with silky black extensions and bright, jangly beads; visited a neighboring orphanage where children slept in a barn full of beds; and ate bowl after bowl of *posho* and *matoke*, corn and plantains boiled in banana leaves and served with gingery beef stew or warm groundnut sauce. The Mamas insisted that I go first, and the cooks filled my plate with the meatiest bones. After each meal, I watched as the Mamas carefully scraped their uneaten food into plastic containers, discovering that it was to bring home to their children.

Some of the women lived in a nearby boardinghouse run by Welcome Home, which provided them with free health care and education. Each morning and afternoon, they arrived at the gate wearing matching checkered-cotton dresses. I enjoyed getting to know them: Doreen, the affable cook who proudly instructed me how to use the indoor gas oven and was delighted to keep the plastic lemonade containers I'd thrown away; Jean, a beautiful young woman who'd witnessed the murder of her parents and bore a fist-sized scar on her chest from a bus accident; and Esther, tall and elegant enough to be a fashion model, who'd married her boyfriend, believing he had a good job, only to find out that he'd lied. When she became pregnant, he left her.

They watched me with special care, these Mamas—especially when Ruth fussed, like the day I sat with her in the garden, trying to coax her to drink her bottle of ultra-pasteurized, boxed milk that I'd brought in my luggage.

"Maybe she is cold?" One offered a blanket even though the temperature hadn't dipped below 90.

"Maybe she is hungry?" Another held out *chapati*, the Indian flatbread served with most meals.

"Maybe." I held the nipple to Ruth's mouth, unable to figure out what was wrong.

"Come." Mama Rose—a strong, angular woman who towered over the others—stared at me in sharp disapproval. Snatching Ruth's bottle from my hand, she marched toward the main house.

I gathered Ruth and scrambled after her, unsure what I'd done to incur her wrath.

Standing at the sink in the indoor kitchen, Mama Rose filled a plastic basin with steaming water and turned to me. "You put the baby's milk in here, like this." She plunged Ruth's bottle inside. Several minutes later, she pulled it out and held the dripping plastic against my cheek.

Only then did I understand how an abandoned baby from a children's home in a developing country could be so picky about the temperature of her milk. The bottle was hot. Like coffee.

During our second week, William drove me back to Kampala, where Peter handed me a sheet of paper declaring me Ruth's permanent legal guardian. Best of all, Dana called to say Ruth's permanent resident visa to return home had finally been approved. Once we had it, Ruth and I would be free to travel to Nairobi, where at the time all East African immigrants had to go for medical tests and to finalize their visas. From there, Ruth and I were scheduled to fly home. Only, when I arrived at the embassy in Kampala to pick up Ruth's visa, no one knew where it was.

"Don't go until you have it," the consular, Mr. Hancon, warned. "Nairobi is very dangerous, especially for an American woman traveling alone. There's been a recent string of muggings and armed carjackings in broad daylight."

With little more than a week until our flight, I didn't know what to do. Continue waiting, and I'd run out of time to complete Ruth's medical tests. Cross the border, and Ruth could be stranded in Nairobi if the missing visa didn't arrive. Frantic with worry, I called Dana every day, but no one knew where the visa was. As our time in Uganda wound down, my anxiety increased until every breath became a prayer: *Do something, Lord. Do something.*

My sole comfort was sitting on the dining room floor with Ruth after breakfast each morning to join the toddlers and preschoolers for songs and Bible stories. It was Ruth's favorite time too. No matter that she couldn't hear their words, Ruth loved being with the children, squealing as the Mamas herded each flock of squirming tots into the room.

"Wel-come, we love you!" sang Baby Justine, the home's preschool teacher, whose delicate features belied a powerful voice. "The Lord will come, and he will say, 'Welcome!'"

Leaping and clapping, the children danced to the rhythm of Baby Justine's fast-flying hands as she sat on the floor pounding a rawhide drum.

"Who is your daddy?" she asked as the children spread out on the floor.

"Jesus!" a chorus of high-pitched voices shouted.

"Who is your doctor?"

"Jesus!" Small fists punched the air.

"Who is your protector?"

"Jesus!"

Eight months pregnant, Baby Justine arrived at the home each morning riding sidesaddle on the back of a *boda-boda* bicycle taxi. "I have a baby in my belly. I have a baby at home. I have babies all around me," she'd explained her nickname with a laugh. The daughter of a witch doctor, she was now married to a local pastor. Sitting on the floor of the babies' breakfast room, Baby Justine pulled out a giant Bible storybook and read to the children about heaven and its streets of gold. Then she pulled the drum back toward her swollen belly. All around the room, children leaped to their feet. Placing their hands on one another's small shoulders, they formed a conga line.

"We are the children, we are the children that the Lord has made, that the Lord has made!" they sang to a familiar tune. Twisting and jumping, they danced their way out of the room as another group filed in. But if these were God's children and he had so much, why did they have so little? How powerless they were, how poor. Yet these abandoned and destitute children possessed a faith for which I grasped: the confidence that God would take care of them no matter what. So did Baby Justine.

One morning, after leading the children in praise, Baby Justine invited me to meet her in the garden. Sitting beneath a canopy, she opened her well-worn Bible to Jeremiah 32:27 and took my hands in hers. "The Lord has brought you here for a reason," she said. "He has given me words to encourage you. Repeat after me, 'Behold, I am the Lord, the God of all flesh.'"

"I am the Lord, the God of all flesh," I echoed uncertainly.

"Is anything too difficult for me?"

"Is anything too difficult for me?"

She flipped to Isaiah 41:10. "Do not fear, for I am with you."

"Do not fear, for I am with you."

"Do not anxiously look about you, for I am your God."

Again, I repeated her words.

"I will strengthen you, surely I will help you; surely I will uphold you with My righteous right hand."

Slowly, as God's word penetrated my anxious heart, fear began to lose its power over me.

Then Baby Justine prayed with the same power with which she beat the drum—rhythmic, confident, resonating.

I knew then what I had to do.

And I knew I wouldn't be alone.

11

A Small Thing

The knowledge steals over me like a horror,
and I hear myself screaming inside.
How can this be?
I hold your picture and see you looking at me with such love
it breaks my heart. Will I ever look in your eyes again?
Each night I crawl into bed and weep.
Child, my child, I would rock you,
take you in my arms,
hold you against my chest,
feel your rigid body relax against mine
and go on rocking you forever.
Daughter, my daughter, I need to know where you are.
Please?
Be somewhere warm.
Be laughing.

"Whenever the bus stops, get out and watch so no one steals what belongs to you," William warned as the sun broke over the red parched earth early on the last Tuesday of July. We stood along a dirt road with Ruth in her travel seat, waiting for the bus to Nairobi. Our flight left the following Monday evening. After one full day of travel, that left just three business days to complete all of Ruth's paperwork and medical tests—including procuring her missing visa. Getting it all done would take a miracle.

"Remember," Esther had warned, arriving at the children's home earlier that morning to pray and hug me goodbye, "if you can't get Ruth's visa, call and I will send someone from the orphanage to bring her back."

Leaving Ruth seemed unthinkable. But what could I do? Once again our tickets weren't changeable, and I lacked money to buy new ones. In retrospect, it seemed foolish to have given ourselves so little time, but with Dana's work—not to mention my desire to return home—three weeks was all I could muster. Miss our flight and I'd have no way home. I didn't even know where Ruth and I would stay in Nairobi, a city so dangerous the United Nations had recently downgraded its security status to below that of Bogotá and Beirut. More than a third of the city's residents had reported being robbed with the threat of violence within a single year, earning it the nickname "Nairobbery."[8] Before leaving home, I'd told Kathy, a friend at our church, how scared I was of traveling to such a crime-ridden city where I knew no one.

"Oh, I know someone in Nairobi!" Kathy had piped up. "A friend introduced me to her at a Bible study while she was here for college. Her dad is a pastor. I'll find her phone number."

Her name? Naomi.

The connection was uncanny. In the Bible, Naomi was Ruth's traveling companion. After the young woman had lost her husband, her mother-in-law, Naomi, led Ruth to a land where Ruth was a foreigner, knowing nobody. There, the older woman watched over the younger, keeping her safe and providing her with a new family. Only, on the many times when I'd tried calling *this* Naomi, she hadn't been home. Her mother, Rose, had promised, however, to have Naomi meet Ruth and me at the bus station.

Beside us in the breaking light stood a handful of locals, somber and silent as they looked down the empty road, and a bubbly band of college girls whose perky blonde ponytails and British accents carried on the early morning breeze. Through the neighboring field, two barefoot girls with water jugs balanced on their heads walked up a path, crossing the road to a nearby petrol station. The smoke of early morning cook fires concealed the distant edge of the field. My own destination was equally hazed. As a hulking red bus roared up beside us, I could only hope that Naomi had got the message.

After helping stow our luggage, William bent down to stroke Ruth's cheek. She grinned up at him, always eager for the next adventure.

"Have a good journey." He reached for my hand, shaking it. "Everything will be okay."

I was so scared, I considered begging William to go with me. Once more, I was being asked to trust without knowing what lay ahead or whether we would succeed. It was my biggest test yet. Fly or fail. There was no other option. To bring Ruth home, I had to keep moving forward, believing that God would go with me. Heaving my pack onto my shoulder and gripping a plastic bag filled with our lunch, I said goodbye to the last person I knew on the continent. Then I drew in the wheels on Ruth's chair and carried her onboard our bus. My one comfort was having splurged on a "luxury" coach ticket. For the next ten hours, at least, I anticipated being pampered. Only our driver didn't seem to appreciate this fact. The moment I climbed the narrow stairwell, he shut the door and gunned the engine. The bus swayed violently, like a ship tossed on a stormy sea. The force threw me against the wall.

"Slow down!" someone yelled as I reached the aisle, struggling to hoist Ruth, still in her chair, above the heads of the other passengers and carry my belongings.

As the bus careened from side to side, I smashed into seats. Hands reached up to keep us from falling. About halfway down the aisle, my flimsy lunch sack ripped open. Biscuits, fruit, and a bottle of juice rolled down the aisle. Our seats were over the rear axle. As soon as I reached them, I dropped Ruth into one and fell into the other. After two weeks in Uganda, I thought I'd grown used to the driving, but this was insane! The bus shook so hard, it felt as if we were being dragged without wheels. As the driver swerved around obstacles and traffic, we hit something so hard my elbow slammed into the metal armrest. Pain shot up my arm, and the seat in front of me fell apart, sending a solid sheet of plastic banging against my legs.

"Jesus!" I screamed, a one-word prayer, as the driver shot into oncoming traffic to avoid a boulder in the center of the unfinished road.

A woman a few rows back began to wail. Some luxury! As I looked around, I realized that our bus didn't even have a bathroom. It did, however, have a television mounted to the ceiling—but only one movie. As we clung to our armrests, barreling toward Kenya, Harrison Ford repeatedly fought to rescue hostages from a hijacked plane. Whether from the brutal jarring or her early wake-up, Ruth quickly fell asleep, completely at peace. No matter what her circumstances, no matter how little control she had, Ruth trusted that everything would be okay. Following her lead, I leaned back in my seat, closed my eyes, and prayed: *Lord, go before us. Lord, make a way.*

❧
....

Uganda's eastern highway cut through rural villages of round, thatched-roofed houses and low-slung towns. Here the traffic was mostly goats and chickens. Next to the road, farmers stood knee-deep in swampy fields of rice. Men scooped mud from watery pits, packing wooden molds to dry in the hot sun beside mounds of finished bricks. In small towns of crumbling concrete, bright signs with colorful names dangled above open doorways—the *Magic Price Shop*, the *Corner Bar & Rest*, and—my favorite—*Fort Jesus*.

A couple of hours into our journey, the bus jerked to a stop. Soldiers blocked the road, and a uniformed officer climbed onboard. While he checked our driver's papers, a money changer walked down the aisle, waving a wad of cash. Believing that this small checkpoint was the Kenyan border, I handed him a wad of Ugandan bills and received Kenyan bills in return, hoping that I hadn't just been cheated. Janet had warned me about Kenya's notoriously high rate of government corruption, but I didn't want to be caught without cash. Soon after, the bus stopped again. Before us rose a huge barbed-wire fence surrounding what looked like a cattle yard. Only it was crammed with people. On the other side, dozens of buses—each identical to ours—filled a vast parking lot.

"Out!" Our driver stood and pointed toward the door. "Everyone out!"

The other passengers stood, threading their way down the aisle, but I didn't move, unsure what was happening.

"Out!" The driver pointed at me.

"She cannot walk." I wrapped my arm around Ruth.

"Everyone out!" His face grew fiery. "This is Kenya. You, OUT!"

Terrified of getting lost, I scurried to my feet, tucked Ruth into her sling, and grabbed my pack to join the swirling throng outside. Where was I to go? I whirled around, recognizing no one. Then, through the mob, I spotted a glint of golden hair. The girls from our bus! I plunged after them. Pushing my way through the crowd, I caught up just as they disappeared inside a dim, stuffy shed crammed with people. I followed them inside. Up front, behind a long counter, a row of immigration officers checked papers and stamped passports. While the college girls stood to the side, I wedged myself in line beside their African guide, relieved to reach adjacent clerks at the same time.

"Where are you going?" a stern-faced official asked me.

"Nairobi." I supported Ruth with one arm while fumbling in my pack for our papers. I was so tense, my hands were shaking. Several papers fluttered to the floor, and I scrambled to retrieve them while one of the college girls offered to hold Ruth. Thankful for the help, I passed her into the young woman's arms.

"You are taking this child?" The officer gestured toward Ruth.

"I am her legal guardian." I slid my letter from the court across the counter.

After examining it, he handed the paper to a clerk and asked for money. "I need to make a copy."

I quickly offered the officer a Kenyan bill.

"It is too much." He waved it away at the same time that the college girls' guide gathered their passports and started toward a side door.

"I have to leave," the young woman apologized and handed Ruth back to me before following their guide out the side door.

"It is the smallest I have," I told the clerk. "I have to stay with my group."

"I cannot take it."

"Please." I begged. "I'll miss my bus."

Still he refused. For the life of me, nothing I said could convince this supposedly corrupt government official to take my money. By now I was frantic, certain Ruth and I would be left behind. Who should I call? Where would I spend the night? Then, from the back of the room, a voice called, "Here."

I turned to see a foreigner, like me, standing at the back of the crowd. He wore a white panama hat and stretched his arm over the pressed-in bodies of the other travelers. I reached over people's heads as he reached toward me, pressing a coin into the palm of my hand.

"Thank you!" I cried, quickly handing the money to the officer.

The clerk disappeared out the door with Ruth's guardianship papers. Minutes felt like hours before he returned with the photocopy. *Chink! Chink!* With two quick jabs of a rubber stamp, the officer issued our visas and waved us on. Clutching Ruth, I raced out the door and into the massive parking lot, which was jammed with people and buses. Through the crush of bodies, I spotted the girls from our bus! Ruth bobbed on my hip as I forced my way after them, clambering back onboard the bus. After finding our seats, I collapsed, thanking God for putting these easy-to-spot girls on our bus. A few minutes later as it pulled away, I spotted a white panama hat on a man moving away through the crowd. For all I knew the man wearing it had saved our lives, and I didn't even know his name.

As our bus roared through the Great Rift Valley, zebras grazed in tall grass beside the road under flat-topped acacia trees. Men and women with enormous baskets slung on their backs picked tea leaves on a green hill in the sweltering sun. And the shore of a distant lake glowed pink from the feathers of millions of flamingos feasting in its algae-rich water. Along the way, we stopped in a remote town just long enough for everyone to get out and use a pit latrine—like an outhouse, but with only a hole in the ground. On my way to use it, I threw away my unopened breakfast tray, which apparently came with my ticket. Not knowing when the next bathroom break would be, I didn't dare eat.

Only after reboarding did I see the bus driver's assistant collecting leftover trays from other passengers and passing them out the window to a crowd of children who surrounded the bus with upraised hands. One boy, who looked the same age as Judah, walked away with a nearly full tray, grinning from ear to ear. Then a bigger boy ran up behind him and smacked the bottom of his hands. Sausages, eggs, and pancakes flew through the air and landed on the grass where they were quickly snatched by dozens of eager children. The young boy walked away empty-handed, and I felt ashamed, knowing that my own meal lay in the garbage. Would I ever learn?

The sun was just beginning to set as our bus chugged up a steep hill on the east side of the valley, where we passed an overturned cargo truck. Cardboard boxes tumbled down the grassy bank. I didn't see any people but hoped the driver was okay. As we neared Nairobi, one of Africa's largest cities, the road widened, filling with traffic. Several times the bus stopped to let people off, and I strained to see out the window, searching for the main terminal where I was to meet Naomi. But what did it look like?

When the bus finally shuddered to a halt in an unmarked parking lot, the driver and remaining passengers collected their things and climbed off. I did the same, hoping this was the place. Only when I parked Ruth on the sidewalk and looked in the open bins under the bus, I didn't see our suitcases. Darting to the other side, I yanked open the first bin I came to, unleashing a whirlwind of feathers. Squawking chickens fluttered to the asphalt and scurried across the busy parking lot. Behind their overturned crate, I spotted our luggage. What to grab first? Some unlucky traveler's runaway dinner? Or our stuff? As I waved my arms to keep the remaining birds from escaping, a taxi driver rushed over to help. After returning several birds to their crate, he helped me retrieve my luggage and carry it to Ruth, who sat patiently waiting.

"You would like a ride?" The man gestured toward his taxi as I profusely thanked him.

"I am meeting someone." I looked around, but no one was waiting. Around seven o'clock at night, it was quickly growing dark, and I began to worry. "Do you have a phone?"

The driver pulled a cell phone out of his shirt pocket but explained that he needed to buy minutes. After giving him money, I waited while he ran up the street to a sidewalk kiosk. When he returned, I dialed Naomi's number.

"Where are you?" Rose asked.

I looked up and read her the name on the nearest building, "The Marble Arch Hotel."

"That is the place," she said. "Do not go anywhere. Naomi is on her way."

As soon as I hung up and handed back the phone, someone called my name. I turned to see a stylish young woman with a smooth-shaved head and round metal glasses staring curiously at me.

"Naomi?" I asked.

Her smile was the answer I needed. I held out my hand, incredulous but happy to see her.

"This is my brother, Daniel." Naomi introduced the stocky teenager standing beside her. "Let us carry your luggage. We have a taxi waiting."

It took creativity to cram four people, all of our luggage, and Ruth's bulky travel chair into the small sedan, but soon we were speeding down a brightly lit highway, suitcases piled on our laps. Within ten minutes, an ominous *thump* caused our driver to pull off the road. A flat tire. No matter. I was so thrilled to have found Naomi and her brother, I willingly stood beside the road with all of our luggage while the driver pulled out a spare tire. Half an hour later, we were back on our way.

"Welcome," said Rose, an ample woman with a broad smile. She and her husband, the Rev. Solomon Mwalili, greeted us on the warmly lit porch of their family's small home. "Praise God, you are safe!"

Later, she revealed that a Western woman traveling by bus on this same route one week earlier had been drugged, mugged, and dumped on the side of the road before being rescued.

After a refreshing shower and clean clothes, Ruth and I sat in this family's snug living room, feasting on rice, noodles, seasoned beef, fresh fruit, and steaming mugs of chai—my first meal all day. The hospitality of Naomi's family amazed me. Unknown to me, we'd arrived during peak tourist season. Every hotel Naomi had called on our behalf was full, but two guests at a hostel run by her father's church, the Free Pentecostal Fellowship in Kenya, squeezed in together so Ruth and I could have a room. Naomi had even taken three days off work to escort us around the city. That night, lying next to Ruth between clean sheets at the Free Pentecostal Fellowship in Kenya Kindaruma Guest House, I was overwhelmed with gratitude to find ourselves among friends. God had truly gone before us. Now, if only Ruth's visa was waiting.

First thing after breakfast, Naomi arrived at the guesthouse in a taxi to accompany Ruth and me to the US Embassy. I'd already called, only to discover that Ruth's visa was still missing.

Naomi suggested that we visit the embassy anyway. "Maybe there is something we can do while we are waiting."

While I sat in the backseat of the taxi with Ruth, the driver wound past sprawling mansions with red-tiled roofs tucked behind thick concrete walls topped with spiraling loops of razor wire. The newly built embassy—all reflective glass and shiny metal—loomed large and angular behind a spiked metal fence, American flag flapping in the breeze. With a wide stone walkway curving across a sprawling green lawn, it reminded me of the Emerald City in the *The Wizard of Oz*. Since Naomi wasn't an American and didn't have an appointment, she was brusquely turned away by a female guard. After passing through security with Ruth, I slung my pack over my shoulder and wheeled her through the gate and up the winding path toward the glass doors, hoping we'd find inside the magic we needed to finally go home.

"I don't know what to tell you." Jason, the assistant to the consulate general, shook his head when it was our turn to stand at the counter. "I've searched for the visa under both of your names and found nothing."

"Nothing?" I asked in growing despair. Then I remembered Naomi's suggestion. "Is there anything we can do while we're waiting?"

"Have you completed Ruth's medical exams?"

I shook my head. "Where do we start?"

Jason handed me a list of tests Ruth needed before her visa could be finalized. "Medical exams are required for certain types of United States visas," I read. "Completion of the medical and all related tests require at least one week."

One week! We had three days.

Returning to the taxi, I handed the paper to Naomi. She read through the list of doctors and directed our driver to one of the largest shopping malls in East Africa, Sarit Centre, a modern complex of glass-walled shops connected by a three-story ramp. Dr. Dogra's office occupied the top floor, but his schedule was full. After scheduling Ruth's physical exam for the following afternoon, we enjoyed a lunch of spicy lamb stew and *chapati* in the food court before driving across the city to snap photos for Ruth's visa. Then we headed to a medical lab to complete her blood work. Ruth was such a trooper, smiling at everyone we met—especially the photographer. She loved having her picture taken. Needles, not so much.

"Nurse take your blood," I signed, making a sad face as I held Ruth on my lap in the clinic. "Hurt. Sorry."

When the technician inserted the needle into the thin back of her hand, Ruth clenched her eyes and wailed like a fire engine—*waaah-waaah-waaah!* Since Ruth couldn't hear, whenever she closed her eyes she was shut off from the world. My touch her only comfort, I brushed my lips across Ruth's tear-streaked cheek, holding her close as her blood filled several vials.

"How long will the test results take?" I asked the technician when it was finally over and Ruth stopped crying.

"A few days." He bandaged her skin.

"That's impossible." I said. "We need it tomorrow."

"For an additional fee—" The man shrugged. "It will be here tomorrow."

Worried about our dwindling cash, I paid. Fortunately, Naomi worked at a bank and helped me replenish my money using my credit card. While walking through downtown Nairobi, with its soaring buildings and busy streets, we stepped around a group of men and women sitting on the sidewalk, selling newspapers.

"These are our blind," Naomi explained. "The government sets apart this corner for them to earn money."

Later, walking past a grassy park, I spotted an emaciated man with a crooked body sitting on a cardboard mat. It scared me, wondering what Ruth's life would be like if I couldn't bring her home. That night, as Naomi dropped us off at the guesthouse for dinner, I desperately hoped to find a message from the embassy saying they'd located Ruth's visa—but there was nothing.

"It is a small thing." A guesthouse worker comforted me that night at dinner as Ruth and I shared a long table with a dozen other lodgers. My companions included a Brazilian soccer coach, a college student, a handful of Kenyan pastors, and an American husband and wife adopting a Kenyan teenager whom they'd previously met on a mission trip. After hearing Ruth's story, all of them were praying for Ruth's visa. "God will do it," our server said. "You will see."

Yes, I thought, *but in time?*

I was filled with anxiety, every moment questioning whether God would come through in the way I'd hoped and prayed, while privately fearing the choice I'd have to make if he didn't. Back in our room, with the sounds of the city carrying through our open window, I got Ruth ready for bed and tucked her in. Exhausted, I lay down beside her and opened my Bible, but the words blurred together. I couldn't concentrate. Ruth began to fuss, thrashing her fisted arms and straining toward me. Knowing she hadn't eaten much for dinner, I poured a carton of milk into her bottle and wrapped my free arm under her head, gently squeezing her cheeks. Ruth forced out the nipple with her tongue. A muffin mashed with milk to make it easier to swallow brought the same response.

"Come on, Ruth." I steadied her twisting body with one hand and held a spoon with the other. "Open your mouth," I said, opening mine.

Still Ruth refused. I slipped the spoon between her teeth anyway. As soon as Ruth swallowed, I inserted more. On the third bite she spit out the muffin and wailed. Food and tears dribbled down her face. All of my frustration and fear turned into anger, and I tossed the spoon. What was I supposed to do with this child?

Just hold her, God spoke quietly to my heart.

I was so weary, holding anyone was the last thing I wanted, but I wrapped my arms around Ruth anyway. I pulled her crooked body against mine, rocking her in bed until she began to relax, and I did too. Calmed by Ruth's warmth and nearness, I lay there, wondering what to do as she fell asleep in my arms. Soon after, someone knocked on my door.

"Telephone!" a woman called.

Hoping it was the embassy, I made sure Ruth was safe and followed the guesthouse worker downstairs to the kitchen, where a cook finished scrubbing pots. A telephone dangled above a big stainless-steel sink. I picked up the receiver.

"Did you get Ruth's visa?" It was Dana calling from his office during what was the middle of the day for him.

"No one knows anything about it," I said miserably.

"I don't understand." He sounded frustrated. "I called the immigration office again today, and they keep saying it's been approved."

"Then where is it?" I snapped, as if it was his fault. "I've been running around all day, trying to finish Ruth's medical work, and it won't do any good without that paper!"

"I'll see if I can find someone else to talk to."

"Well, you better." I smashed the phone into its cradle and buried my face in my hands.

Done.

Finished.

The owl mommy wanted to go home.

ॐ

....

After breakfast Thursday morning, I rehashed my options. Call Esther and ask someone from the orphanage to get Ruth? Or miss our flight? Incapable of deciding, I curled up on a couch in the lounge and watched the news while Ruth napped beside me. Suspected terrorists had been arrested in London. Nigerian villagers were starving from famine along with their herds of cattle. A Sudanese government official had been killed in a helicopter crash, endangering a peace deal to end a two-decade civil war. And Ruth's life rested on a missing piece of paper. Did God even care?

"Meadow Merrill?" A receptionist stepped into the room. "There is a telephone call for you."

Ashamed for hanging up on Dana, I followed her down the hall to the office, ready to apologize when I picked up the phone. "Hello?"

"We have the approval for Ruth's visa."

The embassy!

"Come in first thing tomorrow," Jason said. "As long as you have Ruth's completed medical work, we can stamp her passport before we close at noon."

"Thank you. Thank you. Thank you." I slumped in a chair, barely believing it was true.

Unknown to me, after our phone call Dana had left work and driven to the South Portland immigration office to get a list of contact numbers. All afternoon and into the night he'd dialed number after number until someone somewhere located the approval for Ruth's missing visa and forwarded it to Nairobi. Friday, we returned to the embassy with our completed medical forms. One hour after the office had officially closed for the weekend, we received the stamp declaring Ruth a permanent American resident. As I pushed her chair out the front doors and down the path toward the gate, my excitement soared with each step. I felt as if I was propelling Ruth toward freedom.

Saturday, Naomi and Daniel borrowed a friend's sputtering Volkswagen Rabbit and drove us through the Nairobi National Park where I stuck my head out the sunroof to photograph flocks of ostrich, long-limbed giraffes, and sharp-horned buffalo. Although huge signs warned visitors to stay in their vehicles, ours kept breaking down.

Each time, seventeen-year-old Daniel gamely jumped out to fiddle with the engine while I kept a nervous watch for lions. Sunday was for celebrating, and we joined Naomi's family at their stone church in the heart of the city, lifting our voices with hundreds of others in praise to God.

Yet, we faced one final hurdle. To fly home, Ruth needed a new British transit visa, a process that we were warned could take up to a week. Only, without Ruth's visa, we hadn't been able to apply for it. All weekend, it gnawed at me, making me afraid that we might still miss our flight.

"This is an opportunity for you to see God working," Naomi's father, Solomon, said. "Then you will know it was only God who made it possible."

The faith of those I met here challenged me to believe more than ever that God was in control. Not just sometimes. Not just when I understood. But all the time. Even when I didn't. No matter what. Trust. Trust. Trust. Fly. Fly. Fly.

Monday morning, while Naomi returned to work, Ruth and I took a taxi to the British embassy. That afternoon, six hours before our plane was scheduled to leave, Ruth received the final stamp. After nearly one month in East Africa, I was bringing Ruth home! God alone had made it possible, just as Solomon said. That evening, after a final meal together, Naomi's family crowded into their Jeep to drive Ruth and me to the airport.

"How can I ever thank you?" I took Naomi's hands in mine as we stood inside the terminal, saying goodbye.

"Oh, Meadow," she said. "It has been my joy."

A few hours later, as our plane soared into the star-studded African sky, I looked at Ruth, sleeping beside me, and marveled at how—in a city of three million people—God had led us to Naomi, the one person able to help me bring Ruth home. Forty hours later at Logan International Airport, Judah, Gabriel, and Lydia broke away from Dana and ran down the long terminal toward us. Ruth, buckled in her travel seat, squealed with delight as Lydia dove into my arms.

"Oh, Mommy!" She clung to me. "It's you!"

The boys, who seemed to have grown much older and bigger in the month we'd been gone, threw their arms around us while Dana reached over their heads and pulled me close.

"It's a love cookie!" Judah shouted as his little brother and sister squeezed between us like frosting. "We're the sugar in the middle!"

"And Ruth!" Gabriel clutched his sister's hand.

Being together felt so good, so right. Ruth was safe. She was home. Now, we could help her learn and grow. Was Ruth profoundly intellectually challenged as the neurologist said? Or did something else explain her limitations and disabilities? Either way, from now on, my arms would be her arms, my feet her feet, my voice her voice. Wherever Ruth needed to go, I would carry her. Nothing but death would ever part her from me.

12

Talking Hands

Come back to me.
Come rolling up the ramp through fresh-fallen snow.
Run laughing down High Street.
Come any way you want.
In colors.
In dreams.
In songs.
In laughter.
Return all the hours I wasted,
not knowing how few we'd have.

"Name?" asked the gray-haired gatekeeper as he leaned out of the security booth at the entrance of Mackworth Island, hand extended.

Salty October air chilled my skin as I passed my identification card through the van window. Behind us, seagulls dropped fresh mussels on the paved causeway near the mouth of the Presumpscot River, cracking the shells and gobbling the meaty flesh inside.

Three months after returning from Africa, Ruth was well into a new school year. Twice each week I continued driving our kids to the school for the deaf. The setting was spectacular: one hundred acres set like an emerald in dazzling Casco Bay. Lobster boats and luxury yachts swept past on a stiff Atlantic breeze, but the island's swaying pines and pebble beach concealed a brutal history, one that revealed the vulnerability of children like Ruth.

Until 1975, when Congress passed the Individuals with Disabilities Education Act, which forced public schools to admit students with special needs, deaf children as young as five were routinely removed from their families and sent to state-run boarding schools around the country. Nearly two decades earlier, Maine's former governor, Percival Baxter, had donated $675,000 to build a school for the deaf on his family's former island estate, which he gifted to the state.[9]

Originally located in Portland under a previous name, the Governor Baxter School for the Deaf opened in 1957 and is commonly called Baxter in honor of the millionaire bachelor and philanthropist. Tragically, the island's remoteness further isolated students, some of whom were sexually and physically abused by the very people charged with protecting them.

In 1982, the Maine attorney general's office corroborated victims' claims that the staff routinely abused students at the school including during the 1960s and 1970s, but by then no one could be charged because the statute of limitations had expired.[10] In 2001, after two years of lobbying by former students and the police-shooting death of an abuse victim who brandished an unloaded firearm in a Scarborough parking lot, essentially committing suicide to raise awareness of former students' suffering, Governor Angus King apologized to the deaf community for the abuse, and the legislature approved a $17 million victims' compensation fund. Only now, all these years later, was the horror beginning to ebb. One year before I'd brought Ruth to the island, former students had ceremonially burned down an island farmhouse where much of the abuse had occurred. Having interviewed survivors and written about the school's troubled history for *The Boston Globe*, I'd heard students' stories firsthand.[11] Fresh in my mind was the testimony of one victim who told of being tied naked to a tree and left there all night as punishment for refusing a staff member's sexual demands. That anyone could be so cruel terrified me. Statistically, children with disabilities are as much as 70 percent more likely to be abused as their typically developing peers.[12] If someone hurt Ruth, she would have no way to protect herself, no way to tell us.

That was one reason we were so committed to helping Ruth communicate. Another was watching her small fingers curl around the sleeve of a favorite dress she didn't want to take off at bedtime. Or hearing her howl at Gabriel's sixth birthday party when, in sheer busyness, I accidently served every child juice except her. Or seeing her face brighten with glee when Dana signed, "You want bath?" Ruth was determined to express herself.

"What's Ruth's sign name?" asked Tiffany, Baxter's parent-and-infant teacher, who had greeted us with a smile on Ruth's first visit six months earlier. She was young and pretty with long brown hair and a smile that made even shy Lydia crawl in her lap.

To answer her question, I'd crossed my pointer and middle fingers to form an "R" and brushed the tip of my nose.

Tiffany looked puzzled.

"Because of Ruth's cute nose," I explained, knowing that sign names are usually formed by combining the first letter of a person's name with a physical characteristic or personality trait.

Tiffany remained oddly quiet, but when I later repeated Ruth's sign name while introducing the members of my family in sign language class, Rita, our deaf teacher, waved her hands in horror. *Rude*, she wrote on the whiteboard, indicating the sign I'd made. Or . . . she crossed her pointer and middle finger, veered them off the tip of her nose, and wrote *rat*.

Embarrassed, I slunk in my seat as Rita tapped her overlapped fingers from right to left under her nose as if smelling a flower. *Rose*, she wrote, suggesting a more appropriate sign name.

Since we had already considered adding Rose to Ruth's middle name in honor of Naomi's mother, Ruth's new sign name stuck. From then on, whenever we talked about Ruth, we signed "Rose." Thankfully, we found Baxter to be a safe, welcoming community where children were nurtured and loved.

Learning to speak with our hands took practice. My stiff fingers spelled words one painstaking letter at a time, while the hands of those around me flew faster than I could see. I'd still be decoding the first couple of words or letters long after the signer had finished a full sentence. Whenever Tiffany signed "voice off," a request that meant "no talking," my communication skills dissolved into a series of smiles, nods, and finger pointing. Thankfully, Baxter employed interpreters. The one place they weren't allowed was Rita's class.

"What words do you want to know?" our spunky, middle-aged teacher asked when we sat down for our weekly language class that fall. Handing out dry erase markers to the six or so moms and several children gathered in the room, she pointed to the whiteboard and invited us to write down a wish list of words.

Town, grocery store, library, teacher, I wrote, forming the words I needed most. *Bazooka, lasso, explosion, bomb*, wrote Judah and Gabriel, with a little help on spelling. Meanwhile, Lydia, the only child in Ruth's class who could hear, was learning faster than all of us. Assigning herself as Ruth's interpreter, her small hands fluttered through the air like butterflies. Buckled in the van beside Ruth as we drove home from a long morning at Baxter, Lydia later piped up, "Does a smile mean 'I love you'?"

"Sure," I replied, wondering what she was thinking.

"Then Ruffie loves me very much," she said.

Ruth's smile communicated what her hands could not. So did her nose.

"See Ruth wrinkle her nose?" Melinda, a deaf mentor, signed one day while observing Ruth in class. "Does she do that often?"

"Don't know." I touched my fingers to my forehead and turned my hand away.

"Watch." Melinda snatched a plastic banana from the room's play kitchen and held it toward Ruth. "You want?"

Ruth wrinkled her nose and smiled.

"That's a deaf 'yes.'" Melinda indicated. "She's developing language."

After half a year of wearing hearing aids, Ruth was also more vocal. Now, when I pressed my lips against her cheek or held her hand to my throat and said "Mama," she hummed *Mmmm*. Ruth had two types of cerebral palsy—spastic, which stiffened her muscles; and athetoid, which made her head involuntarily weave from side to side. This made even nodding "yes" or "no" too challenging. To give Ruth all the support we could, Dana and I drove her to Boston Children's Hospital to be evaluated for a cochlear implant, a complex surgery that enables the deaf to hear. The program's director wanted to wait one year to see how quickly Ruth learned sign language, but the delay was frustrating. The first four years of life are critical for language development. Waste them, and Ruth might never catch up. And so we and Ruth's teachers set out to teach her everything we could.

"Where Lydia?" I wagged my pointer finger and shaped my hand into an "L," circling it beside my cheek, while sitting across from Ruth in the living room.

Ruth's eyes darted toward Lydia, playing with plastic farm animals on the floor, and she gave a happy squeal. *Learning was fun!*

We also attached family photos to Ruth's eye-gaze board. When we signed a name, Ruth raised or lowered her eyes to stare at the right picture. In the year she'd been with us, her desire to communicate had become much more focused—grasping a crayon to move it across a sheet of paper, wriggling her body when she wanted to be picked up, screeching if someone stood between her and the television. One evening, while I read to the girls on the couch, Lydia stole Ruth's half-finished bottle. A few seconds later, Lydia began to scream.

"What's wrong?" I gasped, seeing that Ruth had slouched sideways, her face against Lydia's arm.

"Ruffie's biting me!" Lydia howled.

Sure enough, Ruth's teeth were clamped onto her sister's arm in retaliation for the stolen milk—and she was smiling.

Another day I sat at the kitchen table feeding Ruth the rare treat of a doughnut. When it was gone, I signed, "What you want?"

Wedged in her wooden high chair, Ruth giggled and stared at the top of the fridge, where I'd stashed the remaining doughnuts. Needless to say, she got another one. Recognizing how much Ruth wanted to participate, I wondered what her life would have been like had she remained in Uganda. One afternoon at Welcome Home, I'd had a glimpse when the *askari* had knocked on my door with a message from Jude, the café owner:

Dear Meadow,

This note is to introduce my friend who has a brain damaged child. She really needs encouragement.

Waiting for me outside the gate was a young mom, Juliet, whose two-year-old daughter, Grace, had cerebral palsy. After introducing Juliet to Ruth, I visited her home, a few blocks away. Inside, I found a plump little girl with round cheeks buckled in a homemade wooden chair. Her eyes stared vacantly toward the ceiling. Without therapy or a proper wheelchair, Grace spent most of her days inside, often alone after being abandoned by caregivers while her parents worked. As a result she slept during the day and lay awake crying most of the night, overwhelming her exhausted parents. Grace loved music—especially the lively worship at her family's church—but without an easy way to transport her, she seldom left the house. Even more painful was hearing of Juliet's anguished prayer after discovering that her daughter was disabled.

"Am I the only mother in the world with a child like this?" she'd cried out to God, having never met another parent whose child was disabled—not because there aren't other children, but because they aren't often seen in public.

My heart ached, realizing how little help there was for children like Ruth in developing countries. Even here in the United States, caring for such a child was tough. Meeting Ruth's needs separated Dana and me from friends we no longer had the time or energy to visit, from family activities we once enjoyed because Ruth couldn't do them with us, and from worshiping together because Dana and I typically took turns caring for Ruth in the church nursery. It even separated us from each other since we could no longer find a baby-sitter who felt comfortable caring for Ruth. Only slowly did it sink in how fully our lives had changed.

"Are you happy, Mommy?" Lydia asked on a day when the laundry piled up and dishes filled the sink and Ruth was fussing to be fed.

"Yes," I said. "Mommy's happy. I'm just tired."

When the kids squabbled, and toys littered the house, and Ruth needed to be changed or fed—again—I lost my patience, ordering the boys, "Be Quiet! Go To Your Rooms!"

Lydia tilted her small head and said, "I thought you were happy?"

On such days, I stood at the front door, keys in hand, waiting for Dana to walk in from work so I could walk out. After aimlessly driving around town, I'd buy an ice cream or a hot chocolate—depending on the season—and park at the waterfront or library park, feet on the dashboard, listening to the radio until I was relaxed enough to return home.

Yet, for all the hours it took to feed Ruth, for all the therapist's visits and doctor's appointments, Ruth was easy to love, crying only when spasms pulled her fingers into hard fists that struck her throat, or when she was hungry but couldn't swallow the food she so desperately craved, or when the kids ran out to play and she couldn't run after them. Then I'd prop a teddy bear into the crook of Ruth's arms to help her relax. Or Dana would pull her onto his lap to gently feed her another bottle. But nothing helped when Ruth simply wanted to play. Then her bottom lip would poke out, silent tears would slide down her soft, brown cheeks, and we rocked her in our arms.

Other days, I was the one crying.

"Be happy, Mom!" Lydia stomped her foot the day she found me sitting on the kitchen garbage can, head in my hands.

Dana left love notes in the sugar bowl and brought me steaming mugs of coffee on mornings I woke early to work in my closet-sized office at the top of our stairs. Judah drew pictures of flowers and stick people with giant smiles that he left on my pillow. Gabriel cleaned up toys, and Lydia pointed to the heart-shaped bowl on the front of a cereal box and suggested, "Cheerios in your heart make you happy."

If only it were so simple. As I drove Ruth to school and appointments and struggled to take care of the kids while Dana went back to working the night shift, I recalled the miraculous ways God had provided for us in Africa, including the words of Caroline, a social worker I'd met at the guesthouse in Nairobi: "The one who has called you to take care of Ruth will take care of you. The hardships will be great but the blessings will be greater." I clung to these words like a life raft, but as winter wrapped us in its thick white coat and Christmas lights glittered from gutters, it was hard to believe that God was still there, still providing. I knew that Ruth belonged in our family, but getting through each day was hard.

In January we received the final papers to complete Ruth's adoption. I called the little brick courthouse down the street to find out whether the clerk had set a date.

"When?" I held my breath.

"February fourteenth," she said.

Of course! Valentine's Day. After all, our journey with Ruth was about love. Our love for her, yes. But also our love for God, and his love for all the hurting, wounded children still waiting to know that they are loved. Part of me wanted the moment of Ruth's birth into our family to be as private as those of our other children. But because so many people had been involved in conceiving her adoption, I invited family, friends, and neighbors to join us—although several couldn't, including my mom, who had returned overseas.

"What if we missed something?" I asked Dana that morning after driving downtown for breakfast at the Starlight Café. The restaurant's gregarious owner, Susan Craney, had contributed money for Ruth's adoption by encouraging customers to sing for their soup. On our way out, she'd tied a pink balloon to Ruth's chair. But as we drove up

Centre Street toward the courthouse, I was nervous. "What if the judge says no?" I asked.

"Everything will be fine," Dana assured me.

The second-floor hall was packed. When Ruth saw everyone, she squealed.

"How's my beautiful girl?" Tracey greeted us, reaching for Ruth, whom I'd dressed in a fuzzy red sweater with a giant silver heart. Pink ribbons decorated her hair, and tiny crystal hearts glittered in her earlobes.

"Excited," I said and signed.

Back home, I'd decorated the dining room with balloons and baked hand-shaped sugar cookies with the middle and ring fingers bent to sign "I love you." Dana bought roses. *My Valentine*, he'd written on the card. *There could not be a better way to celebrate our love.* After what we'd been through, it was hard to believe this day was here. Half an hour later, when a clerk called our name, we packed the judge's chambers. Dana and I sat at the table, each holding a girl, while the boys stood beside us.

"Would you like to introduce everyone?" the grandfatherly judge asked.

"Well—" I looked around the room at our friends' smiling faces, including a large number of kids, many from our homeschool group. "This is Allen and Theresa and their kids, who first took Ruth into their home. And this is Tammy and Tracey, who drove her to Maine . . ." I named everyone I could.

"I thought it might have been a school bus!" the judge joked, smiling at the kids. Then he picked up a pen and signed a paper that declared Ruth ours.

"That's it?" I asked. "She's a Merrill?"

"That's it." The judge handed me the paper. "She's a Merrill."

My heart was higher than the wispy white clouds speckling the clear blue sky as we carried Ruth to our van. After Dana and I each buckled a girl inside, I turned to our kids—all four of them.

"Do you know what this means?" I looked long into their wondering faces. "This means Ruth is your sister. Your *real* sister. It means that no one can take her away. No one. Not ever."

And I truly believed it.

13

Testing

A single green shoot
peeks through the snow-covered garden.
A tulip?
A daffodil?
How you would smile at this first sign of spring.
Then I realize that I will never show you a tulip again—
never prop the garden hose in your sparrow-thin hand
to help you spray the flowers or your siblings,
their heads thrown back in wide-open laughter.
It takes two years to fully process loss, my doctor says.
Two life spans would not be enough.
How do I let go of a soul I never got to fully know?
Words you were never able to form?
Places you never went?
Treasures you never saw?
Like this flower.
Joy and laughter return to me.
Bring life where grief now reigns.
Fresh tulips pushing through frozen ground.

I'd only met one child with a cochlear implant. Eleven-year-old Abby Latulippe lived with her parents, David and Janice, and little sister, Emily, in nearby Freeport. Like Ruth, Abby was born prematurely. Like Ruth, she had cerebral palsy and was deaf. And, like us, a doctor had told David and Janice that their daughter would never walk or talk. Dr. Klop, who was also Abby's audiologist, had given me their phone number. When I'd called them the previous June, David had invited me to meet his family at a nearby cross-country meet, saying, "You can watch Abby run."

"With a walker?" I asked.

"No," he said.

"With a cane?"

"Nope, on her own."

One week later, I'd pushed Ruth in a stroller across a rutted Cumberland field looking for Abby's team. A group of girls in matching Harraseeket Harriers T-shirts stood under a row of pines, stretching their legs before the race.

"Do you know Abby?" I asked a gangly, brown-eyed girl with sparkling eyes.

She laughed. "I'm Abby!"

"You're Abby?" Only then did I see the round, button-sized disk on the side of her head.

"Uh-huh!" She grinned, clearly thrilled to have surprised me.

No way did this bubbly, athletic girl match my picture of a deaf person with cerebral palsy. As Abby bent down to say hello to Ruth, bringing squeals of happiness, I couldn't get over how easy to understand she was, and how chatty—all because of the curved microphone hooked over her right ear. The mic picked up each word I spoke and carried it through a thin wire to the metal disk above Abby's ear. Inside, an electronic processor converted the sounds into an electric pulse before sending it through a transmitter to a microchip embedded under Abby's skin, and from there to her cochlea. Because getting an implant is a life-altering decision, Abby's parents had sent her to Baxter to learn ASL, waiting until their daughter turned six to let her decide whether she wanted one. Although six was well beyond the recommended age of implantation, here Abby was, freely chatting away.

"You like running?" I asked as Janice and Emily wandered across the field to join us.

"I love running." Abby pronounced each word carefully, as if it were a weight on her tongue. "Soccer too." She stuck out her leg to reveal a rough, red scrape from a recent game.

"We have to slow her down," Janice explained, while Abby and Emily played peekaboo with Ruth.

Soon, parents and coaches gathered along the edge of the starting line. David joined us as Abby took take her place in a pulsating row of runners for a one-mile course across the field and through the trees. The timekeeper counted down—*three, two, one!*—and Abby was off, hurtling across the mowed grass in the middle of the pack.

A minute later, they disappeared into the woods. Standing with Ruth and Abby's family, I watched the dark edge of the forest from where the runners would reemerge. Janice swatted black flies as the fastest kids came pumping and huffing out of the forest. Faces red and shiny, they streaked by. The pack thinned. Stretches grew between runners. Eventually, a few stragglers appeared. Still no Abby. David, who often ran alongside his daughter, scratched his neck, beginning to get worried. Janice leaned over the course ribbon, scanning the far trees. Then Emily yelled, "I think this is Abby!"

Legs gliding and arms swinging, Abby burst out of the trees. As she shot into the final stretch, a shout rang out from the sidelines. Suddenly, Abby's legs flew out from under her. Her arms flailed, and she collapsed on the grass with a howl. David and Janice scrambled beneath the ribbon, running toward their daughter with Emily, who threw herself beside her sister, sobbing. As teammates gathered around, a coach rushed to Abby's side. For a few minutes it looked like Abby wouldn't be able to finish the race—the final contest of the season. Then, Abby dried her eyes. With one arm around her coach, she slowly pushed herself up. For several yards, the two stumbled on together until Abby found her strength, her stride, and then began to run again. As the crowd cheered, Abby finished the race.

"When you have a child, you have a special vision of how that child is going to grow up," David said as Abby collected her ribbon. "And when you have a child with special needs, you don't have that vision anymore. You learn to see as you go."

After saying goodbye, I'd pushed Ruth down the grassy slope toward the road, where yellow school buses bloomed like sunflowers. Would Ruth walk or talk? I didn't know, but one thing was certain: after meeting Abby, I wasn't putting any limitations on her.

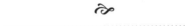

Despite nearly two years of physical therapy, when Ruth turned three she still displayed the physical abilities of an infant. Once, during a rare dinner out at a local diner, Ruth raised her fisted hand to click a spoon against her teeth.

"Did you see that?" I burst out.

The server, taking our order, rolled her eyes, as if asking, "What's the big deal?"

"She can't do that!" I exclaimed.

Another time, during a children's program at our library, I laid Ruth on the floor, and she flipped from her stomach to her back. *Flip, flip, flip*—just like that, she rolled over seven, eight, nine times. A milestone! The smile on Ruth's face told me she was as thrilled as I was, but after that day, I never saw her do it again.

Each night before bedtime, Gabriel continued to clasp his small hands together and prayed, "Dear Jesus, please help Ruth walk and talk."

Ruth tried, lifting her scrawny legs to jerk each foot forward as we held her upright, but walking independently didn't seem likely. Neither did talking. It hurt to see my six-year-old son's prayers go unanswered. The rest of our family's too. Yet perhaps God's purpose was higher than ours. Perhaps instead of healing Ruth, he intended to heal us of our selfishness and pride. Wouldn't that be a miracle?

Had Ruth been able to sign, I'm not sure we would have considered a cochlear implant. Chalk it up to my hippie childhood or my continued prayers for Ruth's healing, but the idea of surgically embedding a computer chip in my daughter's head bothered me—even more so after Rita placed two fingers against her skull like fangs to show me the sign for "implant"—the same sign as "vampire," only pressed against the head rather than the throat. Such is the dread many deaf people feel toward the technology threatening to extinguish their language and culture. While being able to hear may seem preferable to people outside of the deaf community, many within it see the technology as too invasive. Dissensions aside, it was increasingly apparent how much Ruth was missing. While Lydia naturally absorbed language from the constant stream of sound swirling around her, Ruth needed to be directly taught each new word. This became even more obvious the day Lydia announced, "I know where babies come from."

"You do?" I asked, wondering what the boys had been telling her.

"They come from Africa!" she declared.

In contrast, Ruth didn't know what Africa was, let alone that she'd been born there. Even pointing to a map was incomprehensible, because Ruth lacked concepts of countries and continents or of the earth itself—ideas even little Lydia was beginning to grasp. We hoped a cochlear implant would expose this hidden world of sound, but first we had to convince New England's top cochlear-implant team that Ruth was as bright as we believed.

"How are they going to do a psychological exam on a child who can't point or speak?" I asked Dana that May, speeding down Interstate 95 through the pale, budding woods of New Hampshire with all four kids buckled in the van on our second trip to Boston Children's Hospital.

"I don't know." He shrugged. "Ask, 'What do you see in this ink dot?'"

His guess was as good as mine.

Two hours later, we wheeled Ruth into the hospital's Waltham office and met the three people who would decide whether Ruth would hear: Dr. Jennifer Johnston, a speech and language pathologist; Dr. Terrell Clark, a pediatric psychologist; and Susanne Russell, an occupational therapist. Always eager to meet new people, Ruth was grinning.

"Is she always this happy?" asked Dr. Johnston, leading us down a narrow hall.

"Usually," Dana said truthfully.

Laughter was Ruth's native language. I often thought that God had packed her extra full of joy to make up for all the things life had taken away.

While the boys watched a movie in the reception area, Lydia snuggled up on Dana's lap as we sat around the conference table in Dr. Johnston's office, with Ruth sitting snugly in her travel chair. "You've been signing to Ruth for about a year now," she said, as the other team members joined us. "How many words do you think she knows?"

"Twenty? Thirty?" I turned to Dana. "Family names mostly, and everyday objects, like book, bottle, bed."

Dr. Clark leaned forward. "And how does Ruth express herself?"

"With her eyes, but in other ways too." I described how I'd recently let Ruth watch *Babe*, a movie about a talking pig. "Ruth started wailing. I thought she was hurt, but when I ran to check, I realized she was upset because a pack of dogs in the movie were chasing the sheep. Later that night while we were eating, I told Dana about it. The moment I signed 'dog run sheep,' Ruth began crying again."

"Dogs scare you?" Dana asked now, signing each word.

Ruth poked out her bottom lip and tears flooded her eyes.

"Sheep okay," I signed. "Movie pretend."

"Let's see what else she knows." Sue plugged a table fan into an electric box attached to a large, flat button switch that she placed in front of Ruth. When Sue pushed the button, the fan turned on, automatically switching off a few seconds later. "Your turn," she signed.

Thwack! Ruth whacked the button, squinting anxiously as air blasted her face.

"Maybe she'll like this better." Sue swapped the fan for a string of white Christmas lights, draping them over her shoulders.

When Ruth hit the button, the lights flashed and Sue danced. Ruth shrieked with delight. As soon as the lights shut off and Sue froze, Ruth hit the button again to make Sue dance, demonstrating that she understood cause and effect. After an hour of games, the team estimated Ruth's receptive language—what she understood—at eight months old, about the length of time we'd been signing. To track her progress, they asked us to bring her back in July. So began one year of testing during which Dana or I drove Ruth to Waltham every two months while juggling X-rays to make sure Ruth's hips were aligned, braces to straighten her feet, dental work to repair the mysterious ridges on her teeth, a swallow study to ensure she wasn't inhaling food into her windpipe, and getting Ruth measured for a pediatric wheelchair.

I never expected how my throat would clench, how I'd choke on the words "My daughter needs a wheelchair" the day I called our pediatrician. The blue polka-dot chair we picked up a month later was much better for Ruth, but lugging it up the twelve steps to our front door was nearly impossible. Ruth's therapists suggested we move. Instead, with help from a state grant, we built "Ramp Everest," a sixty-foot walkway that wrapped around our front shed before connecting to a thirty-foot stone path, which Dana hand dug and constructed. Before the rails were up, the program manager, Brad, who was blind, arrived to inspect it. I nervously held my breath as he swung his long white cane over the unprotected edge, afraid he'd fall to the bone-crushing rocks below. His slow, steady progress reminded me that we were to walk "by faith, not by sight," as it says in 2 Corinthians 5:7. Faith in God, I was starting to see, began where faith in myself ended. Dana and I couldn't anticipate the obstacles ahead. We simply had to feel our way with faith, one step at a time, trusting God to guide us.

In September, that meant enrolling Judah in fourth grade at a small Christian school in Freeport. Another mom, Libbie, drove him with her own children. Meanwhile, Gabriel and Lydia continued joining me at Baxter, where Ruth now attended preschool four mornings a week. Two days I drove. Two days a van picked up Ruth at our house. After lunch, a bus transported her across the causeway to the Morrison Developmental Center for physical therapy before a van brought her home.

"I wish there were two Ruths," I said to Dana one night. "CP Ruth and Deaf Ruth. The combination is too much."

It was also too much for Ruth, who often arrived home asleep. One afternoon I lay on my bed, my eyes closed, hoping to snatch a nap before Ruth arrived home. Lydia burst into my room. Too tired to speak, I raised my hands and signed, "Go downstairs. Read book."

Quietly, Lydia tiptoed out.

I was feeling quite pleased until she hollered, "Gabey, I think Mom's gone deaf too!"

Dana and I took turns. When I crumbled, my husband took over for both of us—often with characteristic humor.

"Does the food go in your nose?" Dana signed, aiming a spoonful of applesauce at Ruth's nostrils one night at dinner. "In your ear? In your eye?" Shrieking with laughter, Ruth opened her mouth wide. Not only did this frequent game encourage her to eat, it also taught her the names of body parts, which she now readily identified along with the signs for places she liked to go—"school," "library," and "church" being her favorites. Ruth now understood as many signed words as a two-and-a-half-year-old.

We weren't the only ones thrilled with Ruth's progress. During our frequent trips to Boston, Ruth was doing fantastic, beating Sue at a game of memory and correctly identifying with her eyes dozens of new signs—baby, horse, comb, airplane, bird—by gazing at a corresponding toy. But the strain was often overwhelming. "It's too hard," I protested to God one day that fall while driving Ruth home. Was it our fourth visit? Our fifth? They all blurred together. "I give up."

Just keep your eyes on me, an inner voice urged as an image of Christ filled my mind. With one hand on each side of my face, he directed my gaze into his, assuring me of his presence. When I focused on the difficulties, I wanted to quit; but when I focused on Christ I found the strength to keep going.

Having a mother who was a missionary also helped. On difficult days I remembered something she'd taught me from her years in seminary. Each year at the appointed time, the ancient Israelites were to visit God's temple. Only, they were never to go empty-handed. They were to carry an offering, something of value to lay on the altar.

"The temple is an illustration of heaven," she said. "When it is our appointed time to stand before God, we are not to go empty-handed either. We are to bring an offering, something of value to give to God."

And so on days when caring for Ruth was hard, I closed my eyes and pictured myself carrying her up a shining flight of stairs. Staggering, stumbling, I laid her on the altar—one small piece of this broken, pain-pierced world that I could redeem and offer back to God.

In February, as we neared the first anniversary of Ruth joining our family, I scoured newspapers, animal shelters, and online pet adoption sites, hoping to find a family dog to reward our kids for willingly giving up their money to adopt Ruth. I'd searched on and off all year, but the dogs I found were either too young or too rowdy. I'd just about given up when, a few weeks before Valentine's Day, I spotted a newspaper ad by a championship dog breeder seeking a home for a fully trained, two-year-old golden retriever. When I called the owner, Mary, and told her about Ruth, she waived the $500 fee. That's how Sushi, a long-suffering, fluffy-tailed golden retriever whom the kids dressed in bandanas and butterfly wings, became part of our family. In exchange for their meager savings, God had blessed our children with a far better dog than we ever could have afforded.

That spring, after Ruth underwent an MRI and CT scan to ensure she had the correct anatomy to support an implant, we received the news we'd been hoping for: Ruth was approved for a cochlear implant! In May, a few weeks after her fourth birthday, I drove Ruth to Boston for the surgery while Dana worked and friends from church watched our kids.

Worn out from our journey, Ruth was already asleep when I laid her on the operating table—hoping that we had made the right decision. Before stepping out of the room, I kissed the spot behind her left ear where the surgeon would carve a six-inch incision and hollow out part of her skull to slip the microchip inside. Three hours later when I joined Ruth in her recovery room, her gauze-wrapped head looked twice its normal size. That night I slept on a foldout couch at the foot of her bed, waking every few hours as Ruth shrieked with pain and confusion while an IV dripped morphine into her veins.

We also had a surprise visitor: Liz, a mother and missions trip leader from nearby Grace Chapel in Lexington, Massachusetts, who with another church friend had carried Ruth and Yvonne on their journey from Uganda to Boston. They had been working there with a team of college students when Welcome Home asked if they would escort the girls to the States. Without them, I realized, Ruth wouldn't be with us. Two days later, I blearily drove her home. This time, Liz brought pizza, keeping me company while Ruth rested.

Before activating the implant, we had to wait for Ruth's incision to heal. After a month we drove Ruth back to Waltham—this time with Dana and the boys, while Lydia spent the night with friends. Having been warned that hearing sound for the first time can feel painful, like an electrical shock, I'd prayed that Ruth would experience this new sensation like a game, no different from knocking over the block towers Gabriel built on the living room floor or playing High-Ho-Cherry-O with Judah, who held the spinner so Ruth could swat it with her fist. Ruth sat in her wheelchair watching every move as the audiologist, Dr. Jennifer Harris, clipped a tiny microphone to her chair and placed the button-shaped transmitter on her head. Then a computer sent the first soft wave of sound. Ruth's eyes widened. A goofy smile spread over her face. She rolled her eyes to see what was going on. Then, when Dr. Harris increased the volume, Ruth wailed.

Shhh-shhh. I stroked Ruth's face as the audiologist switched off the sound.

"Getting used to hearing will take time," Dr. Harris said as Ruth quieted. Then she programmed the microphone to pick up sounds in the room. "Okay. Talk softly. Ruth can hear you."

"Hey, Ruthie," I said hesitantly. "It's Mommy. Can you hear Mommy?"

Ruth's eyes darted to the side, but she didn't cry.

"Hi Ruth." Dana squeezed her hand. "It's Daddy."

Quietly, Judah and Gabriel joined in, speaking words their sister could hear for the first time. It would be months before Ruth could distinguish between our voices or separate them from background noises. She'd have to learn spoken English from scratch, reacquiring words she now knew only from the shapes of our hands.

"That's enough for now." Dr. Harris turned off the processor. "Ruth's doing great."

To keep Ruth from accidentally knocking off her microphone, we tucked it in an elastic band holding a tuft of her springy hair. After one night at a motel, we returned to the hospital the next morning, and the audiologist readjusted the volume on Ruth's processor, a procedure called "mapping." An hour later, we wheeled Ruth out of the hospital with a shoebox-sized case containing $45,000 worth of equipment. Before returning home, we picked up Lydia, who climbed into the van with a fistful of candy.

"You want—" Lydia began to sign and stopped, holding the candy toward Ruth.

"Candy." I pressed my finger to my cheek, thinking that she'd forgotten the sign.

"I know," Lydia huffed. "But Ruth can hear me now."

Carefully, Dana explained that it would take months for Ruth to recognize common sounds—the bark of a dog or the ring of a bell. Understanding speech would take longer. What he didn't say—but what we'd been warned—was that because Ruth had already turned four, she might never learn spoken language at all.

14

Two Worlds

While Dana is out with the boys, I rip every sheet of wallpaper from the dining area of our kitchen, tearing each jagged strip the way Ruth's loss has torn me.

"Let's see if Daddy notices," I tell Lydia, stuffing fistfuls of gummy paper in the garbage.

When Dana returns, he doesn't.

"Our walls are bare!" I shout.

Dana blinks, blinks, smiles. "Oh, yeah."

"How could you not notice?" I aim a finger at the target of his chest.

Our children's mouths hang as if I've called their father a bad name.

Which I want to.

How can I stay married to such a man?

Over time, my anger morphs into resignation. Rather than tearing my life apart, I desperately need to piece it back together. Abby, our sixteen-year-old niece, arrives for spring break. Together, she and Dana repair our walls.

Safe white paint.

Soft peach paper.

But nothing conceals the pain.

Beneath the bright semigloss, the gouges from the wheels on Ruth's wheelchair still mark the newly painted door frame the way my heart is marked from where her life passed through mine.

"No signing." Cathy, Ruth's new speech-language pathologist, placed her hand over mine at our first therapy session that summer to teach Ruth to understand sound.

"Why?" I asked.

"This is a no-signing environment." The petite redhead frowned. "We want Ruth to recognize sound without depending on clues."

The clash between hearing and deaf culture was exasperating. Dana and I wanted to give Ruth every language clue—signed and spoken—and did so at home. At the time, however, Maine's top oral language program for deaf children was as philosophically distant from Baxter as it was physically. While Baxter then prohibited speech, this center, forty-five minutes inland through Maine's western farmlands, forbade signing—so much so that I was literally instructed to sit on my hands. Unlike children who are born hearing, those with cochlear implants must be taught to identify each new sound, beginning with six: *Mmmm, Ssss, Shhh, Ahhh, Oooo,* and *Weee*. Since Ruth couldn't speak, Cathy associated each sound with a toy, such as a plastic ice-cream cone for *Mmmm* or a snake for *Ssss*. When we said the sound, Ruth's job was to locate the right object, a game she picked up easily.

All summer, we pointed out new noises—the ring of a telephone, the honk of a horn, the buzz of the clothes dryer. Three weeks after activating Ruth's implant, I took her for a walk in her wheelchair along the wide Kennebec River. When a heavy plane droned overhead, I tipped Ruth back and pointed to the sky. "Do you hear the plane?"

Ruth laughed. Had she heard?

Another time, I called Ruth's name and she looked straight at me. A coincidence? Then came the July evening when Ruth lay on the living room floor, watching a movie. From the kitchen, I dashed down the hall and upstairs. Ruth wailed. I ran back down—*thud, thud, thud*—thinking that she had hurt herself. Before seeing me, Ruth stopped crying.

"You heard me!" I raced into the room and fell to my knees, kissing Ruth's teary face. "You heard Mommy go upstairs, and you cried because you didn't want me to go!"

Each day brought a new triumph—matching *moo* to a toy cow, rolling her eyes toward a picture of a clock when I sang "Hickory Dickory Dock," learning the spoken names of everyone in our family—including her own. Now that Ruth could hear, books brought fresh pleasure, especially one about herself.

"This is Ruth," Cathy read a book she'd made one Friday during our weekly session, while the other kids sat in the lobby outside. "Ruth has black hair. Is your hair green?" She waited for Ruth to glance at the "yes" or "no" icons attached to the top of her eye-gaze frame.

Instead, Ruth stared.

"Is your hair black?" Cathy tried again.

Ruth poked out her tongue.

"Did you see that?" Cathy exclaimed. "She's saying yes!"

From then on, Ruth stuck out her tongue for "yes" and gave us a blank look for "no" as in "try again." The further Ruth stuck out her tongue, the more she wanted something, like the day I wheeled her into our old-fashioned candy store, the Bath Sweet Shoppe. While raising money for Ruth's adoption, we'd discovered that the owners, Paul and Joan Fraser, happened to live a few houses down from ours. After they'd donated a huge basket of treats for our raffle and filled a bag with more than sixty candy necklaces for me to give the kids at Welcome Home, Joan had become one of Ruth's favorite people. And with good reason: Joan supplied Ruth with lollipops.

"Watch this!" I parked Ruth in front of the shop's antique display case, filled with fudge and other confections, where Joan stood in her green apron. "Ruth," I began, "do you want a lollipop?"

Quick as a flash, Ruth's tongue reached all the way down to her chin.

Joan's eyes widened.

"Do you want yellow?" I asked.

Blank stare.

"Green?"

"Red?"

Ruth's tongue shot out.

"Oh my gosh! Look at that!" Joan exclaimed. "She understands!"

That fall more than twenty teachers, aides, therapists, and experts from four educational programs crowded around three tables for her semi-annual meeting. Knowing they were all here to help Ruth was awe inspiring, but trying to keep up with all of their goals was nearly impossible. The hardest part of caring for Ruth wasn't Ruth—it was the phone calls, doctor's appointments, school visits, consultations, and tests that caring for Ruth required. Life didn't stop when a therapist ordered a new swallow study or a cable snapped on Ruth's wheelchair. Children still needed to be driven to football and basketball and chorus. People we loved still got sick. Homework still needed to be corrected, papers signed, reports read, groceries bought, food cooked, house cleaned, bills paid, children looked after and loved. It was hard parenting by committee. At one point, I was so far behind I missed three appointments in a single day.

"Why doesn't someone invent 'mommy saving time'?" I suggested as we rolled back our clocks at the end of daylight saving time. "Like adding an extra hour each day so I can catch up?"

I wasn't the only one exhausted. On our mornings at Baxter, Gabriel usually did schoolwork in the library. One morning I couldn't find him. Then I spotted two sneakers poking out from behind a row of books. On the other side lay my recently turned eight-year-old, fast asleep. After that, Ruth rode the van full time.

The strain was too much. Small muscles convulsed under my eye, in my arms, my legs, my back, sometimes twisting in painful knots.

"Stress," my doctor said.

I noticed it in other ways too. Over the three years we'd had Ruth, I'd gained thirty pounds. Not only could I eat off the same spoon, it turned out I could also eat half of her buttery, jam-smothered toast. Gooey brownies were even better. When one disappeared, I simply grabbed another. After years of healthy eating and exercise, I no longer had time or energy.

"What do you do for fun?" my doctor asked during a checkup.

I shifted awkwardly on the exam table. "Fun?"

"You know, something enjoyable just for you."

"I used to go to the gym or read. Does that count?"

"Whatever it is, you need to do more of it," she said, adding a chore to my already-long list.

Dana and I rarely saw each other except on Sunday mornings at church. Photo albums from early in our marriage burst with pictures of the two of us—cheeks together, arms entwined, bodies always touching. Where had we gone? Those two in-love optimists so sure that everything would work out if we just followed God. Our anniversary was the one day we resembled two lovelorn individuals who'd chosen a life together—*two*gether. Most of the time, we were two apart.

One night after tucking the children in bed, Dana and I switched off the lights to watch a romantic movie. As the credits rolled and a syrupy love song flowed from the speakers, he pulled me close.

I stiffened. "No."

"Why not?"

"Because I'm tired of doing everyone's laundry."

Dana's desire felt like one more demand. It was a far cry from that long-ago night snuggled on the couch in his parents' living room, picturing our future. There wasn't enough of me to take care of the children and my work and myself, let alone our marriage. All I could do was struggle through each day and pray, trusting that God would bring us through.

As leaves fell from the trees and frost clung to the windows, Dana signed back up for the night shift. Some of his paycheck filled the Christmas stockings hanging from the hallway stairs. The rest filled the oil tank and refrigerator. Yet each time we had a need, God miraculously met it, like providing money for Judah's tuition.

"Lord," I'd prayed, before registering Judah for fifth grade that summer. "I need one thousand dollars this week if we are going to send Judah back to school."

Within an hour the telephone rang. It was a nonprofit organization that provided money through a free lottery for students to attend private school. From a pool of 1,400 applicants, *both* Judah's and Gabriel's names had been drawn—with just twelve others—providing $1,700 for Judah's tuition and $500 for Gabriel's homeschool books. Around the same time, we needed to replace our badly worn living room carpet. After ripping it out, we had lacked the money to replace it.

"You promised to take care of us," I protested to God while rolling wide swaths of paint over the splintery plywood. "Now look at me."

A few days later, Judah threw a rock through our picture window while trying to kill a squirrel to eat for dinner—his idea, not mine. I marched him downtown to hunt for a replacement at our local Habitat for Humanity Re-Store. Thankfully, they had one. While paying, I asked if they happened to have any wood flooring.

"Funny you should ask." The clerk scratched his head. "We rarely get any, but today we're bringing in an entire truckload."

It was the exact type of flooring we needed—pumpkin pine—for a fraction of the typical price. "And we know that God causes all things to work together for good to those who love God, to those who are called according to His purpose," I recalled the apostle Paul's words in Romans 8:28. Even broken windows, it seemed. Despite our difficulties, God was still providing—and deepening our faith in the process. One of the most remarkable ways was through a teenager named Christina.

Every Fourth of July, our family continued selling Shain's of Maine ice-cream sandwiches—now with Ugandan crafts—to raise money for Welcome Home, providing more than $5,000 along with a jogging stroller for Grace, the child with CP whom I'd met in Uganda. The summer before, a woman had stopped by our booth and mentioned that her seventeen-year-old daughter knew sign language. Were we looking for a babysitter? Were we! Soon, quiet, gentle Christina began watching our children for a few hours each week, giving Dana and me much-needed time together. We also discovered that Christina's congregation had a sign language program. While we were sad to leave our own church, we needed to meet Ruth's needs too. There, under a soaring roof with a classic white steeple, Ruth's hearing and deaf worlds finally came together.

By her fifth birthday, Ruth was doing so well that she knew all the letters of the alphabet, sticking out her tongue as we held up flash cards to indicate that she'd found the right letter. At kindergarten the following fall, she met Fahmo, a pixie-cute six-year-old whose family had moved to Portland from an Ethiopian refugee camp. Profoundly deaf and with no prior schooling, Fahmo raced around the classroom, tearing down posters and knocking toys off shelves. But she embraced Ruth, placing her delicate brown hands on Ruth's cheeks and smiling as if to say, "See, we are the same."

Ruth loved school, but the many distractions made eating a struggle. For lunch, a good day was a few nibbles of a grilled cheese sandwich, a handful of raisins, and juice, squeezed into her mouth with a straw. To add calories, we mixed oil and butter into Ruth's food, but her weight barely topped thirty pounds. Concerned, I made an appointment with our pediatrician.

"Children with CP are often thin," he said, sounding unconcerned.

I asked about supplementing Ruth's milk with a high-calorie shake suggested by one of Ruth's drivers, but our pediatrician said he didn't know anything about it. Several months later, I brought Ruth to a different pediatrician, who calculated her percentage of body fat and immediately recommended a feeding tube. Desperate to avoid another surgery, I stopped at the grocery store on the way home and loaded my cart with peanut butter cups, chocolate-covered raisins, frosted toaster pastries, chicken nuggets, french fries, frozen sausage patties, instant pudding—all of the foods I usually avoided for my family. But now, the more fat and calories a food had, the more I wanted it for Ruth.

"Are we a super family?" Gabriel asked, helping put everything away.

"Why?" I asked.

"Because that's what it says on this hot chocolate." He pointed to the label on a gigantic can. "Super Family Sized."

I laughed, but Ruth's situation was hardly funny. Soon, on top of her other activities, we were driving Ruth to a Portland gastro-intestinologist for monthly weight checks. We hoped the high-calorie protein shake she'd prescribed—like the one I'd previously requested from our pediatrician—would eliminate the need for a feeding tube. Meanwhile, with the help of Ruth's school aides, we began feeding her every hour. The communication between Dana and me condensed to daily e-mails: *Who is picking up the kids? How much money did you deposit?* Most nights he fell asleep with Ruth on the couch, a squeeze bottle of fortified milk in his hand. I fell asleep silently pleading, "Lord, sustain me."

Be grateful. Be grateful. Be grateful, small moments reminded me—when Dana told me I was beautiful, or Lydia drew a picture with giant letters spelling *LOVE MOM,* or Gabriel wrote in his neatest cursive, *Dear Mama, I hope you feel better,* or Judah read to Ruth while I made dinner. Yet, I dreamed of booking a one-way flight to Hawaii. If I disappeared, maybe everyone's needs would too.

"I have been faithful," I cried out to God one night, lying on the floor of my bedroom, face in my hands. "I have tried to honor you. Where are you? Where are you, God?"

The following morning, sleepy-eyed Gabriel staggered into the kitchen. "I had the strangest dream," he said. "Someone shouted, 'Where's God?'"

"Oh." I turned away. "That is strange."

Flipping through my Bible, I read of the boy who'd shared his loaves and fishes with a hungry crowd, of how Jesus had broken the bread to feed five thousand. I knew just what it felt like to be broken, passed from hand to hand, and consumed until there was not one crumb left. That spring the girls turned six. The apple tree blossomed beside our front door, and I discovered that we'd soon have one more person to care for.

I was pregnant.

15

Happiness

"How many children do you have?" a stranger asks at the grocery store.

"Judah, Gabriel . . ." I silently recite, counting fingers.

"Four," I finally reply. "At home."

"It sounds like you have more . . ." Her silence demands an answer.

"We do," I mumble. "In heaven."

She apologizes, but I still can't set the right number of plates each night at the dinner table, chronically counting the wrong number before starting over.

"What will we do with another baby?" I asked Dana in the safe darkness of our bed.

"The same thing we did with the others," he said and then softly sang, "What'll we do with a baby, O? What'll we do with a baby, O? Wrap it up in calico. That's what we'll do with a baby, O."

At thirty-seven, I already felt too old as my body swelled with life. Too old to endure another labor. Too old to stay awake half the night nursing a newborn.

"Many of my patients are in their late thirties," my midwife at our local hospital assured me. But the hollow between my hip bones felt incapable of carrying another human life. As if to prove it, at three months along I ended up in the emergency room of a Massachusetts hospital two hours from home while driving Ruth to a checkup in Waltham.

"Mommy okay," I said and signed to Ruth, who sat in her wheelchair beside my hospital bed, looking worried. "Wait. Wait. Wait. Boring."

Within an hour, a doctor fixed the problem, which involved severe discomfort due to the position of the baby, but we'd missed Ruth's appointment. On the way home I stopped to visit a college friend, Caitlyn, whose family had helped raise money for Ruth's adoption. She and her husband, Greg, had two little girls, the youngest near in age to ours. While we sat in her kitchen sipping tea, Ruth lay on the floor watching cartoons.

"How do you feel about having another baby?" Caitlyn tucked her chin-length hair behind an ear.

"Worried," I admitted. "But I can believe what my mind is telling me, which is 'Panic!' Or I can believe what the Bible tells me, which is that children are a blessing. Whenever I feel overwhelmed, I close my eyes and picture myself physically putting my trust in God the way I'd put something in a cupboard. I give my worries to him. Then I close the door."

Still, I wondered how we would find time to care for another baby.

"How many children will this make?" asked an instructor at a local gym where I'd started getting back in shape.

Embarrassed, I raised my right hand, every finger extended.

"Five?" She gawked.

In the mirror, I caught the wide-mouthed reactions of several tight-muscled women. I crossed my arms to hide my spongy abs and nodded. "But one is adopted."

The instant the words left my mouth, I felt my betrayal—as if Ruth didn't count—and vowed to never repeat them. Five. Dana and I would have five children. Where they came from didn't matter. *Children are a blessing. Children are a blessing. Children are a blessing,* I reminded myself daily. I loved being a mom, loved the tender sweetness of cradling a newborn against my chest, but I'd long believed those days were over. Unsure how to tell our children that we were expecting, Dana gathered them around the kitchen table, and I clumsily mumbled something about how they'd need to practice changing diapers.

"Someone we know is having a baby?" Gabriel asked.

"We are!" I threw out my hands and laughed at the sheer lunacy.

"I hope it's a boy!" Judah whooped. "Then I can teach him how to skateboard!"

"I don't understand!" wailed Lydia.

Neither did Ruth. I pointed to my belly, brought my arms together like a cradle, and said, "Mommy's going to have a baby."

Ruth tightened her whole body and squealed. But did she understand? Now a gangly first-grader with two missing front teeth,

Ruth easily grasped words related to daily living, but less obvious questions mystified her. At school, when her teacher, Christy, had asked "Where does maple syrup come from?" and held up drawings of a tree, a gas pump, and a cow, Ruth had picked the cow.

Explaining life and death had been difficult enough with our other children.

"What's that, Mommy?" four-year-old Judah had once asked, pointing out the car window at a graveyard.

I didn't want to tell him. Growing up on a farm, I'd seen the beginning and end of life early. A lamb slipped into the world on a warm bed of hay. A chicken departed with its head on a chopping block. But in Judah's innocent mind, we all lived forever.

"That's a cemetery," I'd reluctantly explained. "It's a place people are buried after they die and don't need their bodies anymore."

Soon after, while exploring a path up the coast with Dana, Judah refused to walk through an old burial plot in the woods, screaming, "I don't want to die!"

Only after Dana carefully explained did Judah understand that walking through the graveyard wouldn't kill him. "When I die," he later announced, "I'll hold your hand and you hold Daddy's and Daddy can hold Gabriel's, and we'll all go to heaven together."

"What a nice idea," I'd replied, lacking the heart to tell him it didn't ordinarily work that way.

Explaining death to Ruth was even harder. A couple of years before, Dana's curmudgeonly grandfather, Ken, had lain in a Maine veterans' home, dying of cancer. When we brought the kids to visit, I thought we'd walked in the wrong room. The man sleeping on the bed was so serene—so bathed in peace—I didn't recognize him. Then Grampy woke up and smiled his gap-toothed smile. Only later did we learn that Ken had prayed with Dana's father that very week and placed his trust in God, asking Christ to forgive his sins and give him new life. I had never seen someone so utterly transformed. One week later, we gathered in a South Portland cemetery to bury the urn containing his ashes. I wasn't sure Ruth understood. So, when Gabriel's pet hamster died sometime later, I'd asked him to show Ruth. Solemnly, he cupped the shiny mound of black fur in his hands and held it toward his sister.

"Gabe's hamster is dead." I flipped over my hands and frowned.

Ruth eyed the body warily as if waiting for it to move. Then Dana carried her up the hill behind our house to watch Gabriel bury his pet.

Birth was an even greater riddle. Ruth adored the babies at church and grinned at younger photos of herself, but she lacked language to understand where she'd been born. At six, her auditory skills equaled those of a two-year-old—the same number of years that she'd been hearing. To teach her to read, I often wrote words on an easel with a dry erase board at our kitchen table, using the same book with which I'd taught our older children. Ruth was soon identifying sounds and simple words by poking out her tongue and laughing at Lydia's quirky illustrations.

"Do you want a snack?" I asked Ruth one day after school.

No.

"Do you want a movie?"

No.

"Do you want a book?"

Tongue to her chin. No longer content to watch life go by, Ruth yearned to enjoy every minute of it. When we walked up the street to the playground, she strained against the straps of her wheelchair, eyeing the slide. Dana untangled Ruth's twisted body and hauled her up the stairs to send her plummeting through the plastic tube where one of the kids caught her on the other side. As she squealed with excitement, up he carried her again.

What Ruth lacked in coordination she made up for with determination, pinching a lollipop between her knotted knuckles, pushing herself away from the dining room table by kicking her foot, sticking out her tongue to help me seal envelopes while helping pay the bills, and pointing with her tongue to indicate which direction she wanted to go on our walks—toward town, always toward town, with its bright shops and busy library and café with jars full of cookies. If we didn't have time to walk the full mile, she cried. Ruth also adored watching movies. The fantasy world of the screen allowed Ruth to fully participate in a way her body did not. Whatever the characters did for one brief hour or episode, she was doing too—in her imagination. A favorite was *The Secret Garden*, which is about a boy, Colin, who uses a wheelchair. When Colin stood and took his first steps, Ruth squealed with excitement. It was the same watching

Heidi, when frail Clara pushed away her wheelchair and stood on a Swiss mountainside. Did Ruth expect such a miracle? Much as I believed God could heal Ruth, I no longer believed he would.

"How come God never answers my prayers?" Gabriel asked one evening.

"What do you mean?" I said.

"About Ruth." He slumped at the table, head in his hands. "Each night I ask God to let her walk and talk, but he doesn't."

"I don't know." I struggled to answer. "But I know God hears, and I know he wants us to keep praying. And even if he doesn't heal Ruth here, I know he will in heaven."

Heaven was another puzzling concept—one I'd avoided telling Ruth about for fear that she'd think it was a place we could drive, like visiting my mom, who'd bought a small cottage in Connecticut. Strap Ruth in the van, cross a border, and—voilà!—she'd be well. If only. While I valued my Pentecostal roots, my ideas about healing were now much more complex. Rather than limiting God to a prescribed way of acting, I was learning to trust him beyond the bounds of my desires or expectations. God—not me—controlled the future. My job was to simply keep flying.

That autumn, the children stretched their arms around my rapidly growing belly to see if their fingers still touched—all except Ruth, whose arms didn't stretch beyond her chair. Instead, I held her hands to my swollen stomach while we cuddled on the couch.

"Is the baby a boy?" I asked.

No.

"Is it a girl?"

The tip of a tongue.

Ruth was so sure we were having a girl, her teachers thought we'd found out the baby's gender, but we wanted to be surprised. Meanwhile, we kept working to help Ruth gain weight.

After months of daily supplements, Ruth had gained a few pounds, but no sooner did we find a food she liked—chocolate shakes mixed with half-and-half—than she tired of the flavor. Adding to our difficulties, when I was about six months pregnant, the economy crashed. Dana's employer slashed his hours. While he scrambled to find more work, I prayed for help, sending up a heavenly SOS. That same week our neighbors, Paul and Joan, marched down the sidewalk between our houses, toting two huge cardboard boxes filled with food.

"I know how tiring it can be to take care of a large family while you're pregnant." Joan, a petite powerhouse who'd raised five children, slid a box onto my kitchen counter, unloading a still-warm pan of chicken parmesan. "You need a break."

She and Paul filled our fridge with ready-to-bake casseroles, tossed salad, steamed vegetables, and a plate piled high with brownies. They even included ice cream, fudge sauce, and whipped cream. Over the months ahead, we gratefully welcomed many of Joan's home-cooked meals. And that wasn't all.

"What do you think the kids would like for Christmas?" Dana asked one evening that December, after returning to the night shift, as I hung laundry beside our living room woodstove.

"We can't afford much," I said.

"I know." He picked up a shirt and laid it over the wooden drying rack. "But what would they like?"

I pictured Lydia standing on tiptoe at Renys, a downtown department store, to stare longingly at a veterinarian play set, and thought of the wooden dollhouse I hoped to buy Ruth. Choosing gifts for the boys was harder. With a new baby on the way, we had to be extra careful. Even so, Dana encouraged the kids to write letters to Santa. Christmas Eve, my mother arrived. After church, we gathered by our brightly lit tree to read *A Visit from St. Nicholas*, followed by the second chapter of Luke, and tucked our happy, squirming children in bed—me hoping they wouldn't be too disappointed in the morning.

"Ready?" Dana wrapped my wool cape around my shoulders when I came downstairs.

"For what?"

"I'm taking you for a drive."

"On Christmas Eve?" I couldn't imagine. "Everything's closed."

"I'll stay with the kids." Mom smiled from the couch, where she sat crocheting a blanket with yarn she had spun from the wool of sheep she had raised on our farm.

Dana ushered me into the chill December dark, and I climbed in our van, truly perplexed as he backed into the road. One block away, he pulled into Paul and Joan's driveway. The white lights decorating our neighbors' snow-covered porch twinkled like the stars of

Bethlehem as Dana led me up their rough granite steps to the front door and rang the bell of their white farmhouse.

"Merry Christmas!" Joan opened the door and greeted us with a hug, pulling us inside.

A beautiful Christmas tree, decked in bows, filled the candlelit parlor. Carols jingled on the radio, and there, in the center of the room, was a giant pile of bags filled with brightly wrapped boxes.

"These are for you." Their grown daughter, Sarah, pointed to the boxes.

"For us?" I gasped. "You did all this?"

"Not just us," Joan said. "A few friends and downtown businesses pitched in. But this is from me." She handed me a giant shopping bag filled with chocolate Santas, hand-rolled candy canes, caramels, mints, gumdrops, and plenty of Ruth's favorite lollipops.

"And a gift certificate for the two of you to go out for dinner," Paul said as he stood from his chair by the brick fireplace and handed Dana an envelope.

"You knew?" I turned to Dana. "This is why you had the kids write letters to Santa?"

He grinned.

The country was in the greatest financial slump since the Great Depression. Work was down, cash scarce, and comfort hard to come by, but God was still providing, still showing us his love—this time through our neighbors. As we poured ourselves out, God poured himself in. Everything Christ said about loving others was right here, right in this room. We—all of us—are loved with an everlasting love that reveals itself through flesh and blood, just like on that first Christmas. That was the answer. Wasn't it? Not just for us, but for children sniffing glue and sleeping in airports and nursing empty breasts and sobbing alone in their cribs. God loves others through us; we love others through him. Inhale. Exhale. Like breathing.

That night, after driving home with our van full of gifts, Dana and I were like kids ourselves. After Mom went to bed, we sat on the living room floor, trying to guess what was inside each brightly wrapped package, including several marked *Baby Merrill*. By the time we finished, the space under our tree was filled. As the first waves of light rippled through the woods early the next morning, the children huddled at the top of our stairs in their pajamas. Feet kicking, Ruth squirmed in Judah's arms while Lydia and Gabriel pranced behind him like reindeer.

"Can we go down? Can we go down?" they begged.

"Hang on!" Dana stumbled from bed as groggy as a hibernating bear. "No going downstairs until I make coffee."

"Dad!" The children howled—all together, all laughing, all well.

"You know." I followed Dana downstairs. "Life doesn't get any better than this."

"I know," he said.

That morning, Dana sat on the floor with Lydia, snapping together her new veterinarian set. Ruth whacked her wooden dollhouse, and Judah raced a red, remote-controlled Mustang, while Gabriel read the instructions on a wooden airplane kit. I marveled at God's goodness. For months, I'd been begging God to remove our difficulties. Instead, he had blessed us right there in the middle of them, just as he blessed us on a dark night two months later when I wrapped my arms around the newborn baby lying on my emptied-out abdomen and laughed at discovering we had another son. We named him Asher, which means "happy," and—unexpectedly, crazily, beyond our wildest dreams—we were.

16

Hope and Holding On

How impossible for your Ugandan mother to know what became of the frail, gasping-for-breath daughter she gave birth to.

I imagine she thinks you died all those years ago. Was she thinking of you on this day too? How surprised she would be at the life you lived. The places you went. The people who loved you—us most of all.

We are sisters in our sorrow.

Sisters in our loss of you.

Sisters in our need of knowing.

Today is the beginning of Holy Week. Holy and unknowable and filled with hope. Oh, hope! That I will hold you once more, hear you laugh, wrap my arms around you, bless you for all the years you blessed me.

Happy birthday, beautiful girl.

What I would give to sing to you again.

"Is Asher a boy?" I cradled our rosy-cheeked son in my hospital bed as our children gathered around.

Ruth pondered this curiosity from her wheelchair. *No. Try again.*

"Is Asher a girl?"

She poked out her tongue.

"Asher's a boy." I laughed and signed. "Surprise! You have a baby brother!"

"Do you want to hold him?" Dana asked.

Ruth's feet flew up with excitement. Gently, Dana laid Asher on the tray of her wheelchair so his corn-silk hair rested on Ruth's elbow.

"Isn't he soft?" Lydia stroked Asher's head.

To find out, Ruth licked him.

"Is Asher a boy?" I repeated.

No. Try again.

It took Ruth a week to concede that Asher was a boy. Even so she adored her little brother, squealing the night Dana brought us home to the streamer-festooned dining room that the kids and Christina had decorated. For Ruth's return to school a couple of days later, I printed a photo of her holding Asher with *I'M A BIG SISTER!!!* scrawled across the top. Then I tied together a handle made of ribbon and uncurled Ruth's fingers to slip it inside. Ruth carried the picture all day before letting me hang it on the wall of the pink-flowered room where she now slept downstairs. When we'd moved her, I worried that Ruth would feel alone, but after a few nights Lydia marched downstairs with her pillow and curled up beside Ruth in her queen-sized bed. From then on, they slept together.

With six pairs of arms to hold him, Asher smiled early and drew our family together around my father's wooden cradle. At night, while he slept in a crib beside my bed, I watched his chest rise and fall and marveled at how I'd doubted what to do with another baby. Dana was equally delighted, and we quickly dubbed Asher our "bonus baby," the reward we'd never expected.

"Are you going to have more?" Questions cannonballed in.

"Who knows?" I said.

Hadn't we chosen to trust God? And hadn't he blessed us? But when I counted the number of people in our family—seven—I realized we'd reached the biblical number of completion. Seven days of creation. Seven days in a week. Seven times seven, the Jewish year when bond slaves—all those who were bound, dependent, or held captive—were set free. Seven times Jesus spoke from the cross, ending with "It is finished." Complete. Nothing to be added. Purpose achieved. Work done. Time to rest, you who have labored long and suffered much. Take your rest.

That winter, before Ruth's seventh birthday, Dana drove her to Portland for a routine weight check. Despite a year of butter-fried bananas, calorie-rich protein shakes, and peanut-butter-smeared treats, her weight barely topped thirty-five pounds. Her twig legs and burl knees resembled undernourished saplings. I'd recently sewn darts in the waists of all her size-four pants to keep them from slipping off her thin waist, which they had once—when Dana helped her stand up to sing in church.

"Time to eat!" I announced, sitting at the kitchen table with Ruth one day after school, holding out a spoonful of chocolate pudding.

She eyed the spoon warily.

"Come on, Ruth," I coaxed. "First eat. Then I'll read you a story."

She wouldn't open her mouth.

"Just one bite." I held the spoon closer. "Please?"

The corners of Ruth's mouth dipped, making her long face even longer.

"Don't you like chocolate pudding?"

No.

"Is chocolate pudding yucky?"

The tip of a tongue.

"Do you want yogurt?"

No.

"Toast and butter?"

No.

"Cheese?"

No.

"Oh, Ruth." I sighed. "What are we going to do?"

We scheduled the surgery for Ruth's feeding tube in March. Feeding her would now be as easy as pouring gasoline into a car, the surgeon assured us. But Ruth wasn't a machine, and I hated putting her through one more operation. Dana drove her to Portland while I stayed home with six-week-old Asher. The next morning, Christina arrived in a swirl of calico and lace to watch our kids, and even let me borrow her car so I could visit Ruth at the hospital. When I arrived, she lay in bed watching TV. Her belly was bandaged, and a painful-looking IV protruded from her arm, but when Ruth saw me, she squealed, *Eeeeeeeeeeeeeeee!*

"I brought you a gift." I held out a brightly colored bag from a new toy store, Papa Geppetto's, where I'd stopped on the way down. "Is it a toothbrush?"

Ruth giggled.

"Chocolate pudding?"

She glared.

"Want to see?" I held the bag closer. With Dana's help, Ruth reached inside. The moment she pulled out the brown baby doll with black curly hair, she grinned and laughed, sticking out her tongue to lick the doll's hair the way she had her baby brother. The next day, Dana drove Ruth home, but it took more than a month for the skin bulging around the valve-shaped nozzle poking out of her belly to heal.

Each night, Dana changed Ruth's bandages and poured two vanilla shakes into the plastic pouch hanging from a metal pole beside her bed. The artificial smell turned my stomach, but Dana never balked as he programmed a pump to drip the syrupy fluid through the long tube he attached to Ruth's stomach. For the first time, Ruth awoke drenched in urine. Occasionally, she vomited in her sleep. *Love endures all things*, I repeated Paul's words to the Corinthians when the sorrow seemed too much. For the most part, Ruth seemed to like the feeding tube, sticking out her tongue when Dana asked if she wanted "milk in her button," but I wanted only to remember the feel of her baby-soft belly beneath my hand.

Dana or I would climb in bed between the girls to read them a story at night, often from a children's Bible. But God was another mystery I wasn't sure Ruth understood.

"Do you see the trees?" I pointed out the window one evening as the sun slipped behind the western pines. "God made the trees. Do you know who made the sky?" I pointed to clouds and rocks and stars, before ending with, "And who made you?"

Ruth beamed.

"God made you," I said. "We can't see God, but we know he's there and that he loves us because we see all the good things that he made."

After praying, I'd sing a lullaby while tucking them in bed: "Good night Lydia, good night Lydia, good night Lydia, it's time to go to sleep."

I repeated the song for Ruth, touching the tips of my fingers to my chin and turning my hand over like the setting sun. I did it fast. I did it slow, the change in speed inducing peals of laughter. "God loves you," I added, repeating these three simple words to the same tune. Then I kissed my daughters, flashed the sign for "I love you," and switched off the light.

A few minutes later, Lydia hollered, "Ruthie won't stop kicking me!"

Hands on my hips, I stood in their doorway and signed, "No kicking."

In the green glow of her electric pump, Ruth's teeth flashed a mischievous grin.

"She's still kicking me!" Lydia called a few minutes later.

This time, I scooted Ruth toward the edge of the bed. Soon, Lydia's protests turned to girlish giggles, and I smiled.

By the end of first grade, Ruth was doing so well that she could count to twenty, add simple numbers, and spell her name along with more obscure words such as *Alaska*, which she'd learned about while studying the Iditarod Trail Sled Dog Race. At home, I continued teaching Ruth at the kitchen table.

"Find *cat*." I moved my finger between two columns of words on her dry erase board, hovering by each word for three seconds before touching the next. When I got to the right word, Ruth stuck out her tongue. "Find *ball*." I started over.

Ruth was now hearing so well, some of the same experts who'd insisted she would always need sign language now claimed she no longer qualified for a deaf education. Knowing how much Ruth loved her friends and teachers, Dana and I wanted to keep her at Baxter, but—as with many parts of Ruth's education—the decision wasn't ours. The following year, Ruth would attend Dike-Newell, the public elementary school across Bath.

To make sure she was ready, we replaced Ruth's wheelchair. After five years, the front wheels wobbled, the hand brakes had failed, and the foot- and headrests were secured with duct tape. Dana repaired as much as he could—even fashioning a new headrest from sheet metal in our basement—until our insurance company finally agreed that Ruth deserved a new chair. She picked the color herself: fire-engine red. It arrived for her final day of summer school at Baxter. After tying helium balloons for her classmates to the cushioned handle and buying flowers for her teachers, I slipped my camera in

Ruth's backpack. That afternoon when she arrived home, I sat with her at the table, scrolling through photos. When I came to one of her and Fahmo, Ruth squealed. They were cheek to cheek, and Ruth's best friend grinned from beneath her flowing headscarf.

"Do you love Fahmo?" I asked.

Ay-eeeeeeeeee! Ruth stuck out her tongue.

It broke my heart to know they wouldn't be together. Would Ruth make friends when she repeated first grade at public school? Or would she be an outsider, someone whose appearance and gestures were too different for others to understand? The possibility was too painful to imagine. Ruth loved shopping for clothes, the flowery aprons I sewed for her to wear at lunch in place of bibs, and sitting for hours in the living room while a stylist braided long extensions into her hair, but she frowned when I explained that her new classmates wouldn't know sign language.

"Do you want only talking?" I asked.

No.

"Do you want only signing?"

No.

"Do you want signing and talking?"

Yes!

As Baxter had denied our request one year earlier when we'd asked that Ruth be placed in a signing and speaking classroom, our regional school district now denied our request to provide Ruth with an ASL interpreter. Too tired to fight, we decided to wait and see how Ruth did, knowing that Katie, Ruth's aide from Baxter, would be with her at least part of the time. When Katie wasn't there, Ruth would have only her eyes and her implant to communicate.

Judah and Ruth began new schools on the same day. Now a burly eighth-grader, our oldest son eagerly caught a bus across the river to a small Christian school in nearby Woolwich, but Ruth's transition was rough. Three times in a single day, the school asked me to come in when Ruth wouldn't sit, wouldn't eat, wouldn't stop crying—something she rarely did at home. When I arrived, sweat blistered Ruth's forehead, dampening her curls the way it often did when she couldn't relax. She was so upset, three adults—including her long-time physical therapist—were unable to bend her rock-rigid body into her wheelchair.

"Does your head hurt?" I asked.

Ruth arched backward, squinting through tears while trying to keep her eyes on me.

"Your throat?"

A wide wail.

"Your belly?"

I went through Ruth's entire body without a single *Yes*.

Worried, I drove Ruth to her new pediatric neurologist, who prescribed an antacid and muscle relaxant. She screamed the whole way there and all the way through her appointment. I debated driving her to the hospital, but we were already in a doctor's office. The medications seemed to help, but Ruth spent much of each school day lying in a beanbag chair because she was too uncomfortable to sit in her chair. Even so, by the end of September she could spell the names of all fourteen kids in her class plus the twenty-five words her classmates had all year to memorize. And she'd made a friend. One day early that fall, I unzipped Ruth's blue-flowered backpack to find a construction-paper book bound with staples. Wobbly letters stretched across two pages: *ruth fond a frend namede kennedy. Me and ruth saw a ranboe.*

Monday afternoons, Christina—who had taken a class and become certified as Ruth's personal support specialist to provide additional care at home—volunteered to babysit our other kids while I helped in Ruth's class.

"That's Sean!" A group of giggling girls surrounded me on my first day, pointing at a brown-eyed, brown-skinned boy. "Sean is Ruth's boyfriend!"

"Ahh—" I smiled and quickly changed the subject, not wanting to embarrass him.

"It's true!" another girl insisted. "Sean loves Ruth!"

In quiet moments, I occasionally allowed myself to imagine what would happen as Ruth grew older. Would others love her as much as we did? She'd already fallen hard for Matt, a baby-faced seventeen-year-old at church who stopped by our pew each Sunday to tell her she was beautiful. If Ruth couldn't see him, she'd shriek until we turned her chair so that she could. But Matt had left for the Marines a few months earlier, making Ruth cry. Best to leave boyfriends for later.

Only once did I miss a Monday volunteering in Ruth's class. That afternoon, Ruth arrived home with a note in her pack: *Ruth cried and cried all afternoon. We couldn't figure out what was wrong.*

"Were you sad at school today?" I asked.

Big tongue.

"What day is today? Sunday?"

No.

"Monday?"

Yes.

"Is Monday the day Mommy goes to school?"

Sad eyes. So sad.

"Were you sad because Mommy didn't go to school today?"

Ruth clenched her eyes and wailed.

I wrapped my arms around her and our tears ran together. Never did I miss another day without telling Ruth first.

Having all of Ruth's services under a single roof greatly simplified our lives; but in October, just as we were settling into this new routine, Dana lost his job. After two years of cutbacks, the company where he'd worked for a decade let him go with two weeks of unused vacation pay.

"What are we going to do?" I asked.

"Keep praying," he said. "Keep moving."

While searching for work, he painted our house, cut firewood, got Ruth ready for school, and washed dishes. But our reduced income and overlapping schedules created new conflicts, such as the afternoon Dana grilled hamburgers before Gabriel's football practice.

"I expect you to be looking for a job, not making hamburgers!" I snapped.

"I'm trying to help!" Dana snapped back.

I remembered kissing those stubble-rough lips, coarse against my cheek, and now felt that coarseness inside me. I knew I wasn't being fair, knew finding a job would take time, but I was scared.

Dana stretched out his arms. "Come here."

It looked like a trap. Step into his embrace and I'd lose time to return a phone call, finish a story, change a diaper. *Hurry! Hurry! Hurry!* Believing our future depended on me, I flew from one task to another without ever completing them all. *Relax!* an inner voice whispered, but everyone's needs were so everlastingly urgent that my husband's fell last of all. In November, a global mapmaking company offered Dana a job.

"How much?" I asked hopefully.

"Ten dollars an hour."

"How are we supposed to survive?"

Lord, do for us what we cannot do for ourselves, I prayed. *Provide what we cannot provide for ourselves. Open doors we cannot open ourselves. Keep safe my precious ones—more precious than life itself.*

As winter approached, I took more writing assignments. Dana began working from home. And Ruth was a rabbit in her school Thanksgiving concert. What a rabbit had to do with Thanksgiving, I didn't know, but Ruth loved dressing up. She and Lydia often spent afternoons modeling hats and gloves and shawls, their faces "painted" with pretend makeup that Lydia crafted from cardboard. Using curtain rods and a towel, she even transformed Ruth's wheelchair into a royal carriage, pulling her squealing sister through the house on all fours while pretending to be a horse.

The day of the performance, we pressed into the crowded school cafeteria to find a giant white bunny with a brown face sitting in a wheelchair at the front of the stage.

"I see you!" I signed and waved.

With one floppy ear covering an eye, Ruth grinned while her turkey- and vegetable-clad classmates belted out a song. Unable to sing along, Ruth could have easily been angry. Instead, she was beaming, reminding me that despite our own tough circumstances, we could be happy too.

I never figured out what a bunny had to do with Thanksgiving—but we had plenty to be thankful for. Judah loved his new school. Gabriel's football team finished the season undefeated. Dana's flexible schedule gave me more time with Lydia and Asher. And Ruth's comprehension was now so good that one day I skipped our regular reading lesson and propped a cardboard map on the dining room table and pointed to Africa. Knowing it was time, I gathered the wooden dolls from the house she'd received the previous year for

Christmas and rolled her wheelchair up to the table. Usually, we played with her house too, talking as we decorated the rooms. We'd even written *Ruth's House* on a banner taped to the roof, but today there was only the map.

"When you were born," I said, holding the dolls as Ruth eyed me curiously, "your Africa Mommy loved you *sooo* much. She rocked you and rocked you, but she couldn't take you home." I made a sad face as the black doll held her wooden baby. "All the way across the ocean, Mommy and Daddy wanted a beautiful baby from Africa." From the center of the table, I grabbed two pasty scarecrow figurines with straw hats. "We prayed and prayed. So your Africa Mommy kissed you goodbye and put you on an airplane." The baby flew across the wide blue Atlantic on top of a toy plane to the waiting scarecrows. "The airplane brought you to us! We were so happy! We hugged you and kissed you and made you part of our family. God answered our prayers. Do you like that story?"

Yes! Ruth squealed.

"Do you want to hear it again?"

Ruth's tongue touched her chin.

I hoped that Ruth would soon be telling stories of her own. In December, after months of working with her previous therapist, Colette, at Baxter, and with Mark Hammond, one of the state's top augmentative communication specialists, Ruth received her first computer. By kicking a switch attached to her wheelchair, she could choose pictures on the screen to form words that the computer would then speak. Dana was at school the day Ruth wrote her first sentence: *I want Mom.*

"Mom's not here," said Mark. "What else do you want?"

I want book.

This was it, the beginning of everything we'd hoped for. Finally, instead of merely responding to our words, Ruth would be able to say whatever she wanted—her needs, her hopes, her dreams. What thoughts lay hidden in her heart? What questions and fears had she been silently aching to share? What stories? What jokes? At seven years old, Ruth finally had a Voice—the name she gave her computer. For now, her voice would stay at school, while she and the staff trained to use it. Until it came home, I continued working with Ruth using her easel at the kitchen table. One day I wrote, *Ruth goes to school on the bus.* After reading each word aloud, I erased it, rewriting the words out of order and asking Ruth to put them in order again, which she did. Then I asked her to write the same sentence from memory, which she also did, picking out letters one at a time from her alphabet board.

"Good job!" I exclaimed, but Ruth was still staring at the letters on her board. "Do you want more words?"

Yes.

I touched each letter, but Ruth didn't pick any.

"What do you want?" I moved my finger to a row of punctuation marks. "A period?"

No.

"A question mark?"

No.

Finally, I touched the exclamation point, which I'd explained means "Wow!"

Yes! Ruth's tongue shot out.

"Is going to school on the bus exciting?"

Yes!!!

I added the exclamation point. "Is your sentence done now?"

Yes.

When Christina tried a similar experiment, Ruth wrote a sentence of her own: *Ruth likes Fahmo!*

Nearly five months had passed since Ruth had left Baxter. The following week, I dressed her in a hot pink cardigan and matching twirly skirt, clipped bright green bows in her hair, and drove her to the island. Fahmo stood at the door, waiting. She threw her arms around Ruth, who squealed, and insisted on pushing her to class. Hands waved and fingers flew as Ruth rolled through the door. An interpreter tried to keep up, but with so many children signing at once, she quit. To settle everyone down, the teacher set a time limit. Each student could sit next to Ruth for five minutes. Then they'd switch. In all my years of school, I'd never been so popular. Ruth looked happier than ever, knowing how deeply she was loved.

For Christmas, our children filed to the front of our church in bathrobes and scarves with curtain ties wrapped around their heads. Judah as a wise man. Gabriel as the angel, proclaiming words of great joy. Lydia as Mary. Asher as a baby angel. And Ruth as a wise woman in a wheelchair with a construction-paper crown. Some of her favorite people filled the pews, including former teachers, aides, and our dear friend Tracey. Ruth shrieked when she saw them, as she did a month later when baby-faced Matt returned from the Marines to kiss her forehead and tell her that she was beautiful.

But on this night, a two-year-old with a coat-hanger halo stole the stage. Long after the other children had returned to their seats, little Alex stood by the manger. He didn't see his mother coaxing him away. He didn't see the congregation standing for the final song. All he saw was the baby—a plastic doll—lying in the hay. And that is where he stayed, beside the sheep, under the star, until the last strains of "Joy to the World" echoed out the candlelit windows and into the cold street beyond—a reminder to stay close to Christ during the darkest time of the year.

17

Heartbreak

My heart is too fragile a house
to hold all these people inside,
people who fall down stairs
and ride the bus to far-off basketball games
bouncing over long, lonely roads
through ice and snow,
without blankets to keep them warm
should the engine seize and stop;
seize and stop like a child's heart,
one night in winter.

Winter heaped snow on the roof, bent the lofty tops of the pines, and raised white mountains alongside the road. Our older kids tromped up the back hill, sledding past trees and rocks at breakneck speed to slam into the house before dragging their sleds back up the hill again, while Ruth often remained inside with Asher and me.

"Watch the baby." I laid eleven-month-old Asher beside Ruth on the futon we kept on the living room floor. "Make sure he doesn't go anywhere."

Eeeeeeek! Ruth shrieked with laughter as her brother flipped onto his tummy and skedaddled away.

"You get back here!" I scolded, pretending to be angry and making Ruth laugh even harder as I chased Asher across the room, scooped him up, and plopped him back beside his sister. "No crawling away!"

Other days, Asher pulled himself to standing by grabbing the sturdy rungs of Ruth's wheelchair. He had long ago surpassed Ruth in agility. Another month and he would walk and talk, passing her entirely. Although Ruth couldn't say how this made her feel, I wondered. CP wasn't something we really talked about. How do you explain to a child with limited language that she'll most likely never walk? One day, sitting with Ruth at the kitchen table during our daily lessons, I tried.

"I know it's hard." I signed and spoke. "Not everyone can walk, but you can smile! Not everyone can talk, but you can stick out your tongue! You are a smart girl, and Mommy is so proud of you!"

Ruth grinned as I raised my thumb toward my chin to sign "proud."

Each morning after feeding Ruth and getting her ready for school, Christina, Dana, or I pushed Ruth's wheelchair across the street to catch her bus in the parking lot of a neighboring gym. In warm weather, the arrangement worked great, but in winter, layers of ice and slippery snow made the crossing treacherous. Several times I'd phoned the bus company and the school, requesting to have her bus stop directly in front of our house. Each time I was told that our street was too busy—drivers would grow angry, and police and fire trucks wouldn't be able to get by. I considered driving Ruth to school myself, but her new wheelchair was backbreaking to lift. Plus, riding the bus was one thing Ruth could do just like everyone else, and she loved it—grinning as her elementary school classmates, who also struggled with disabilities, greeted her each morning.

That final Friday afternoon of January, I climbed aboard Ruth's bus, high-fiving kids who struggled to speak or to control their actions, or whose difficulties lay deeper than I could know. They were always excited to see me as I made my way to the very back of the bus where Ruth sat, grinning. After unbuckling the straps that secured her chair to the floor, I pushed Ruth toward the side door where a platform lowered us to the ground. The snow, where passing trucks and boots had not beaten it into slushy batter, was ankle deep. More was quickly falling. Fat flakes clung to Ruth's curly eyelashes and melted on her warm brown skin as the lift slowly raised behind us.

"Ready?" I asked.

Ruth stuck out her tongue.

To keep her front wheels from pivoting, I turned Ruth's chair around and dragged her backward through the sludge. Cars churned around us, and she skidded from side to side in the slippery parking lot. We would have been better off with a sleigh, I thought, or maybe an old-fashioned baby buggy with runners instead of wheels. After waiting for a break in traffic to pull her across the street, I turned Ruth around in our driveway and pushed her up the ninety-foot ramp to our back door. This time I'd had it. After wiping melted snow from Ruth's face and parking her at the kitchen table, I picked up the phone and called our school superintendent, William Shuttleworth. For five minutes, I described the danger of crossing our street—all the while steeling myself for a fight.

Instead Mr. Shuttleworth said, "Monday morning I will make sure that bus stops at your door."

That was it. Problem solved. Only on Monday, Ruth awoke with a fever. I gave her ibuprofen and tucked her in bed with a movie. The next morning, her temperature was normal, but she had upset digestion—a common side effect of her medication. When she woke up with the same problem on Wednesday, I kept her home again.

"Is Ruth okay?" someone from school called to ask.

"She's fine," I assured her. Ruth didn't have a cough, something we vigilantly watched for, or even a runny nose.

I was more worried about my mom. A week earlier, while walking with friends at night in a western Asian city, she'd stepped on a manhole cover that had flipped, pinning her between the heavy metal lid and the opening to the sewer system. After being rescued by her friends and undergoing X-rays at a local hospital to make sure she hadn't broken any ribs, she'd flown back to her apartment in Israel. The following night she'd woken up in so much pain that she couldn't sit up to reach the phone. Another friend, who happened to be spending the night, called an ambulance. It turned out that my mom had ruptured her spleen, a life-threatening emergency that had required immediate surgery at a Netanya hospital. I'd been on the phone all week, checking on my mom and updating family and friends and asking them to pray.

So I was grateful for a few quiet mornings without having to get Ruth on the bus. By Thursday, she seemed back to normal, but when Dana asked whether she wanted to go to school, Ruth poked out her bottom lip. It was the same on Friday. Since the week was almost over, we let her stay home and watch movies in bed. What was one more day to rest? That morning, Dana worked from home while I drove to Portland to research a story. On my way back, I stopped at a resale shop and bought a wooden push-bike for Asher, who was about to turn one. Dana's parents were coming for his birthday party on Sunday after church, and I mentally planned my grocery list, trying to decide what to serve. But when I arrived home that afternoon, Ruth seemed oddly warm.

I called Dana over. "Feel Ruth's forehead. I think her fever is back."

"It doesn't feel very high." He joined me beside Ruth's bed, where she lay propped with pillows on top of her covers while Barney, the big purple dinosaur, danced and sang on the screen of a laptop.

"But why would her fever come back? We should take her to the doctor."

Whether from the concern on my face or something else, Ruth began to wail.

"Your head hurt?" Dana signed.

Ruth cried louder but didn't stick out her tongue.

"Your throat? Your button?"

No.

"Do you feel bad?" I asked.

Yes. Ruth howled.

The sound was so fierce, Ruth's breathing so rapid, that I panicked. "Call an ambulance!" I gathered Ruth in my arms. "Or put Ruth in the van. We should drive her to the hospital!"

"Why don't we call her doctor first?" Dana suggested.

Carrying Ruth, I raced into the kitchen, followed by Dana. I wasn't even sure that our pediatrician's office was open. We'd switched practices a few months before, and it was nearly 4:30 p.m. Dana held Ruth while I dialed our doctor's number and left a message. When he called back, I described Ruth's symptoms.

"Give her Tylenol," he said. "Then send some water through her feeding tube. If she stops crying and her fever goes away within an hour, she should be fine. But if she's still uncomfortable, you might want to bring her to the emergency room and see if they can find anything wrong."

Within fifteen minutes, Ruth's fever vanished and she stopped crying. Crisis over. Or so we thought. Saturday morning Ruth seemed fine. Christina arrived and spent several hours reading to her. Gabriel played basketball at the YMCA. Judah was headed to a friend's birthday sleepover, and his mom had invited me to join them for dinner, but a late afternoon storm pelted the coast with ice and snow, so I asked Dana to drive Judah instead. While they were gone, I gave Lydia and Ruth a bath. Ruth loved baths, twisting her head to lap the warm water with her tongue—the one time she could feed herself. But on this night, she strained against the straps on her bath seat, unable to relax. Still needing to bake Asher's cake, I wrapped Ruth in a towel, tucked a blanket around her, and laid her on the foot of her bed to watch the fish swimming in the glass tank the boys had given her for Christmas.

Get Ruth! An inner voice urged as I walked down the hall. *Ruth loves to cook!*

It was one of her favorite activities, measuring ingredients hand over hand and stirring the batter together. Ruth grunted as if she wanted me. I took two steps toward her room and stopped, realizing that I'd first have to get Ruth dressed and in her wheelchair. But it was late, and I was tired, so I turned back toward the kitchen.

"How are the roads?" I asked when Dana stomped through the back door a short while later.

"Slippery." He shook off melting ice. "I'm glad you stayed home."

"Well, I'm not." I rinsed a bowl in the kitchen sink and set it on the rack to dry. "I was looking forward to going out. Lydia's upstairs getting into her pajamas, and Ruth's on her bed. Can you dress her?"

While I finished washing up, Dana headed down the hall. Lydia gave me a hug before scampering off to join Ruth for a story. I pictured the girls curled together with their favorite dolls beneath the construction-paper-and-Popsicle-stick name signs Lydia had made and taped to the wall, while Dana read and prayed before turning out the light. I felt too weary to join them. As if bearing an immense weight, I sank into a chair at the kitchen table—the same table where I'd sat with my mom eight years earlier when she'd revealed her dream. Sushi, our golden retriever, snuffled up beside me, brown doggy eyes staring into mine.

Dana found me like that, head in my hands. "What's wrong?" He stood behind me, kneading my shoulders.

"Do you realize that Sushi is going to die?" I asked.

"What are you talking about?"

"I mean, how could God create dogs just to let them die?" The apparent emptiness of life overwhelmed me as I imagined our happy-go-lucky golden retriever loping through the woods, then pictured her lying in a grave. "Do you realize how terrible that is? What's the point of living?"

Dana shook his head. "You know that's not the way it is with us." He started talking about God's promise of eternal life for those who put their trust in him.

But I didn't want to hear it. Pulling myself up, I climbed the stairs and fell into bed. As ice pelted the windows, I curled up in the dark, wrapped my arms around myself, and rocked with grief as I imagined burying our dog.

"Meadow, call 911!" Dana shouted.

Dark. Early morning. Silence outside my window. The storm was over. Had a car slid off the road?

"It's Ruth!" Dana burst into our room.

"What do you mean 'It's Ruth'?" I shot up in bed.

"She's not breathing." He tried to control his voice, but I felt his panic. "Meadow, I think she's dead."

"No, God! No!" I lunged for the phone beside our bed. Hands shaking, I punched numbers, but all I got was static. Dana rushed back downstairs. I followed, still yelling, "No, God!"

"What's wrong?" Gabriel staggered into the hall, hugging his chest.

"Ruth!" I shouted. "Wait in my room!"

"What's happening?" Downstairs, Lydia huddled in a corner of the hall, where Dana had shooed her from bed.

"I don't know! Go upstairs. Get in my bed."

I couldn't look in Ruth's room, afraid that if I did, what Dana had said would actually be true. While he ran back to her, I grabbed the phone in the entryway around the corner and dialed again.

"Nine-one-one. What's your emergency?"

"I need an ambulance. My daughter isn't breathing. She has cerebral palsy."

"Are you with her?"

"My husband is."

"Where is she?"

"In bed. Is someone coming?"

"An ambulance is on the way. Have your husband lay your daughter on the floor."

"Lay her on the floor!"

"Can he feel a pulse?"

"Can you feel a pulse?" *Please, God. Please let him feel a pulse.*

"No!" Dana cried.

"Can he see anything in her mouth? Is anything blocking her airway?"

"Is anything in her mouth?"

Why hadn't we taken Ruth to the hospital?

"No."

"Have him tilt back her head."

"Tilt back her head!" *Oh, God. No. Please, no!*

"Pinch her nose tightly closed."

"Pinch her nose!"

Four EMTs walked around the back corner of the house. Two carried a stretcher. Horror engulfed me as I threw open the door and pointed to Ruth's room. "In there!"

Then I fled to the living room. On the street below, two ambulances were parked in front of our house, bright strobes lighting up the inside walls. *Please, God,* I begged, falling to my knees beside the couch. *Please, do a miracle. Please, don't let Ruth die.* Hadn't I read about children who'd slipped beneath frozen ponds or been born without breath and been miraculously saved?

"Can we come down?" Lydia called from the top of the stairs.

"No!" I hurried toward the back hall as a man carried Ruth toward the door. Arms and legs limp, her head rested on his sweater, black curls dark against the blue sleeve.

"Can I go with her?" I asked.

Eyes filled with compassion, the man shook his head and carried Ruth outside.

"Mom? Dad?" Gabriel called down the hall.

"Wait!" Dana returned to Ruth's room with the remaining paramedics, answering their questions.

After they packed up, it was just us.

"What happened?" I moaned.

"I don't know." Dana pulled me against his chest. "I came down to let Sushi out, and when I checked on the girls, Ruth wasn't breathing."

"Had she tangled in her sheets?" I thought of the warm flannel I'd bought her for Christmas a little more than a month before.

"She was on her side, just like I'd tucked her in. Only—" his voice cracked, "her sheets were soaked with sweat."

A vision of Ruth's damp curls lying on her sweat-darkened pillow filled my mind. I'd seen her. I didn't remember looking in the room, but somehow I had seen her.

"Mom?" Lydia called again.

"Coming!"

While Dana called his parents and someone from church to come stay with our kids, I herded Lydia and Gabriel from where they stood at the top of the stairs to our room. Down the hall, Asher lay in his crib, still sleeping.

"Is Ruthie okay?" Lydia asked.

"We don't know," I answered honestly. "Do you want to pray?"

Two golden heads nodded. As we knelt together beside my bed, I began with the only words I could think of: "Our Father, which art in heaven, hallowed be thy name. Thy kingdom come, thy will be done, on earth as it is in heaven."

A few minutes later, Dana joined us, entreating God for a miracle, "Show us your strength. Show us your divine power."

Minutes felt like hours as we paced in the living room, waiting for someone to come so we wouldn't have to bring the children to the hospital. After about fifteen minutes, unable to wait any longer, I grabbed the van keys and asked Dana to borrow someone's car and meet me at the hospital as soon as he could. When I stepped outside, everything was covered with ice. It took several minutes just to scrape the windshield.

"Show me a sign," I begged God, driving as fast as I dared as the sun broke through the glittering trees. "If Ruth is really gone, I need some sign to know that you were in control."

It was so early, the hospital waiting room was empty.

"My daughter is here," I told the receptionist. "She wasn't breathing. An ambulance just brought her in."

"Her name?"

I crossed my fingers and touched my mouth from right to left. "Ruth," I said, realizing that I'd forgotten her processor at home. "She's deaf."

A nurse appeared and put her arm around me, leading me to a small sitting room. From the look on her face, I knew that Ruth would no longer recognize her name whether I signed it or not. When I was ready, she ushered me to her room. Ruth lay on a hospital bed, surrounded by people and wires. Hands pumped her chest. A doctor stepped forward. They'd tried everything, he said, without getting a response. They were all looking at me, waiting.

"It's okay," I said, realizing what they were waiting for. "You can stop."

I stroked Ruth's head, holding her hand as nurses removed the electrodes from her body. Her hand still felt warm. But when I mentioned it, a nurse said the heat was from my own body. Slowly the room emptied, until only the doctor and I were left. Stunned with shock and grief, I went over every detail from the week before, everything I could remember, including Ruth's sweat-soaked sheets.

"Could her fever have come back?"

"Possibly," the doctor said. "Sometimes with CP these things just happen."

Gently, he told me to take as much time as I needed, stepping out. As I had in hospital rooms so many times before, I stood beside Ruth's small body. Around her neck sparkled the plastic necklace Lydia had given her while playing dress up the day before. Bending to lay my head beside hers, I continued to hold her hand and stroke her hair.

"I am sorry. I am so sorry." I cried, unable to fathom how this had happened. *How could a mother not know her own daughter was dying?* With crushing despair, I recalled the past week, ending with the unaccountable grief I'd felt the night before. Then I remembered something else. Friday morning, while Asher napped, Ruth had whimpered in her chair.

"Do you want to read?" I'd asked.

No.

"Do you want to watch a movie?"

No.

"Do you want Mommy to hold you?"

Yes.

Unbuckling her straps, I sat on the living room futon, cradling Ruth in my lap. Body stiff with tension, she lay against my chest. As I rocked back and forth, the words of an unknown melody filled my mind. "There is a place," I sang, "with no more tears, where Jesus will take away all your fears." Ruth breathed deeply, beginning to relax. "There is a place where you will run and dance with joy under the sun. There is a place where you'll be free, a place with no more pain and suffering. There is a place where you will know all the love we have for you here below." Tears spilled down my face and onto Ruth's as the words kept coming, verse after verse filled with hope and the promise of heaven.

A few minutes later the song ended. *Wow!* I thought as Ruth rested comfortably in my arms. *Where did that come from?*

That same day, I'd had a sudden impulse to reorganize Ruth's bedroom. Pulling down art and drawings she'd made at school, I carefully folded and tucked each one into a keepsake box I'd bought one week before to store mementos from her adoption. *When Ruth came, all she had was a ripped backpack with secondhand clothes,* I thought. *But when she goes, she'll leave this box full of all the things she got to do and all the gifts from the people who loved her.*

Then came the most extraordinary experience of all. That night, while falling asleep, I'd suddenly felt as if I were floating. Arms crossed over my chest and eyes closed, I saw myself lifted like a boat by a sea of love that surrounded me like an ocean. I was in the love and the love was in me, filling me with warmth and absolute peace. *What is this?* I'd wondered. *This is so wonderful!* Had God let me glimpse the love Ruth was experiencing now?

Even so, I couldn't fathom how she could be gone. Deep down, I felt certain I'd failed. *If not, wouldn't she still be alive?* Face pressed against Ruth's cheek, her hand in mine, I waited with Ruth for about an hour, crying and praying. Only later would I learn that Dana had been too overwhelmed by shock to join me. Not wanting to leave, but knowing I must, I bent and kissed my daughter one last time.

"I love you," I said, hoping that Ruth could somehow hear.

Just before leaving, something made me pause. I stopped and pulled back the sheet covering Ruth's body. She wore the pink-flowered pajama bottoms Dana had dressed her in the night before. Then I noticed her shirt, which I'd given her for Christmas more than a year earlier. It was so big, she hardly ever wore it, but the bold, swirly letters on the front made me gasp.

God's girl, they said.

And I knew she was.

18

Winter Bare

"Do you think I don't have regrets?" Mom once asked. "Of course I do. Everyone has regrets. But I am not going to spend the rest of my life dwelling on them."

"I don't have regrets," I said.

"What a ridiculous thing to say!"

It was true. I was in my early twenties, married to a good man, pursuing a promising career.

"I always knew what I wanted, and that's the road I took," I said. "So, I don't have regrets—not big ones."

"Just wait," Mom said. "You might not make the same mistakes I did, but you'll make plenty of your own."

Time proved her right. Sharp words. Teary faces. A million ways I am less than the mother I want to be.

But nothing—nothing—compares to the regret of irreversible loss.

What if I'd tucked Ruth in?

What if I'd checked on her during the night?

What if I'd woken up?

I was her mother.

It was my job to save her.

And I failed.

Stop the earth on its axis. Turn the calendar back one day. Climb the stairs and crawl back in bed. Could I relive a single day, the Sunday Ruth died would be the one. How much easier to believe that God had brought her to us than to believe he'd taken her away. Or, worse, that we'd failed. I agonized over every detail of Ruth's final week, blaming myself for not realizing that something was wrong. Overcome by loss and grief, I was engulfed with guilt. Why hadn't we taken Ruth to the hospital?

"Had she been my own child, I would not have brought her in," the emergency room doctor told Dana later that terrible morning when someone accompanied him to the hospital.

While they were gone, his parents arrived. His mother, Pat, threw her arms around me with a wail that let me know how deeply this woman, who had sewn matching pajamas and Easter dresses for Ruth and Lydia, loved her granddaughter. In the chaos, I sat on the kitchen garbage can and phoned the friend at whose house Judah had spent the night, asking her to drive him home. Reaching my mom, who was still recovering from surgery in Israel, was harder, and I was forced to leave a message. Huddled in the living room after Dana arrived home, we tried explaining to our children what had happened, although we didn't know. As friends and family arrived, the front door opened and closed, opened and closed, and I found myself answering questions and offering comfort, while desperately craving answers and comfort myself.

"If only I had woken up," I sobbed on the phone to Mandy. "If only I had known something was wrong."

"When I sent Yvonne and Ruth to America, I knew their lives would be a struggle," Mandy said. "My prayer was simply that they would live long enough to know they were loved. God answered my prayer. Your family gave that little girl the best life she could've had, and I truly believe that Ruth lived as long as she was meant to. She was ready to go."

"But I wasn't," I groaned.

Wanting to be alone, I slipped into Ruth's room. A construction-paper card lay on her bureau. *Happy Birthday Asher!* it said in Ruth's shaky scrawl. Inside, Christina had helped Ruth draw two smiley faces and write her name. And so, one of the happiest days of our lives—the day on which we'd welcomed Asher—became the saddest. Gradually, bright morning light gave way to cold evening shadows. Asher explored his gifts. Dana's family left, and the door stayed closed. The walls seemed to close with it. The roof as well, trapping me with the horror that Ruth was gone. The house felt too silent, my arms too empty, my hands—with nothing left to sign—too still. *I want Ruth back,* I silently pleaded. *God, I want Ruth back.* But it was too late. That night Dana rocked and rocked me, our tears soaking the bed.

To push the horror of Ruth's death far from me, I organized her dresser, separating her pleated pants and striped socks and flowery dresses into a small pile to save and a larger one to give away. In place of clothes, I packed Ruth's drawers with books and hair bows and the hundreds of cards that overflowed our mailbox, many from people we had never met. One wrote that he'd followed Ruth's adoption in the newspaper. Another said her daughter was in Ruth's class at school. One afternoon I looked out the living room window to see a boy, clutching a bouquet of pink roses, and his mom standing on the sidewalk below. I went out to meet them and recognized the boy, Titus, from Ruth's bus.

"I miss her smile," he said, struggling to form each word.

"Me too."

Only slowly did we understand how many people Ruth's life had touched. The funeral home, just down the street, donated its services. Mandy and Lukas's church, three thousand miles away, paid for her burial. The café, where Ruth loved to buy cookies, sent over steaming carafes of coffee. Church friends and neighbors brought meals and shared memories, as did Ruth's teacher, Ms. Buotte.

"I wanted to tell you how sorry the children are, how sorry we all are," she said, standing in my kitchen with a loaf of freshly baked bread. "Do you remember Sean?"

I nodded, recalling the handsome boy, who I learned had also been adopted—the one the children had called Ruth's boyfriend.

"When I called to tell Sean's family about Ruth, his mother shared a story I thought you'd like to hear," Ms. Buotte said. "Last fall, Sean came home from school and said he had a girlfriend.

"'Oh?' his mother asked, 'What do you do together?'

"'We don't do anything,' Sean said.

"'What do you talk about?' she asked.

"'We don't talk,' he said.

"Sean's mother thought he had an imaginary friend," Ms. Buotte chuckled. "'Then, what *do* you do?' she asked.

"'When I jump up and down on the playground, she smiles at me and laughs!'"

Ms. Buotte shook her head. "I don't think Sean ever saw Ruth's disabilities. He saw her smile, and it made him feel so good that he loved her. On Monday as we walked back to our classroom from recess, Sean stepped out of line to kiss Ruth's picture in the class photo outside our door."

So Ruth had a boyfriend after all. Such stories dulled the pain, but nothing filled the aching emptiness of Ruth's loss. I wasn't the only one hurting. That week, I opened Ruth's dresser to discover a pile of neatly folded doll clothes.

"Have you been cleaning out Ruth's doll's clothes?" I asked Lydia. She nodded. "Are you going to get me another sister?"

"Oh, Sweetheart." I wrapped my arms around her. "It doesn't work that way, but you were the best sister Ruth could've had."

The boys had their own questions.

"Why did Ruth die?" Judah asked.

Desperate to know myself, I called the neurologist who had treated her several months before. "Birth related," he said. "Genetic predisposition . . . almost unheard of in this country."

Sitting at Dana's desk, I frantically scribbled notes on a yellow legal pad, catching bits and phrases. One word, *kernicterus*, stood out from the rest. Having never heard of it, I wrote it twice—each time with a different spelling.

"In all my years of practice, I've only seen one other patient with it," he said. "She was in her early teens when she died in her sleep at summer camp. They found her the same way that you found Ruth— lying in a pool of sweat. She wasn't even sick."

Caused by the buildup of bilirubin, the same neurotoxin that causes newborn jaundice, kernicterus occurs in the first days of life when the deadly poison passes from an infant's bloodstream to the brain. It is most common in premature babies—like Ruth—and hardest to diagnose in those who are black because the yellow hue of jaundice doesn't show up as clearly in their skin. When untreated, it causes the two types of cerebral palsy that Ruth had, deafness, poor eye muscle control, and—most shocking of all—malformed baby teeth, often while leaving a child with typical intelligence. Ruth had every single indicator, yet not one doctor over nearly seven years of medical tests from Maine to Boston had ever mentioned the word. Kernicterus, her neurologist now explained, can also damage the hypothalamus, the part of the brain that regulates body temperature. His other patient had once been rushed to the hospital with a temperature of 107.

"She'd been sitting in her wheelchair when her caregiver noticed sweat pouring off her," he said. "Only, when it happened in her sleep, no one knew. Not even people sleeping in the same room. She died without a sound."

Horrified, I recalled the beads of sweat that sometimes dappled Ruth's forehead and pooled in her ears, notes from Baxter saying that she'd arrived "drenched in sweat" or to "send lighter clothing," and how she often seemed hotter than the rest of us. But never did we imagine that this could be dangerous. I pictured Ruth lying awake, sweating under her carefully tucked in covers, waiting for me to come.

"Would Ruth have been awake?" I asked. "Would she have been in pain?"

"No," he said. "The result would be similar to heatstroke. As Ruth's temperature skyrocketed, she would have lost consciousness. Her muscles would have stopped working. Then her brain. She would have suffered heart arrhythmia, and she would have died."

That night I crawled into Ruth's bed. Lying on her pillow with my eyes closed, I felt my arms and legs and toes, trying to measure whether I was too hot. Had we given her too many blankets? But all I felt was comforting warmth. Weeping, I wrapped my arms around Ruth's favorite doll, which she'd named Rose, the faint smell of vanilla clinging to her hair.

Friday night, our family set up for Ruth's memorial service. Arms full of flowers, we stumbled into the darkened sanctuary of our church. A basket on the altar caught my eye. I thought it was full of pinwheels until Dana flicked on the light to reveal a giant arrangement of tissue-paper blossoms. *With much love from the students and staff at Dike-Newell School*, read the tag. Beside them stood a vase with fresh-cut branches decorated with construction-paper hearts and hair bows.

Too young to go from us, was written on one heart with a frown.

Ruth, I love you, said another.

Then I spotted a sparkly purple heart signed, *Fahmo*.

"Who are they from?" Dana and our kids gathered around.

"Ruth's friends," I said, astonished.

On an empty table, we placed the ripped brown backpack that had arrived with Ruth from Uganda, the red dress I'd sewn for her first Christmas, the birthday card and dolls from Welcome Home, a few favorite books, Titus's pink roses, and a watercolor I'd helped Ruth paint of her school a couple of weeks before by sliding a floor-sized easel over the arms of her wheelchair. After all we had done to trust God and give Ruth a home, after how much we had loved her, this was not how Ruth's life was supposed to end. I wanted to claw a hole in the earth and die.

"How do people get through this?" I asked Dana.

"Drugs," he said. "Alcohol."

For the first time, I understood pain so deep you'd swallow razor blades to kill it.

Saturday morning, tulips, roses, and daffodils dotted the altar. Our family arrived at the church early, joining hands around Ruth's open casket in the otherwise empty sanctuary. So many times when the days had seemed too long and Ruth's needs too many and my strength too small, I had envisioned laying her on God's altar, but never, ever had I imagined this. Dana thanked God for bringing Ruth into our family. Together we closed the lid. Then we covered it with the red woven blanket that had arrived with Ruth from Uganda, laying a single white rose with a pink ribbon on top.

An hour later, the church was packed. Twice, the minister asked people to squeeze together in the pews. Ruth's former teachers and aides from Baxter, along with an interpreter, lined the front. A dozen Boy Scouts from Judah and Gabriel's troop skipped a winter derby to fill the balcony. In all, more than five hundred people came to honor a little girl who'd never spoken a word.

Dana walked down the aisle with Lydia, her small hand gripping his, while I carried Asher. The boys, always Ruth's biggest advocates, now thirteen and eleven, followed behind. We sat in our regular pew at the front of the sanctuary, beside Ruth's empty wheelchair. Five generations of Dana's family filled the seats behind, but my mom was still too sick to travel. *God, you have to help me,* I prayed as the worship team sang and photos of our family flashed on the screen—Judah reading to Ruth on the couch, Gabe dancing with her, Lydia sleeping by her side. It was almost my turn to talk, and I wasn't sure I could. The minister looked at me. Thumbs up and I'd speak. Thumbs down and he'd read my notes for me. Hesitantly, I raised my thumb and took my place at the altar.

Looking out at all those faces, my sorrow was overwhelmed by gratitude. Many had donated money for Ruth's adoption or dropped off secondhand clothes at our door or watched our children while I drove Ruth to appointments or shuttled the others to school or Scouts. Some had just been there to listen or laugh or share a cup of tea. But as I saw them all gathered together, I knew that even in the hardest moments, we had never been alone. Our family and neighbors had embraced Ruth right along with us, and now they were here to help us let her go. Unfolding words written in the darkest hours of the night, I took a deep breath and began, "What a privilege to have Ruth in our family . . ." I shared about Ruth's laughter, her remarkable determination, and how close we'd come to saying no to adopting her, but what a blessing we would have missed! All the sacrifice, all the struggle now seemed as nothing compared to the joy Ruth brought us, the joy of loving her.

Tammy, Tracey, Theresa, Christina, Dana's parents, and several others who had linked their hearts to ours, joined hands with us around Ruth's coffin as we prayed and offered our precious daughter back to God. Then, as "Release me, Oh Lord" played over the speakers, Dana clasped a hot pink helium balloon—Ruth's favorite color—and led everyone outside. Mourners poured down the church steps, crunching across the snow-crusted lawn to line the street.

"Ready?" Dana asked as our family took hold of the string dangling from Ruth's balloon.

"One, two—" Dana counted, and I could almost see the grin spread across Ruth's face that bright fall day as she sat in the backyard swing more than six years earlier, black-buckle shoes rocketing past my head. "Three!"

We all let go.

But instead of soaring into the heavens, the balloon bobbed over the street and across a neighbor's lawn. Would it snag in the bushes?

"Come on," someone urged as it struggled along.

With one arm around Asher, I raised my free hand as if to give it a lift. Then an unseen breeze caught the balloon up, up through the winter-bare bones of an outstretched tree, higher and higher until the single, solitary sphere became a shining pink speck against a cloudless sky—and just like that, it was gone.

19

What Remained

I dream that I am digging and digging, a huge trench filled with toys. On top lies Ruth's favorite doll. I pull it from the dirt only to realize Ruth herself is what I am searching for.

I am not the only one disturbed in sleep.

At night, Dana climbs from bed and tiptoes down the darkened hall. I hear him creep from room to room. A few minutes later, he slides back under the covers, only to rise again.

"What are you doing?" I ask when he returns.

Dana doesn't answer.

In the morning I say nothing.

He repeats this strange ritual a few nights later.

"What's wrong?" I question.

"I was afraid." My husband shudders.

So begin Dana's nightly walks to lay his hand on the chests of our sleeping children to make sure that they are still breathing in their beds.

"Get him! Get him!" I yelled.

"What's wrong?" Dana shot up in bed beside me.

"Asher!" I shouted as our son's small face slipped beneath a lake. When I realized it was only a dream, I turned away, sobbing. Dana stroked my hair, falling back to sleep, but I lay awake for hours, his hand the only thing holding me to Earth.

In the month after losing Ruth, Asher took his first steps. Lydia painted trees and raced through the house riding an invisible horse. Judah turned fourteen and spent most of his time in his room strumming guitar or riding down the street on a skateboard. Dana went back to work, drafting for an engineer from church. And Gabriel played piano, the same song over and over.

"This is when you and Dad got married." He hunched over our aged upright, fingers playing a bright, happy tune. "Then you had

Judah." He picked up the pace. "And me." The keys danced the way his little legs had once danced for Ruth. "And Lydia." Even faster. "When we had Ruth, it got hard." His hands slowed. "And then Ruth died." Each finger dragged as if made of lead.

Above, Ruth smiled from a silver frame, long braids tickling her shoulders—her first-grade school photo. Regret crushed me. I hadn't just lost a daughter. I'd lost their sister. Surely, this was not God's plan. At meals, I found myself reaching toward Ruth's empty place at the table, opening and closing my fingers as if to feel her own small hand in mine. Each morning I peeked in her room, where Lydia now slept alone, not because I expected to see Ruth, but because I wanted to. Some days the ache was so strong my lips hurt from wanting to kiss her, my arms from wanting to hold her. Instead of lessening as the days rolled into months, my pain seemed to intensify. My heart was a sieve. Only so much sorrow could seep through at a time. If only I'd loved Ruth more, I was convinced, she'd still be here. Yet, pain was the proof. We had loved Ruth fiercely.

Only once did I forget that she was gone. Standing in the kitchen, holding a wooden pizza board in front of my face, I played peekaboo with Asher, who was sitting in his high chair at the kitchen table. He was laughing, laughing—bright eyes shining, white teeth flashing. I popped my head out from one side of the board. "Boo!" Then the other. "Boo!" Glancing over to catch Ruth's reaction, I felt a physical jolt when I saw she wasn't there.

"What are we going to do?" I asked Dana—ten, twenty, thirty times a day.

"Keep trusting. Keep moving."

But my faith was in free fall. Wings tucked against my chest to protect my broken heart, I plunged toward the bone-crushing rocks below, where no unseen hand seemed poised to catch me. *Where was God now?*

That spring, I drove our children to Baxter for an assembly in Ruth's honor. Fahmo raced up to me. "Ruth dead?" she signed, turning over her fairy-light hands.

I nodded, making a sad face, and signed, "Ruth with God."

"What 'God?'" Fahmo asked, dark eyes questioning.

Surprised she didn't know the word, I began to sign, "God made the trees . . ." and stopped. After losing Ruth, it was as difficult for me to believe in God's presence as it was to accept my daughter's absence. My one comfort was Asher. During the long days and dark nights, the baby I hadn't known what to do with became my sole reason to hope that God still existed, to believe he might even be good. Snuggling my growing son in bed, I marveled at how wonderfully he fit into my arms—his downy head nestled on my elbow, his diapered bottom the precise span from my hand to draw him to my breast, his eyes the exact distance to focus on mine. What else but God could create such perfection? Surely not the random collision of energy. Yet, if God existed and he was good, then why hadn't he healed Ruth? Why hadn't he woken me during the night when her temperature soared? Why hadn't he restored her to life?

"How long has Ruth been gone?" Lydia asked one night that spring while I made dinner.

"Almost three months," I said.

She hung her head. "I guess I'm getting used to it."

"It feels like an empty spot in my heart," I said.

"It feels like an empty spot in my bed," she said.

To cope with my grief, I straightened Ruth's blankets and arranged the furniture in her wooden dollhouse and ripped the paper from our kitchen walls. And we chose Ruth's grave marker—evidence undeniable that Ruth was no longer our laughing, loving little girl . . . but what? A princess? A spirit? A streak of light? I knew Ruth was not her body. She was always so much more than her body—more like a light shining through a lantern than the lantern itself. Yet what is a lantern without a flame? What is a spirit when the body has died? From the time I'd first entrusted my life to Christ on our Oregon farm, I'd believed in heaven, believed God would welcome me when I died. So why did heaven now feel like a lie? As Easter came and went, petals of once-answered prayers wilted into despair when I saw Easter lilies.

I thought I was handling Ruth's death well until I realized I'd given away her favorite pink slippers. Should I phone the clothing bank and explain my mistake? Maybe I'd take back Ruth's ruffled shirt as well, the one she'd picked for school. Dana shook his head when I told him my plan. And I knew he was right. Our house wasn't big enough, my arms not long enough to hold it all. Yet what were we to do with all that remained?

The processors for Ruth's implant we mailed to Boston Children's Hospital, which passed them onto two girls with outdated equipment, allowing them to hear a wider range of sound. Her computer we gave to an eleven-year-old girl, Berleeann, who was losing her voice, along with other physical and cognitive abilities, to a degenerative disease. When her mother and father invited Dana and me to visit their Scarborough apartment a couple of months later, the young girl with a slow smile offered us pie and gave me a sticker: a single pink rose. But what to do with Ruth's flashy new wheelchair? For months, it sat in the mudroom gathering skateboards and jackets and dust.

I'd long dreamed of bringing Ruth back to Africa—of our whole family traveling the red, dusty roads to where she'd been born. Now that was impossible. But could we send her chair? Sitting at Dana's computer, I typed *Joni and Friends*, the name of a California ministry that distributes wheelchairs to people with disabilities around the world. While driving back and forth to Baxter, I'd often heard Joni Eareckson Tada, the founder and CEO, speak on our local Christian radio station. When I was eight, Mom had taken Sunny and me to see the movie about her life, how she'd gone swimming with friends as a teenager and broken her neck after striking her head on a rock, becoming paralyzed from the neck down. Joni wanted to die, but a friend shared God's love with her, helping her find his purpose for her life. Now, nearly five decades later, she is one of the longest-living people with her type of spinal cord injury. She was also an internationally known author, artist, and speaker, delivering wheelchairs and God's love to thousands of people in impoverished countries every year.

"Wouldn't it be amazing if Joni and Friends had a team going to Africa this summer?" I asked Dana that night when he came home. "Maybe we could bring Ruth's chair?"

When I called the organization's New England office, I was amazed to discover that they did. The *first ever* Joni and Friends Cause 4 Life team to Uganda was heading to Kampala—the very city where Ruth was born—in July. Dana and I applied to go. So did Christina and a minister from our church. Only, there was a glitch. With roughly seven thousand chairs then going to twenty countries annually, Joni and Friends didn't let donors decide a wheelchair's destination. Many chairs first need to be cleaned and repaired—work done by inmates in American prisons. But because Ruth's chair was so new and we were willing to carry it, the team leader made an exception.

Dana, Christina, and the minister were quickly approved to join the team of college students, physical therapists, medical workers, mechanics, and special education teachers preparing to deliver one hundred wheelchairs to Uganda. But I wasn't. The leader was concerned that both Dana and me going would be too hard on our children. And so Dana, who'd spent many nights repairing Ruth's chair, would go for both of us.

I dreamed of Ruth just once, the week before Dana left for Uganda. Only, instead of carrying Ruth's wheelchair on a plane, I carried our daughter, wrapped in a veil of white lace.

"I don't know what I'm going to do if I have to place another child in Ruth's chair," Dana confessed the night before leaving.

Despite the many times we'd talked, this was the first time I understood how much my husband was hurting. At the Portland airport the following morning, Dana checked in while Lydia climbed on the armrest of Ruth's chair, the way she often had with her sister. Sitting on her sister's lap like a spider, Lydia would place her feet on the wheels of Ruth's chair, wheeling them around the house while Ruth squealed. Soon another child would sit there. But who? Dana filled out a destination sticker and looped it around the padded handle. Then I bent and kissed the inside curve of Ruth's headrest goodbye.

Thirty hours later, Dana and the team arrived in Uganda—but Ruth's chair didn't. Somehow it had been lost during a layover in Holland. When my husband e-mailed me this unhappy news, I imagined Ruth's chair crisscrossing the Atlantic in the dark hold of a plane and prayed someone would find it. Meanwhile, Dana and the others prepared to distribute wheelchairs at the Kampala School for the Physically Handicapped, a boarding school begun in 1969 for children with cerebral palsy, designed to teach them gardening and handcrafts such as cloth dying and woodworking. When the team's bus pulled up to the concrete and gardened compound, children with twisted limbs and withered bodies sat on the ground, cheering. Those who were able clapped. They were so excited, Dana said it was like someone had hit a home run at a baseball game.

Christina assisted children in the school, the way she'd often helped Ruth. Dana and the other mechanics assembled wheelchairs under a sprawling tent, helping the therapists lift children from the dirt and place them in custom-fitted chairs. With an added footrest here and a harness there, every child in need soon had a safe, comfortable way to get around. Some children spun around the dirt, racing their new wheels, while others happily tottered with walkers and crutches. But Ruth's wheelchair was still missing. Dana and several other team members were preparing to move on and distribute wheelchairs five hours north in Gulu, an area devastated by the Lord's Resistance Army. Would Ruth's chair arrive in time? Two days before they left, it was delivered in the trunk of a taxi. Back home, the kids and I eagerly waited to discover who would get it. It had to be a girl, I prayed. It just had to be a girl. At last, an e-mail from Dana flashed on my computer screen:

I was praying we would be able to find a girl that would be the perfect fit for Ruth's chair. All of our physical therapists were looking too, but most of the kids were either too little or they were somewhat ambulatory, so Ruth's chair would not be a good match. Then in comes this mom with her little six-year-old girl in pink tights with stars (a lot like the ones we used to put on Ruth). She had a great smile with all of her front teeth missing.

Her name was Madrine. Because Dana couldn't access a phone and Internet service was spotty, we had to wait until he returned to hear the rest. One week later, we stood with others from our church as three weary travelers rode down the airport escalator in Portland, but I saw only Dana. Thinner and ragged looking with dark circles under his eyes, he hugged our children and me.

"Welcome home." I wrapped my arms around his broad shoulders.

The drive to Bath was filled with questions as our kids begged to know what Dana had brought them. An hour later, he emptied his luggage in the middle of our living room floor, doling out gifts—a hand-forged knife to Judah, a carved elephant for Gabriel, jewelry for Lydia, a zebra for Asher.

"Bring me back something of great beauty," I'd said when Dana had asked what I wanted. The swirling blue skirt sewn by the students in Kampala was lovely, but not as beautiful as the story he told me after our children were in bed. We sat at a lace-covered table in the front shed, a former candy store that we'd converted into my office. Earlier that afternoon, Joan had stopped by with a gourmet dinner in a box. "Dana's going to need to talk when he gets back," she said. "Feed the kids dinner early. Once they're in bed, take a little time just for the two of you. Promise?"

I promised.

So there we sat, eating shrimp cocktail by candlelight, while classical music played on the radio.

"Did it help?" I asked in the flickering light. "Putting another little girl in Ruth's chair?"

"Yeah." Dana looked drained. "One of the therapists put her in the chair, but I made the adjustments."

"Was it hard?"

"I was bawling the whole time," Dana said as he wiped his eyes.

I asked him to tell me the story again, once more from the beginning. I wanted every detail, to fill my mind with the firm, clear knowledge that Ruth's life—and our love for her—had made a difference.

Madrine's mother had heard a rumor about people giving away free wheelchairs. In a country where such equipment cost more than a year's salary, could such a thing be true? Hardly daring to believe it, she had carried her daughter to the school on the final day of the outreach to find that most the chairs had already been given away. The rest were the wrong size. Unable to sit upright, Madrine needed head and foot supports as well as a harness. But one final chair had just arrived.

"I could have lined up all one hundred children, and it wouldn't have fit any of them," Dana said, "but Ruth's chair fit perfectly, right down to the footrest and buckles. It was just like it was meant for her."

After tucking Ruth's favorite purple bear in Madrine's arms, Dana told her grateful mother about our daughter through an interpreter. Then he showed her Ruth's picture, which she asked to keep.

"Only the interpreter didn't tell her Ruth had died. He said the chair was a gift from our daughter."

"What did she say?"

"She took my hand and said, 'Thank your daughter for me.' "

20

Wisdom in the House of Mourning

Certain patterns are discernable only from a distance, like gazing out an airplane window at a blanket of forests and fields far below.

When driving, one sees only jagged boughs and blowing hay, but from above, a larger design appears.

A Massachusetts farmer, living along an international airplane route, once planted soaring evergreens in the shape of a cross.

From the ground, the trees resemble a random wood, but passengers flying overhead clearly understand their meaning.

The difficulty of gaining a higher perspective is that we are stationed below.

The sorrows and disappointments that perplex earthbound travelers reveal a higher purpose only when viewed from heaven.

There are many ways a heart can break, but only one way to heal it. You can take all the grief and sadness and hold it as tight as you can, or you can open your arms to spread the love and joy you remember as far as you can.

My instinct was the first.

"I will always blame myself," I told Dana in bed, one of the few places we talked. "I will always feel responsible for Ruth's death."

"You can't think that way," he said.

Oh, but I could. What if I'd been less tired? Or busy? Or stressed? Every day I relived the night Ruth died, and every day I reached the same conclusion: I should have known. When I thought this way, I was sure that life was hopeless, that no matter how hard I tried or whom I loved, it would never be enough.

"What are we going to do?" I asked for the umpteenth time.

"What we've always done. The best we can."

"Our best wasn't good enough," I said flatly.

"How can you say that?" He shifted, so even in the dark I knew he was looking at me. "We may not have done it perfectly, but we gave Ruth everything we had. That's all God was asking. And you know what? She knew the difference. That girl knew we loved her."

Deep down, I knew he was right. But if we'd loved Ruth so much, why wasn't she still here, riding the bus to school? Picking words on her computer to tell me what she'd learned that day? Why wasn't our love enough to save her?

One day, I sat at the computer and typed *kernicterus*. What I found shocked me. Photo after photo filled the screen, photos of kids just like Ruth—with big grins and crooked bodies and cochlear implants. Only a blood test taken during the first weeks of life can conclusively diagnose kernicterus, but Ruth had every symptom. When I recalled Ruth's sometimes rigid and other times floppy muscle tone, her oddly indented teeth and wandering eye, I knew our neurologist was right. Even more heartbreaking was learning that kernicterus is 100 percent preventable with a one dollar blood test. In other words, Ruth never had to suffer. Had someone tested her bilirubin level after birth and taken steps to reduce it, she would have been as healthy and active as Lydia.

How many other children in Uganda suffered this way? Did Grace, whose mother had knocked on the gate at Welcome Home? Or Madrine, the little girl now riding around Kampala in Ruth's wheelchair? I didn't know. But many fathers in sub-Saharan Africa carry a gene that puts their children at high risk for the condition. So does Rh disease, an easily treated incompatibility in blood types between a baby's mother and father. A lack of prenatal care also increases the risk by contributing to a greater number of premature births. As a result, the world's poorest countries, particularly in South Asia and sub-Saharan Africa, have both the highest rates of kernicterus and the fewest resources to care for children affected by it. Yet even in America, with some of the best medical care in the world, hospitals don't universally screen bilirubin levels, despite the fact that jaundice affects 60 to 80 percent of newborns. Instead, many doctors gauge a child's bilirubin levels by eyeing the color of his or her skin, a technique that has been proven inadequate. Despite intense lobbying from parents of children affected by kernicterus, the Centers for Disease Control doesn't currently track the number of new cases. However, lead researcher and advocate, Dr. Steven Shapiro, chief of the Division of Neurology at Children's Mercy hospital in Kansas City, cites statistics estimating that more than one hundred children in the US are impaired by the condition each year.

One North Carolina mother I spoke with, Miriam Iliff, questioned her pediatrician about the yellow hue of her four-day-old son only to be told to expose him to sunlight. Four days later, he had orange skin and chicken-soup-colored eyes. Miriam drove him back to the doctor. "It's only jaundice," he assured her. By day nine, her son wouldn't stop screaming. Eyes rolled down in their sockets, he was literally dying in her arms. Miriam and her husband, John, rushed their son to the emergency room, where he was assigned the lowest priority. By the time they saw a doctor two hours later, their son was in respiratory failure, body arching backward, eyes fixed on the ceiling. Blood samples revealed a bilirubin level of 46 mg/dL—twice the amount at which permanent brain damage occurs. Since it was too late to airlift their son to a larger hospital for a blood transfusion, Miriam and her husband clung to each other and prayed while a doctor ran tubes from their baby's groin to his heart, hand-pumping in clean, healthy blood with a syringe and extracting the deadly blood with another. But it was too late. Like Ruth, their son, nicknamed "Blue," is an otherwise-typical kid who is deaf, has severe cerebral palsy, relies on a wheelchair and cochlear implant, and communicates with a computer while requiring constant care—all because his bilirubin levels rose too high.

As Miriam shared her story I grieved, imagining tiny, motherless Ruth wailing in an overcrowded, poorly equipped hospital with no one to intervene as bilirubin slowly damaged her brain.

As the months passed, the shock of Ruth's death began to fade—a mark that burned and blistered like a brand before deadening to a scar. But my faith was seared. When Ruth died, my dream of helping orphans in Africa died with her. For the first time, I had no idea what came next. Searching for answers, I picked up my Bible, starting with the most melancholy books I could find, including the Psalms, which are full of suffering. "I am completely discouraged," my soul cried with King David in Psalm 119:25–27 (in the Living Bible translation). "Revive me according to your word. I told you my plans and you replied. Now, give me your instructions. Make me understand what you want. For then I shall see your miracles." Like Israel's ancient poet, I too needed to be revived, to hear God's instructions, to understand what he wanted. I needed a miracle. As never before, I recognized my need for grace—the unshakeable knowledge that God loved and accepted me despite my limitations. "Nothing is perfect except your word," David wrote in verse 96 of that same psalm. Not me. Not my knowledge. Not my actions.

Continuing my search over the following weeks, I turned to Ecclesiastes, which begins by stating that all life is meaningless—my suspicions exactly. Yet as I continued, I came to the words in the fourth verse of the seventh chapter: "The mind of the wise is in the house of mourning." I stopped and read the verse again. Then I underlined it. Mourning joined with wisdom? Could God use something as shattering as grief to bring about something good? I thought of Ruth's abandonment and disabilities and of how they had brought her to us; of our great loss in letting her go, but of her great gain as a child of God, now completely well and surrounded by the perfect love of his presence; and of all the wheelchairs Dana had helped deliver to hurting people—all because of Ruth. In that way, God used Ruth to redeem others just as she had been redeemed.

Lastly, I turned to Lamentations—a funeral dirge proclaiming that the same God who allows loss also brings healing. In verse thirty-two of the third chapter, it reads:

For if He causes grief,
Then He will have compassion
according to His abundant loving-kindness.

Grief is not God's end plan. While we all experience loss and death, God's compassion does not leave us there. His plentiful love is enough to restore our broken hearts and dreams and fill us to overflowing. This was the love I needed. But where could I find it?

My mom suggested CFO—Camps Farthest Out—an ecumenical prayer retreat with gatherings around the globe, which was where she'd first accepted Christ in Oregon. Afterward, she often packed Sunny and me into the back of our Datsun pickup to drive four hours south to the camp held on California's Mount Shasta. There I learned to hear the voice of the Holy Spirit under the whispering ponderosa pines, lying on my belly beside a murmuring brook. In October, I looked up the nearest retreat and discovered that it took place the following weekend.

"Should I go?" I called and asked Mom.

"Only if you want to be completely encircled by love," she said.

Rain pelted our van the night we pulled up to the warmly lit inn a few hours north in the coastal village of Southwest Harbor. Since Judah and Gabriel were away on a Scouting trip, only Lydia and Asher came along with Dana and me. Stepping from the van into the chilly downpour, we raced for the covered porch of the old-fashioned inn. Strangers greeted us like friends as we registered in the firelit parlor and made our way to the dining room. Everyone seemed so happy, but we picked a table by ourselves, too sorrowful to join in. As soon as dinner was over, we retreated to our room, laying Asher in his playpen. While Lydia slept on the pullout couch, I stretched out on the bed beside Dana with a book. Then, through the sound of the rain, I heard singing.

I looked up from my book. "Is there a service tonight?"

"I don't think so." Dana was already half asleep.

I flipped open our welcome folder. There, under the first night's schedule, I read *Vespers*. Standing at the window, I stared through the drizzly dark toward a lighted room. The glow was so inviting, the sound so full of hope, I had to find out what was going on. Making my way downstairs and crossing the damp grass, I followed the music through the doors of a converted carriage house and slid into a chair near the door, embarrassed at being late. When the music ended, Ellen Stamps, a grandmotherly woman with silver hair and radiant warmth, spoke of growing up in Holland during the Holocaust where she was abandoned at age four by her parents, who couldn't afford to take care of her. After sharing her own story of loss and sorrow, she talked about the healing power of God's love. Opening her Bible to Psalm 42:5, she read, "Why are you in despair, O my soul? And why have you become disturbed within me? Hope in God, for I shall again praise him."

Hope. Something that seemed impossible now that Ruth was gone. What was left to hope for? I could barely believe in God, yet alone hope in him. The following morning, Dana and the kids joined me after breakfast as Ellen spoke again, this time about forgiveness. "The longer you hold a burden," she said, "the heavier it becomes. To let go of a painful experience is sometimes the hardest thing. Let the sadness and pain come out in a beautiful way."

I couldn't hold back my tears. For months, I'd been carrying Ruth's death like a burden—crushed by the weight of pain I felt for not being able to save her. But until I forgave myself, I'd never let go of the pain. Later that morning, when we broke into preassigned prayer groups, I found myself sitting beside Ellen in a cozy den as the glassy waters of Somes Sound mirrored the rugged mountains outside.

"What would you like to pray about?" she asked.

I shared about Ruth. "I don't know how to keep going when I don't know what is ahead."

"Jesus," Ellen said simply. "Hope is ahead. It is around the next curve."

There it was again, that thing I'd lost: hope.

"May I share a poem?" asked a white-haired man, Jack, as he cleared his throat.

I nodded.

He closed his eyes. Then, in a voice as deep as my suffering, he spoke:

Weep not, weep not,
She is not dead;
She's resting in the bosom of Jesus.
Heart-broken husband—weep no more;
Grief-stricken son—weep no more;
Left-lonesome daughter—weep no more;
She's only just gone home.

From memory, Jack recited the entire poem "Go Down Death," by the African-American poet James Weldon Johnson. In the poem, God looked down with pity on one who was tired and weary and commanded Death to ride his fastest horse to where an old woman tossed on her bed in pain. "I'm going home," she whispered, unafraid. Then she smiled and closed her eyes. Death lifted her like a baby and brought her to Jesus, who wiped her tears and rocked her in his arms, saying, "Take your rest. Take your rest."

"Weep not," Jack finished. "Weep not. She is not dead; she's resting in the bosom of Jesus."

For the first time, I saw Ruth no longer weary, no longer suffering, but at home with God. The following morning, during Communion, I wanted to curl up on the floor and weep as I joined others in line to receive the bread and the wine. So great was my anguish, I didn't think I could stand as those around me sang, "He wraps me safely round in his infinite love and wisdom. With love, with love. With infinite love and wisdom."

I followed the feet of those in front of me as I lifted my face to gaze upon a portrait of Christ.

"The body of our Lord Jesus Christ, given for you." A priest held out the plate.

With open hands, I received the gift of broken bread.

"The blood of Christ, the cup of salvation." A woman offered the chalice.

And I embraced it, this blood shed for me—for my humanity and limitations and lack of knowing. For isn't this what ultimately separates us from God? As I returned to my seat, a sense of lightness filled me and the heaviness lifted. In that moment, I knew that God's love was great enough to redeem Ruth, even when ours wasn't. We were just part of her journey. Our job was simply to continue sharing that love with the needy and broken—even though we were needy and broken too.

Driving home on Sunday afternoon, we passed a straggling procession of runners completing the Mount Desert Island Marathon. Those huddled around the finish line stretched sore muscles and wrapped themselves in foil blankets. But miles beyond, we came upon runners who limped along so stiffly that each step looked excruciating.

"It's hard coming back," I said to Dana that night back home in bed.

"You mean, thinking about tomorrow?" he asked.

"And the day after that, and after that, and after that . . ."

Beneath the blankets, his fingers clasped mine. "Take my hand," he said and then softly sang the words of an old tune that had been a favorite when we were dating. How long ago they seemed, those simple days of innocence and untried dreams.

I pulled my hand away.

"No." My gentle husband held on tighter, reciting lyrics about a couple struggling down the long road of life together. "Please," he said. "Will you try?"

I pictured the final runners we'd passed that afternoon, a man and woman. Gray-haired and stooped, they had held hands while plodding down Route 3 together. *You're almost there!* I'd wanted to shout. *Keep going!* But I was afraid to interrupt their slow, steady pace.

"I'm not sure I can," I said.

Dana stopped singing and rested his cheek against mine. "It's hard, but we'll make it if we walk together."

Hesitantly I filled in the next verse, pledging not to quit.

With Dana's hand clutching mine, I saw how far we had come, and I knew that we'd make it.

21

Waiting for Spring

*From my office chair, I gaze through a narrow window at
our backwoods, my view limited by walls and framing.
Standing, nose against the glass, I see more.
Yet, the back hill obstructs the path that winds beyond.
Ruth lies over such a horizon.
I cannot see my daughter through the narrow window of
humanity through which I peer.
We glimpse eternity through such a slender frame.
Yet someday I will not only see Ruth but also be with her.
Oh, child, you have transformed my heart.
I miss you achingly, but I release you into the care of the
One whose child you were before you were mine.
Go.
But be not absent from my heart and mind.
Go!
But leave me with the knowledge that I will hold you again.*

Climbing out of grief is a slippery slope. Each time my hands
gripped the edge, I slid back in. On the mornings when I sat in my
shed to write, I stared up the snow-covered ramp to our front door,
imagining Ruth sitting at the kitchen table, waiting for me. Knowing
she wasn't was devastating. But not all memories are sad.

"Remember when Ruth would lick you?" Lydia asked, after carrying her pillow back upstairs to sleep in her own bed when Ruth had
been gone for nearly one year.

"And I would tell her to stop, and she'd laugh?"

"Oh, yeah!" Lydia giggled.

The sound coming from my throat surprised me. How long had
it been since I'd laughed?

I missed Ruth so much that when Dana came home from work I
often crawled in bed rather than face another family dinner without

her. Once, Judah trailed after me. He didn't talk. He simply stretched his broad, almost fifteen-year-old body beside me and opened a book, letting me know that I wasn't alone. Through small moments like these, God began to mend my aching heart. One morning, Lydia pulled me into the kitchen to show me four names she'd spelled with magnets on our refrigerator: Judah, Gabriel, Lydia, and Asher. It hurt to see Ruth's name missing, but the names that remained reminded me that our other children still needed me. And so I asked God to take care of the one only he could, while praying for strength to care for the ones I could.

That winter, the leaves on the rhododendron outside my shed curled from the cold, their fragile limbs layered with snow. The tight, unopened buds pointed sharply toward the sun, waiting for the tilting of the earth, the coming of spring, when they would bloom with radiant color. So it was with Ruth, I realized. I saw the bud, but God sees the flower. Scripture offers a glimpse—but only a glimpse—of our future splendor. Or as the apostle Paul wrote in 1 Corinthians 2:9, "No eye has seen, no ear has heard, no heart has imagined the glory that awaits those who love God."

As I'd often told my children, there is nothing of value that may be lost here that will not be redeemed in heaven. Everything life takes, love restores. Everything. Broken bodies. Broken hearts. Broken dreams. No matter how painful. No matter how devastating. God can transform even our greatest sorrow into something good. We simply have to keep beating our wings, keep trusting, to discover what it will be. In the meantime, he gives us the hope to keep living. Ruth's life didn't end the way I wanted, but God had not promised how long we would have her. He had not promised to spare us from pain. He had simply asked us to love her. And we did. The same way he loves us. Unconditionally. Each morning was a new day to believe that God was still there, still in control, still fulfilling his plan.

Instead of teaching Ruth, I began to see all that she had taught me. The value of people the world often overlooks. The power of a smile. How that which requires the greatest sacrifice can also bring our greatest joy. Such joy is not found in meeting my own needs, I discovered, but in trusting God to meet my needs while I pour out my life to meet the needs of others. In other words: loving them. And even when the object of such love is taken away, the seed it produces yields a vine that wraps its twisting tendrils around everything it touches until it bears a heavenly harvest.

After bringing Ruth's wheelchair to Uganda, I thought our work was done, but Dana was so inspired that he signed up to return to Uganda with Joni and Friends through its Wheels for the World outreach the following summer—this time to train as the team's lead wheelchair mechanic, sharing God's hope with other children waiting to know his love. If our hearts could hurt so much from the death of one child, how God's must break every day over the millions of orphaned, neglected, and disabled children still waiting for someone to show them his love. Despite her limitations, Ruth really was an ambassador, leaving her homeland to represent those who could not advocate for themselves, all without speaking a word.

"You are going back to Uganda someday, and you are going to preach," Dana had said on that first weekend we brought Ruth home. "You are going to walk. You are going to talk."

Through the nearly seven years we shared with her, Ruth never walked or talked independently, but her life preached volumes about God's love for people with needs we'd never considered. I marveled at the places Ruth took us, the people she'd introduced us to—places and people we never would have gone or seen, people we didn't even know existed before welcoming her into our hearts. Here we thought that we were transforming Ruth's life, and she had transformed ours. When the needs are many and our resources small, it's easy to believe we can't make a difference—the way we were told that adopting Ruth wouldn't make a difference. But God calls us to love anyway. He calls us to stop, like the Good Samaritan, to use whatever resources he has given us to help those we meet along our way.

During that last week in Uganda when Ruth and I were at Welcome Home, Esther, the social worker, was driving when she spotted an injured kitten lying in the middle of the road. In the nearby field, a pack of wild dogs was hungrily approaching. Esther stopped and rescued the kitten, only to discover that its back legs had been crushed. It was so skinny, its soiled fur barely covered its jutting bones. Maggots infested its skin. Determined to help, Esther scooped up the kitten and carried it toward her car, only to be stopped by an old man sitting along the road.

"Where are you taking my kitten?" he called.

"Your kitten?" Esther asked, incredulous. "If this is your kitten, then why aren't you taking care of it?"

Instead of answering, the man shrugged. "If you pay, I will let you have it."

Esther paid. Then she took the kitten home, bathed and fed it, handpicked the maggots from its fur, and laid it in a clean, soft bed. Too wounded to be saved, the kitten died anyway. It would be easy to assume that Esther's actions didn't matter. After all, the kitten died. But she wasn't responsible for the outcome. She was simply responsible to love—the way we all are, each one of us, to help whomever God puts in our path. The empty hole in my heart—and the spot at my dinner table—tempts me to believe that our love for Ruth didn't matter. Then I remember the joy in her eyes, the sparkle of her laughter, the brightness of her smile, and I know that Ruth knew that we loved her. Instead of dying forsaken and alone—as many abandoned children and people with disabilities do in the developing world—Ruth knew she was beloved upon this earth. And that made all the difference. Because no matter how and when life ends, only love is guaranteed to last.

There isn't a price I wouldn't pay to spend one more day with Ruth. To gallop up the road with her in wild abandon as she yelped at our speed. To spin her around the basketball court at the YMCA or carry her up the slide at the playground and send her plummeting down. To curl up beside her in bed and finish the story we were reading—*Rebecca of Sunnybrook Farm*—the week she died. Or to glimpse her smile as I sang and signed one last time, "Good night, Ruthie. Good night, Ruthie. Good night, Ruthie, it's time to go to sleep."

Neither would I trade anything in exchange for the days we had. Yes, the price of adopting Ruth was high. Yes, the pain of losing her was great, but the blessing of each day we were privileged to share with her was far greater. Since losing Ruth, Dana and I have met other families who have lost children with cerebral palsy or kernicterus in similarly sudden and devastating ways. Such pain, I believe, lasts for a lifetime, but so do the memories, the happy ones. So even if you love and lose, keep sharing God's love anyway. Love in the face of suffering and grief and heartache and loss. Love beyond racial and religious and physical borders and barriers. Love like a fool, without considering what such love will cost. You won't have to look far to find someone who is hurting, someone without a voice, someone waiting to know that they are loved.

"What are the flowers for?" Lydia asked the following April on what would have been Ruth's ninth birthday.

"Something special." I pushed two-year-old Asher in his stroller through the leafy rows of a local greenhouse, trying to choose between a pot of purple "Johnny-jump-ups" and a delicate "bleeding heart" plant with drooping heart-shaped pink flowers. The first was the wrong color; the second too sad. I settled on red pansies and bright yellow daffodils. Because it was so beautiful and smelled so sweet, I added a single white hyacinth covered in bell-shaped blooms. After loading the van, we headed down Route 1 toward Topsham for nine-year-old Lydia's homeschooled art class. By now, both Gabriel, who was in seventh grade, and Judah, in ninth, rode the bus over the river to their school in neighboring Woolwich.

"I wonder what kind of birthday party Ruth is having in heaven?" Lydia asked. "Maybe one with a twenty-six-foot cake!"

"Maybe a nine-foot cake," I said, remembering how Ruth loved birthdays. "One foot for each year."

"I thought Ruth was turning eight?"

"No." Had she forgotten they were the same age? "Ruth died when she was seven."

Nothing to be added. Purpose achieved. Work done. Time to rest, you who have labored long and suffered much. Take your rest.

After dropping Lydia off for class, I steered toward the interstate and headed north, knowing I had just enough time.

"Where we going, Mama?" Asher pulled his two favorite fingers from his mouth to ask.

"We are going to plant flowers."

Chains blocked the road through the cemetery, so I parked along the side and buckled Asher in his stroller, handing him the hyacinth.

"Hug it to your tummy tight so you don't drop it," I said, loading the bottom of the stroller with a jug of water and the remaining flowers while I carried a shovel. Then I started down the rutted lane; but as soon as I found the pink granite marker, I heard a sharp *Snap!* Looking down, I saw the stalk of white flowers leaning sideways between Asher's hands. Sap oozed from the broken stalk.

"Why don't we put it here?" I sighed and set the damaged flower on the grass.

"I get down and play?" Asher leaned forward, rocking the stroller, as I planted the tip of the steel shovel in the hard-packed earth, leaning down with all my weight.

"Not here. Do you want to sing?"

"I don't want to sing." He poked his fingers back in his mouth.

Clearing a narrow strip of grass, I knelt and gently coaxed the pansies from their cramped container, pressing them into the cold earth. After planting the daffodils, I covered the bare soil with chunks of grass before pouring out the water. Only the single white broken blossom remained. Since the hyacinth was still as beautiful and sweet as before it was injured, I laid it beside the name etched on the stone. *Ruth Alyssia Merrill, 2003–2011,* it said next to the image of Christ carrying one little lost lamb.

"I love you," I whispered, placing my hand beside Ruth's name. Then, because once didn't seem enough, I said it again, adding, "You changed my life."

"Mama!" Asher called, eager to get going.

God's plan didn't end here. Not for Ruth. Not for any of us. Standing, I picked up my shovel and steered Asher's stroller down the rutted road toward home.

Epilogue

It's crazy to go from the red, dusty streets and open-air markets and noise of Africa to the quiet coast of Maine in little more than a day. There should be a mental quarantine. Regardless, when I heard the car door slam that hot July afternoon in 2013 and looked out the window, there was Dana, standing in our driveway after his third trip with Joni and Friends delivering wheelchairs to Uganda—this time as the lead mechanic.

"Guess who's home?" I shouted.

"Daddy!" Ten-year-old Lydia bolted from the living room, where she'd been lying on the floor doing math after her first day at school with her older brothers.

"Yes!" I scooped up eight-week-old Ezra, the baby God had unexpectedly blessed us with two years after losing Ruth, and ran down the back hall, which was finally finished.

Three-year-old Asher, just finishing his bath, raced outside and down the front stairs wearing nothing but Band-Aids. And just like that, Dana was home. Laughing and talking, we paraded inside, eager to hear about his latest adventure. Judah and Gabriel, sweaty and tired from soccer practice, lumbered up the porch steps soon after. Seeing their dad, their weary faces brightened. As Dana pulled gifts from his luggage, dinner, delivered by Joan, was already in the oven. Ugandan necklaces and flags lay scattered around the living room as Dana described the challenges and triumphs of his trip to set up a wheelchair distribution clinic in Gulu. The old men and children, pulling themselves over the ground, wearing homemade shoes on their hands. The knees flattened and swollen like the pads of a camel's from their constant burden. The grandmother, afraid to trade in her worn walking stick for a sturdy pair of crutches as she hobbled along. The children, being carried in by relatives, from different tribes and families and villages, all bearing the same last name: Ojok.

"Why do so many children share the same last name?" he asked an interpreter.

"It means 'cursed,'" the woman explained. "Or 'little demon.'"

"That's the way many children with disabilities are seen in Uganda." Dana shook his head, repeating the story to us. "Because they don't know why these kids can't walk or talk, they blame evil spirits."

Tears filled my eyes as I recalled the scars on Ruth's arm, knowing God loves us regardless of where we are born or how well our bodies work or what we accomplish. He loves us despite our brokenness, the way we loved Ruth—simply because we are his.

Sitting around Dana's computer later that night, looking at pictures from his trip, I spotted several children in wheelchairs with quilts sewn by Lesley, a woman from our church. To pray for them, she'd asked for a photo of each child with his or her name. One little boy, with weak arms and legs and a beautiful smile, held a paper printed with his name, *Joseph*. Bold letters beneath proclaimed his last name: *Blessing*.

My eyes filled with tears, knowing someone understood. Some may have called Ruth cursed, but—like this little boy with yet-undiscovered hopes and dreams and gifts—she was a blessing.

Author's Note

I began writing Ruth's story in 2006 when she was three, never imagining where it would lead. After many starts and stops, the unfinished manuscript sat in a drawer gathering dust. Someday I hoped that Ruth would be able to finish writing her story with me. What a gift that would have been! Heartbroken after Ruth died, I completed her book to honor her life and help other abandoned children and people with disabilities in Uganda. As a journalist for more than two decades, I have made every effort to recreate events and conversations as they occurred. No names, facts, or time sequences have been changed. I relied heavily upon journals, e-mails, calendars, school and medical records, and personal interviews to write the truth as accurately as possible.

Since Yvonne's and Ruth's adoptions, more than one hundred and sixty children have been adopted from Welcome Home Ministries, Africa—including tiny, malnourished Agnes, who is now thriving, and curious little Timothy, who received lifesaving surgery in America to correct his damaged heart. Four-year-old twins Cissy and Juliet were reunited with their father, who now supports them with a business he began with a loan from the children's home. Raymond, who loved playing telephone, lives in a group home for children with AIDS and remains healthy.

Following the gift of Ruth's chair, Dana helped deliver more than five hundred wheelchairs to Uganda. In 2014, Joni and Friends— which has served a total of 141 countries through all of its programs— celebrated the delivery of its 100,000th donated wheelchair. Since then, donations have increased so much that it anticipates delivering 100,000 more chairs by 2020. Yet, for each child who finds a family, for every person who receives a wheelchair, many more are waiting. Worldwide, an estimated 153 million orphans need support, with nearly 18 million having lost both parents.[13] Children with disabilities are often the most neglected. Adoption is one way to help. Due to recent changes in Uganda, the process to adopt a child is now more involved; however, travel to Kenya is no longer necessary and more US agencies work in Uganda.

Another way to make a difference is to encourage others to buy this book, as all personal proceeds from it will benefit orphans and people with disabilities in Uganda. To support Welcome Home Ministries, Africa, become a sponsor at www.welcomehomeafrica.com. To help Joni and Friends send wheelchairs to Uganda and other developing countries, contact them at www.joniandfriends.com. And to help prevent kernicterus, visit Parents of Infants and Children with Kernicterus at www.pickonline.org.

From our family to yours, thank you. Your support makes a difference in the lives of people like Ruth.

Author's Thanks

"If you climb a mountain, and you did it all by yourself, you didn't climb a very tall mountain," Sir Edmund Hillary once said. Early in writing Ruth's story, I taped this quote to my desk, little knowing that *Redeeming Ruth* would take a decade to complete and publish. Whenever I came close to quitting, many supporters kept me reaching for the next hold.

Thank you to my family, with great love and appreciation to my husband, Dana, and our children for giving Ruth a home and me the time and space to write her story. I am so proud of you for sharing Ruth's journey with great humor and grace and love. You are the best!

Thanks to my mom, Lucy Lincoln, who passed from death to eternal life in December 2014, for living a life that shows what it means to lay down your desires, pick up your cross, and follow the Master. Thank you for faithfully sharing your dreams and always encouraging mine. Thanks to my brother, Sunny Day Morgan, of Kauai Creative, for his inspired web design, technical support, and stunning photography, and for great memories growing up on the farm; to Roger and Patricia Merrill, for your steadfast faith and love, for accepting Ruth as your own, and for raising such a kind and faithful son; and to my sister-in-law, Cindy Merrill, for beautifully producing Ruth's first book trailer.

Thanks to the Mamas, volunteers, and supporters of Welcome Home Ministries, Africa, and especially to Jackie Hodgkins, Janet Mulford, William Edema, Justine Mukalazi, Esther Osborne, and Mandy Sydo for giving hundreds of children like Ruth a loving home; to Tammy Cutchen, Tracey Peck-Moad, and Allen and Theresa Jackson for bringing Ruth to us; and to Naomi Kariuki and her family for rescuing us in Nairobi.

Thanks to the many doctors, therapists, educators, and specialists who embraced Ruth and helped her succeed—Peggy Vance, Lisa Jaskowski, and Jan Giroux at Child Development Services of

Brunswick; Jill Andrews, Christy Callahan, Julie Clark, Patty Cook-Stewart, Rita Deschaines, Tiffany Downs, Sammy Hargis, Katie Hudak, Christie Leech, Colette Merritt, Melinda Meyers, Margaret Ryan, Ann Scarponi, Gail Strattard, and the other fabulous teachers, aides, and students at the Maine Educational Center for the Deaf and Hard of Hearing, who gave Ruth her first language; to the staff at the Morrison Center, who helped Ruth learn and grow; the drivers who transported her when I could not; to Lindy Ost and her super-bouncy therapy balls at Movement Matters; to Drs. Terrell Clark, Jennifer Harris, and Jennifer Johnston, and Susanne Russell and the cochlear implant team at Boston Children's Hospital, who gave Ruth the chance to hear; to Cathy Janelle at Hear Me Now, who taught her what those sounds meant; to Mark Hammond at Mark R. Hammond & Associates, who gave Ruth her Voice; to Catherine Buotte and the staff and children at Dike-Newell Elementary, who made Ruth feel so welcome; and to the other families of children with cerebral palsy, deafness, and kernicterus who shared their stories with us.

Thanks to our community in Bath and the many friends who kept us going with your love, prayers, casseroles, hand-me-downs, car pools, child care, and chocolate-covered caramels, especially: Paul, Joan, and Sarah Fraser, more family than neighbors; Beth York, who never once called me crazy; Bill and Wendy Mracek, who said, "Of course you're adopting her"; Charlie and Rachel DeTellis, for hospitality and abiding friendship; Christina Dumont, babysitter extraordinaire, who, along with her generous family, gave Ruth and our whole family a picture of Christ's love; Jamie Dorr, of Seaside Web Design, for launching me on the Internet; to Jacqueline Zimowski for her beautiful photographs; to Joel Dobbins for writing and recording Ruth's song; to Lilly Murphy, for uncommon kindness; to Greg and Caitlyn Thomas for coming alongside us; and for my behind-the-scenes prayer team: Caitlyn, Christina, Debbie, Jenny, Kelly, Laura, Naomi, Susan, and Wendy.

Along the way, I received much inspiration and knowledge of craft from the community of Maine writers, who listened to early drafts of Ruth's story and affirmed that it needed to be told; with gratitude to: Milena Banks, Janis Bolster, Jeanette Cakouros, Deborah Gould, Raye Leonard, Judy Maloney, Lin Riotto, Lisa Schinhofen, and Bonnie Wheeler; and the Redbud Writers Guild, a vibrant and diverse movement of Christian women who create in community to influence culture and faith.

Thanks also to Joni and Friends for helping us bring Ruth's wheelchair to Uganda; my agent Karen Hardin of Priority PR Group & Literary Agency, for wisdom and unwavering determination; and for the visionary team at Hendrickson Publishers, especially my editor Patricia Anders, for saying "Yes!" and sharing Ruth's story with the world.

So many others have made this journey possible. This book would still be in a drawer without your love and support. Most chiefly, thanks to God for answering our prayers; to Fahmo, for being Ruth's best friend; and to Ruth, for blessing us with your life. You will forever have a home in our hearts. We love you, beautiful girl. This is your story. Thank you for sharing it with us.

Reader's Guide

From childhood, I've kept a journal—a huge help when writing a memoir! But *Redeeming Ruth* is as much your story as it is ours. Why? Because God wants to use each of us to help redeem those he puts in our path. The following guide is designed to help you discover your own story, the one God wants to write through you as you share his love with others. Maybe you don't know what that is yet. Maybe this is your first time considering God's purpose for your life. Have faith! As you step from the nest, he will be with you. Simply start by inviting him into your life. Surrender your will to his. And ask God's Spirit to guide you. The following chapter guides can be used to start your own journal or for discussion. All Scriptures are from the New American Standard Bible.

1   The Danger of Dreaming

"Delight yourself in the Lord; / And He will give you the desires of your heart." (Psalm 37:4)

> It's natural to focus on my desires—what I want, or dream, or hope. Yet God promises a fulfilled life only when my highest aim is pleasing him. As I delight in God, he satisfies my heart.
>
> 1. *What are your dreams or desires?*
>
> 2. *Pray and give these to God, asking him to help you shift your focus from what you want to wanting to please him.*

Application: As I seek God, he becomes my highest desire.

2   Twins?

"Trust in the Lord with all your heart / And do not lean on your own understanding. / In all your ways acknowledge Him, / And He will make your paths straight." (Proverbs 3:5–6)

Your dreams may not come about the way you expect—the way I didn't expect a child with disabilities. Be open to new possibilities. Ask God to direct your thoughts and imagination as you learn to trust him.

1. *Describe a situation or area in which you struggle to trust God.*

2. *What is one small step you can take to deepen your trust?*

Application: When I am unable, God is able.

3   Two Dark Eyes

"The steps of a man are established by the Lord, / And he delights in his way." (Psalm 37:23)

Bringing Ruth home required risk, like following an unknown path. God is a caring Father who remains near to keep you from falling as you take your first wobbly steps of faith.

1. *How do you feel about trusting God as you follow his path? Scared? Excited?*

2. *How do you think God feels?*

Application: Wherever God leads, he is with you.

4   Considering the Cost

"Whoever does not carry his own cross and come after Me cannot be My disciple." (Luke 14:27)

As great crowds began to follow Jesus, he warned that following him comes with a price. The cross is a symbol of sacrifice. Jesus asks us to die to our own desires so that we might live a sacrificial life devoted to him.

1. *How do these words of Jesus frighten or inspire you?*

2. *What fears keep you from fully following Christ?*

Application: Following Christ comes with a cost.

5   A Jar of Faith

"And without faith it is impossible to please Him, for he who comes to God must believe that He is and that He is a rewarder of those who seek Him." (Hebrews 11:6)

I was afraid to adopt Ruth without knowing how hard it would be. Yet Scripture says that faith—action before evidence—is essential to pleasing God.

1. *Look up the meaning of "faith" in a dictionary, and then write your own description.*

2. *In what area do you most struggle to have faith or confidence in God?*

Application: God wants us to confidently trust him.

6   A Raw, Choking Wail

"And do not neglect doing good and sharing, for with such sacrifices God is pleased." (Hebrews 13:16)

On our own, we lacked the financial resources to adopt Ruth. God wants to use all of us to bless others. Such giving helps those in need and is pleasing to God.

1. *What gifts or resources has God given you?*

2. *How can you share these with others?*

Application: When you give, God rejoices.

7   Reservations and Preparations

"For we are His workmanship, created in Christ Jesus for good works, which God prepared beforehand so that we would walk in them." (Ephesians 2:10)

God created each of us with a purpose: To do good. He equipped you with specific gifts and interests and abilities to bless others. As we walk, he leads.

1. *What does it mean to be God's workmanship?*

2. *In what areas of service do you sense God leading you?*

Application: God made you with a purpose.

8 Soaked

"Create in me a clean heart, O God, / And renew a steadfast spirit within me." (Psalm 51:10)

When I was younger, I loved travel and adventure. As an adult with a family to take care of, it terrified me. Like the psalmist, I needed a steadfast spirit. Sometimes God uses trouble—like our difficulty getting Ruth on the plane—to renew our resolve.

1. *How has God used tough circumstances to help you grow?*

2. *What fears keep you from following the desires he's put in your heart?*

Application: Trouble is an opportunity for God to transform your heart.

9 Welcome Home

"Be strong and courageous . . . the Lord is the one who goes ahead of you; He will be with you. He will not fail you or forsake you. Do not fear or be dismayed." (Deuteronomy 31:7–8)

Moses spoke these words to Joshua, who led the nation of Israel from captivity to freedom. To bring Ruth home, I had to trust God to do what I could not. When confronted by fear, remember who is with you.

1. *In what areas do you struggle to believe that God will take care of you?*

2. *Rewrite this verse by making it personal, inserting your name at the beginning. Then read it out loud to yourself.*

Application: Where God leads, he guides.

10 Waiting

"But as for me, I will watch expectantly for the Lord; / I will wait for the God of my salvation. / My God will hear me." (Micah 7:7)

While waiting for Ruth's visa, I discovered the children at Welcome Home were also waiting. Yet while I fretted, these vulnerable, innocent children fully trusted God to rescue them.

1. *When you are in a place of waiting, what helps you stay focused on God?*

2. *What does it mean to "watch expectantly"?*

Application: While you are waiting, God is working.

11 A Small Thing

"For nothing will be impossible with God." (Luke 1:37)

We often limit our dreams to what we think is achievable based on our own strength, knowledge, resources, and abilities, while forgetting that God is all powerful. Faith is the key that unlocks the door to God's strength, knowledge, resources, and abilities.

1. *What dream would you pursue if you knew it was possible?*

2. *Whose abilities do you trust more: yours or God's?*

Application: God is greater than any obstacle.

12 Talking Hands

"Seek the LORD and His strength; / Seek His face continually. / Remember His wonderful deeds which He has done." (1 Chronicles 16:11–12)

When confronted by difficulties and doubts, remind yourself of all that God has done in the past to get you this far. Strength comes as you continue to seek God, despite the hardships.

1. *Make a list of ways you have seen God work on your behalf.*

2. *Write a prayer, thanking God for his help.*

Application: When you feel stuck, remember God's provision.

13 Testing

"Let us run with endurance the race that is set before us, fixing our eyes on Jesus, the author and perfecter of faith." (Hebrews 12:1b–2a)

When we are worn out and exhausted, it's easy to lose faith. But as we focus on Jesus—rather than our problems—we find the strength to keep running.

1. *What obstacles or difficulties cause you to doubt?*

2. *Rather than focusing on the problem, make a list of what you are grateful for, thanking God for his provision.*

Application: God's strength is enough when ours fails.

14   Two Worlds

"God causes all things to work together for good to those who love God, to those who are called according to His purpose." (Romans 8:28)

God promises to take care of you. Even in hardship, he is in control. Our purpose is to live out our love for him as we pursue his plan.

1. *Recount a time when God brought something good out of a difficult situation.*

2. *How did this strengthen your faith?*

Application: God's desire is for your good.

15   Happiness

"In God I have put my trust, I shall not be afraid." (Psalm 56:11)

It's easy to get discouraged and give in to fear, especially when prayers seem to go unanswered. Trusting God is an act of faith. So is choosing to fear. Only we can decide which we will believe.

1. *What fears are you facing today?*

2. *Imagine putting your trust in God—the way you'd put something in a cupboard—and close the door, leaving the results to him.*

Application: You can either trust God or trust your fears.

16 Hope and Holding On

"[Love] bears all things, believes all things, hopes all things, endures all things. Love never fails." (1 Corinthians 13:7–8a)

The better you know someone, the better you understand their hurts and struggles. And the more you love someone, the more it hurts to see them hurting. This is the same love God shows us: an intimate love that knows us well, yet loves us anyway—a love willing to be wounded.

1. *How has God shown this type of love to you?*

2. *Name three specific actions you can take to show God's love to someone you know is hurting.*

Application: Love never quits.

17 Heartbreak

"'For My thoughts are not your thoughts, / Nor are your ways My ways,' declares the Lord." (Isaiah 55:8)

Our efforts don't always bring the results we hope. After losing Ruth, my choice was to trust God or turn away from him. The challenge, in the midst of heartbreak, is to continue trusting that God is still in control, still carrying out his plan.

1. *When has God disappointed you?*

2. *What helped you hold on to your faith?*

Application: When God's ways seem unclear, it is an opportunity to trust.

18 Winter Bare

"Even though I walk through the valley of the shadow of death, / I fear no evil, for You are with me." (Psalm 23:4)

Some valleys are so deep that only God can walk through them with you. Dark days may come, but God promises to be with us.

1. *When have you most needed to experience God's presence?*

2. *How has he revealed himself to you in the valley?*

Application: God's presence overcomes the deepest darkness.

19   What Remained

"Have I not commanded you? Be strong and courageous! Do not tremble or be dismayed, for the Lord your God is with you wherever you go." (Joshua 1:9)

Even when we don't understand where God is leading, he tells us to be strong. Wherever we go—or whatever we go through—God is with us.

1. *As you follow God's path for you, what challenges do you find most concerning?*

2. *Imagine God standing beside you. How does his presence change the way you feel?*

Application: With God, I am never alone.

20   Wisdom in the House of Mourning

"The Lord's lovingkindnesses indeed never cease, / For His compassions never fail. / They are new every morning." (Lamentations 3:22–23a)

Death will cease. Sorrow will cease. Darkness will cease. But God's love will never cease. Nor will it fail.

1. *List or share the ways you have experienced God's love today.*

2. *How does this comfort you as you face tomorrow?*

Application: God's love is as reliable as the sunrise.

21   Waiting for Spring

"This is My commandment, that you love one another, just as I have loved you." (John 15:12)

God calls us to a life of love. As we walk with God and come to know his Son, his love will flow through us to reach others.

1. *How are love and obedience linked?*

2. *Spend a moment in prayer and ask God to show you one thing you can do in obedience to him today, not from duty but from your love for him.*

Application: My obedience to Christ is fueled by my love for Christ.

If reading the Bible is new to you, or you aren't sure what to do next, I encourage you to find a local church where you can be encouraged as you get to know God and pursue his purpose for your life. Welcome to the adventure—and the blessing!

Notes

1. http://archive.bangordailynews.com/2001/03/16/jury-awards-8-9-million-in-malpractice-lawsuit-oxygen-deprivation-left-girl-without-motor-skills/.

2. http://www.unicef.org/infobycountry/uganda_statistics.html.

3. http://www.census.gov/population/international/files/ppt/Uganda94.pdf.

4. http://travel.nationalgeographic.com/travel/countries/uganda-facts.

5. http://news.bbc.co.uk/2/hi/africa/1523100.stm.

6. http://data.worldbank.org/indicator/SP.POP.0014.TO.ZS.

7. http://www.unicef.org/infobycountry/uganda_statistics.html.

8. http://www.nytimes.com/2001/11/29/world/un-study-says-nairobi-is-inundated-with-crime.html.

9. http://abacus.bates.edu/muskie-archives/ajcr/1969/Gov%20Baxter%20Death.shtml.

10. http://www.pressherald.com/2012/12/09/shoot-man-tormented-by-sex-abuse-appears-to-commit-suicide-by-cop/.

11. http://deafed-childabuse-neglect-col.wiki.educ.msu.edu/file/view/ex-pupils_seek_payback_for_abuse_at_deaf_sch.pdf.

12. http://www.thearc.org/what-we-do/resources/fact-sheets/abuse.

13. https://cafo.org/wp-content/uploads/2015/06/Christian-Alliance-for-Orphans-_On-Understanding-Orphan-Statistics_.pdf.

Picture of Ruth, 19 months old, for first "Rally 'round Ruth" fundraiser
(November 2004; used with permission of Jacqueline Zimowksi)

Dana and Meadow with Ruth and Lydia, both 19 months old; Gabriel, age 5, and
Judah, age 7 (November 2004; used with permission of Jacqueline Zimowski)

Ruth's home therapy session with Peggy Vance, left, and Jan Giroux, right
(March 2005; used with permission of Jacqueline Zimowski)

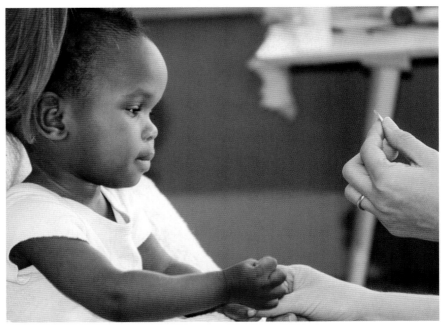

Ruth undergoing therapy with Peggy and Jan (March 2005;
used with permission of Jacqueline Zimowski)

Welcome Home Ministries, Africa, main house (July 2005)

Mandy Sydo, director of Welcome Home, with children (used with permission of Welcome Home)

Mandy Sydo and William Edema, former driver and now manager of Welcome Home in Uganda (used with permission of Welcome Home)

Welcome Home children (used with permission of Welcome Home)

Ruth with Mama Joy (July 2005)

A Mama cooking in God's Glory Kitchen

Drying cloth diapers

The Nile River as seen from Bujagali Falls near Jinja

Bicycle delivery in Uganda (used with permission of Welcome Home)

Houses in Uganda (used with permission of Welcome Home)

Daniel and Naomi with Ruth, returning from safari in Nairobi, Kenya

Family reunion after Meadow and Ruth's return from Africa: Dana with
Ruth, 2, Judah, 8, Gabriel, 5, and Meadow with Lydia, 2, at Popham Beach,
Maine (August 2005; used with permission of Sunny Morgan)

Dana with Ruth, 2, at Popham Beach, Maine (August 2005; used with permission of Sunny Morgan)

Ruth, age 3, graduates from infant program to preschool at Baxter (Spring 2006)

Lydia and Ruth, both age 3, cuddling with their twin dolls (Summer 2006)

Lydia and Ruth, both age 5, painting (Summer 2008)

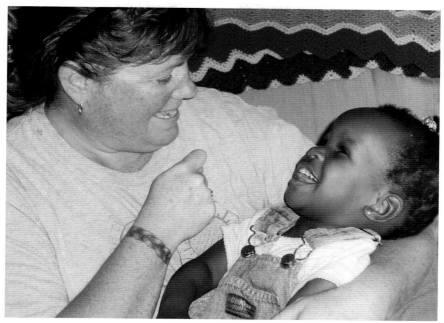

Tracey Peck-Moad signing her name "Mama Tracey," with Ruth, age 3 (July 2006)

Selling Shain's of Maine Portland Seadogs Biscuits (ice-cream sandwiches) during Bath Heritage Days (July 2006; used with permission of Jacqueline Zimowksi)

Gabriel, age 6, dancing with Ruth, age 3 (Summer 2006)

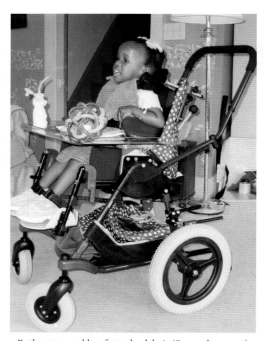

Ruth, age 3, and her first wheelchair (September 2006)

Judah, age 10, with Ruth, age 4 (Fall 2007)

Dana with Ruth, age 6, post-implant surgery (Spring 2009)

Ruth, age 6, holding newborn Asher (February 2010)

Ruth, age 7, with her best friend, Fahmo, during Ruth's final week at Baxter (Summer 2010)

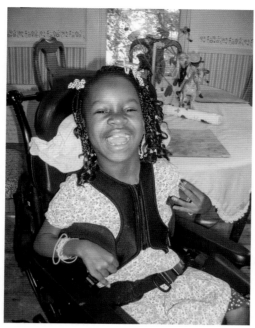

Ruth, age 7, with new wheelchair and fancy hair, ready to start first grade
at Dike-Newell Elementary, Bath, Maine (August 2010)

Christina on Cause 4 Life trip at Kampala in Uganda (August 2011;
used with permission of Joni and Friends)

Loading wheelchairs at Kampala to deliver to Gulu (used with permission of Joni and Friends)

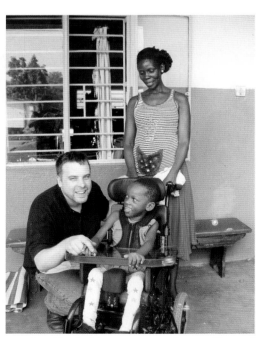

Dana with Ruth's wheelchair recipient, Madrine, and her mother
(August 2011; used with permission of Joni and Friends)